Steeltown U.S.A.

CULTURE AMERICA

Karal Ann Marling
Erika Doss

Series Editors

❖ ❖ ❖ ❖ ❖ ❖ ❖ ❖ ❖ ❖ ❖ ❖ ❖ ❖

Steeltown U.S.A.

WORK AND MEMORY IN YOUNGSTOWN

Sherry Lee Linkon and John Russo

UNIVERSITY PRESS OF KANSAS

To the steelworkers of Youngstown and their families

Published by the University Press of Kansas (Lawrence, Kansas 66049),
which was organized by the Kansas Board of Regents and is operated and
funded by Emporia State University, Fort Hays State University, Kansas State
University, Pittsburg State University, the University of Kansas, and
Wichita State University

A webpage with many color images related to this book is available on the
Center for Working-Class Studies Web site, www.as.ysu.edu/~cwcs.

Library of Congress Cataloging-in-Publication Data
Linkon, Sherry Lee, 1959–
Steeltown U.S.A. : work and memory in Youngstown / Sherry Lee Linkon
and John Russo.
p. cm. — (CultureAmerica)
Includes index.
ISBN 0-7006-1161-4 (cloth : alk. paper)
1. Youngstown (Ohio)—History.   2. Youngstown (Ohio)—Social
conditions.   3. Youngstown (Ohio)—Economic
conditions.   4. Deindustrialization—Ohio—Youngstown—
History.   5. Memory—Social aspects—Ohio—Youngstown.   6. Group
identity—Ohio—Youngstown.   I. Title: Steeltown USA.   II. Russo, John,
1946-   III. Title.   IV. Culture America.
F499.Y8 L56 2002
977.1'39—dc21   2001006342

British Library Cataloguing in Publication Data is available.

Printed in the United States of America

10 9 8 7 6 5 4 3 2 1
The paper used in this publication meets the minimum requirements
of the American National Standard for Permanence of Paper for
Printed Library Materials Z39.48-1984.

CONTENTS

ACKNOWLEDGMENTS / vii

Introduction: Remembering Youngstown / 1

1. Reading the Landscape:
Conflict and the Production of Place / 9

2. Steel Town / 67

3. Deindustrialization and
the Struggle over Memory / 131

4. From "Steel Town" to
a "Nice Place to Do Time" / 190

Epilogue: Community Memory and
Youngstown's Future / 239

NOTES / 251

INDEX / 275

ACKNOWLEDGMENTS

One of the great pleasures of studying local culture is that so much of the research takes the form of talking with people whose memories represent the most useful, interesting archive about the community. While we can't mention everyone, we want especially to acknowledge the assistance of Fred and Josephine Ross, Dan Pecchio and Mary Frances Carol, members of the Youngstown Fire Department, Homer Warren, Harry Meshel, Joe Gavini, Sam Camens, Staughton Lynd, Charles McCollester, and Leo Jennings. Our colleagues Tom Marraffa, Donna De Blasio, Bob Bruno, Bill Hunter, Rick Shale, and C. Allen Pierce talked with us about their own research, helping us to develop some of the key ideas for this book. Mark Peyko, Mary and Steve Salpukas, and Donna DeBlasio provided important materials from their own collections. Dale Maharidge, Michael Williamson, George Dombeck, and Bryn Zellers talked with us about their work as creators of representations of Youngstown.

Our research assistants, Sean Kalic, Jim Meese, and Rebecca Finnick, spent many hours on-line and in the library gathering materials for us. Throughout the project, Martha Bishop at the Youngstown Historical Center for Industry and Labor helped us locate materials on the steel industry, and she provided support and encouragement along the way. Melissa Wolfe gave us access to the archives of the Butler Institute of American Art, and she pointed us toward supplementary research in art history to help us analyze what we found there. William Lawson and the staff at the Mahoning Valley Historical Society, especially Pam Pletcher, helped us find a variety of historical documents and representations. The staff of Mahoning County Public Library helped us locate news reports and local historical data, and Bob Yossay at the *Youngstown Vindicator* provided copies of old photographs. Dean Chance created custom maps, and the staff of the Youngstown State University Media Center, especially photographer Carl Leet, provided valuable help with producing the illustrations.

Before we had even fully imagined this book, Nancy Scott Jackson from the University Press of Kansas and series editors Erika Doss and Karal Ann Marling encouraged us to explore our ideas about images of steelwork and to develop a book-length project. As we moved through the writing process, Erika Doss, David Stephens, Don Mitchell, Dale Maharidge, and Michael Frisch read drafts and provided helpful comments. Throughout the journey, Jack Metzgar served as critic and friend. He read every chapter multiple times, and he was unstinting with both criticism and encouragement. He deserves a lifetime of bacon cheeseburgers and our gratitude.

Youngstown State University provided three research assistant grants and funded two research leaves to support this project. Our administrative assistant, Patty LaPresta, helped us find time to complete the book by handling many tasks around the office and just being a remarkably cheerful, positive presence. We would also like to thank Linda Adler-Kassner, Raymond Lepore, and Teresa Lepore for their friendship and support throughout this process. Finally, Frank Bongen, Susan Russo, and Alex Russo have allowed us to devote huge amounts of time and energy to this project, and they tolerated and even joined in many dinner table conversations during the past three years. We thank them for their acceptance, support, and love.

INTRODUCTION

Remembering Youngstown

From the Monongahela Valley
To the Mesabi Iron Range,
The coal mines of Appalachia,
The story's always the same.
Seven hundred tons of metal a day
Now sir, you tell me the world's changed.
Once I made you rich enough,
Rich enough to forget my name.
—Bruce Springsteen, "Youngstown"

In 1995, Bruce Springsteen released the song "Youngstown," an evocative personal narrative of one family's history in steelmaking. The song emphasized the significance of work and the pain of loss as fifty thousand local workers who had given their lives to the steel mills saw the work disappear and their own value fall. The chorus is addressed to "my sweet Jenny," not a woman but a blast furnace—the Jeannette Blast Furnace at Youngstown Sheet and Tube's Brier Hill Works. Like most of the mills in the Youngstown area,[1] the Brier Hill Works closed at the end of the 1970s, but while most mill structures were torn down in the 1980s, the Jenny remained standing until 1997, one of few markers of the community's past as one of the steelmaking capitals of the United States.

"Youngstown" was released almost twenty years after the mills closed, yet the community was still struggling to reconcile its steelmaking history with its as yet uncertain future. In the mid- to late 1990s, while the community debated whether to preserve the Jenny as a monument to Youngstown's history, four new prisons were being built in the Youngstown area, a locally grown business was facing the national embarrassment of its founder's embezzlement trial, and a major FBI investigation yielded a long series of indictments of local officials for involvement with organized crime. At the same time, local political and business leaders kept seeking new opportunities for economic development, turning to warehouses, telemarketing, prisons, and minor league sports in hopes of revitalization. All of these developments occurred against a backdrop of local debate about how Youngstown's past would shape its future. Springsteen's dark and nostalgic elegy to steelmaking appealed to some because it recognized the commitment of the community's workers and reminded them that they had once been important economic contributors. Yet others rejected the song as too negative and too concerned with history.

As the mixed response to Springsteen's song suggests, memory is a significant source of conflict in Youngstown. For many years, the area had a clear sense of itself as one of the most important industrial communities in the United States. Youngstowners were proud not only of what they produced, but also of the benefits brought by their efforts—high rates of home ownership, impressive cultural resources, and a deep sense of hometown loyalty. At the same time, especially among Youngstown's working class, the community took pride in its history as a site of struggle for workers' rights. Some of the most important battles in American labor history were fought here, ultimately bringing greater prosperity and increased status for steelworkers, which in turn increased wages and improved working conditions for other jobs in the area. The tale of Youngstown's rise as an important industrial site can be seen as the community's "constitutive narrative," the story that provided a unifying image of the meaning of this place for most of the twentieth century.[2] When the mills shut down, those proud memories were brought into question. Not only did Youngstown lose the work that had long been its primary source of identity as well as income, it also wrestled with questions of why the shutdowns had occurred and, eventually, why the community was not recovering as well as some other deindustrialized cities. Community pride gave way to widespread doubt as both local and national critics asked, "What's wrong with Youngstown?" All this led to the fragmentation of Youngstown's constitutive narrative as locals began to argue about how to think about their shared history.

Steeltown U.S.A. explores the struggle over memory in Youngstown. Memory is important because it helps to shape both personal and communal identity, and how individuals and communities see themselves influences their behavior and their sense of what is possible. Put simply, how Youngstown remembers its past plays a central role in how it envisions its future. In their 1985 work, *Habits of the Heart: Individualism and Commitment in American Life,* Robert N. Bellah and his colleagues explained that communities "have a history—in an important sense they are constituted by their past—and for this reason we can speak of a real community as a 'community of memory,' one that does not forget its past." Communities of memory continually retell their stories, and this process creates a sense of shared history and identity, out of which they develop vision and hope for the future. What we see in the past provides a "context of meaning" that helps people link their personal hopes with the goals of the community and thus to understand individual efforts as "contributions to a common good."[3]

The potential power of a healthy community of memory was made clear at a December 2000 symposium on "The Role of Civil Society in Countering Organized Crime: Global Implications of the Palermo, Sicily, Renaissance," sponsored by the United Nations. Youngstown sent a delegation of twenty individuals—by far the largest—representing the media, education, law enforcement, religious organizations, and community groups. The symposium examined the relationship between the erasure of community memory and the rise of a culture of criminality in Palermo, and it showed how the community's systematic reclamation of its past had helped build a new culture of lawfulness. For the Youngstown delegation, the idea that civic culture is undermined by the loss of historical memory, the shift of population from the city to the suburbs, the destruction of historic sites, and a crumbling sense of community had great resonance, for they had seen a similar pattern at home. The symposium also suggested that for a fragmented community uprooted by deindustrialization economically, culturally, and geographically, the recovery of a positive memory of itself is the first important step toward reconstructing a sense of place, belonging, and ownership.[4] Yet even as those who attended the conference saw it as an important opportunity to explore strategies for community development, not everyone was persuaded. In fact, Youngstown Mayor George McKelvey called the trip "a terrible idea" because it would "only call attention to Youngstown's seedy past."[5]

As this story suggests, Youngstown's powerful constitutive narrative as a productive steel town obscured conflicts and divisions. Beneath the apparent unity, competing versions of the Youngstown story reflected the experiences of different communities of memory within the larger community. When the constitutive narrative came into question, however, the conflicts that had always existed gained significance and eventually challenged any illusion that there was a unified community of memory. Separate and conflicting communities of memory emerged, based largely on differences of class and race, but also on the very problem of how to relate the past to the future. While Bellah et al. note that "a genuine community of memory" will tell stories of both success and failure, in Youngstown conflicting communities of memory tell very different tales about what matters, what counts as success, and what explains the failures.[6]

In this book, we explore the origin of the constitutive narrative of Youngstown, and we consider how that narrative fell apart during the years after deindustrialization. Throughout, we emphasize the underlying conflicts that, over time, became increasingly divisive. These divisions, especially the community's struggle to deal with its own past, left Youngstown in an especially vulnerable position at the end of the twentieth century. As we argue, until Youngstown addresses its internal conflict over how to remember its past, it will continue to falter in its efforts to build a new identity for the future.

Most of our discussion focuses on the representations that both reflect and perpetuate how Youngstown understands itself as a community and its past. This book is built around a wide range of representations, starting with the landscape of Youngstown and moving on to written texts, visual images, sculptures, films, songs, and interviews, both oral histories and our own conversations with people who have lived and worked in Youngstown. Together, the physical space of Youngstown and representations of this place form a cultural landscape. We have mapped this landscape using the huge body of stories and images created in and about Youngstown during the twentieth century, most of them focused on ideas about work and community. We have emphasized stories and images that were produced or readily available locally, but we have also examined nationally distributed representations, especially for the later periods, when the national media played a more significant role in providing Youngstown residents with ways of seeing their hometown while also creating a national image.[7]

As the Springsteen song illustrates, representations operate in complicated ways. Any single representation may offer multiple meanings, and audiences bring their own perspectives to their interaction with representations. Former steelworkers, who had a stake in remembering the importance of their work, almost certainly heard different things in "Youngstown" than local business leaders, who may have worried that the song put too much emphasis on failure or class conflict. Because everyone involved in the creation and use of representations comes to the process from an interested perspective, with an investment—though not always a conscious one—in the disputes around them, representations are inherently conflicted. Consequently, images and stories reflect power relations by highlighting some patterns and masking others.

Both those who hold the most power and those who were less powerful contribute to public discourse, but the representations of the powerful tend to be the most visible. This is true partially because the most easily accessible representations are published, public images, and most of them were produced or financed by, and thus reflect the perspectives of, people who were not workers. It is not surprising, then, that our study includes fewer stories and images from working people and even fewer that reflect the experiences and perspectives of women or people of color. Given Youngstown's history of racial and ethnic conflict, this absence is significant. It reminds us of how representations can redefine reality, presenting a monolithic vision of the community, though such images almost never really worked to quell conflict. While compensating for this absence is difficult, we have turned to oral histories and interviews as well as images from worker-centered sites such as churches and union halls to try to learn more about workers' experiences and stories. In addition, given our understanding of how representations both perpetuate and attempt to manage conflict within the community, we have considered the multiple ways of reading images as well as the possible interests of those who created them. Though it is impossible to know exactly what these representations meant to their audiences, reading in this way provides a more complex understanding of how local people experienced the contested cultural landscape of everyday life in Youngstown.

At the same time, we are attentive to the ways that representations are linked with each other. Springsteen's "Youngstown" is an especially telling example because it was based on a 1985 book about deindustrialization and homelessness, titled *Journey to Nowhere: The Saga of the New Underclass,* which opened with several chapters on Youngstown. The song was also the basis for further representations, such as a 1996 report on *CBS This Morning* and a number of newspaper articles, and it was subsequently used in several documentaries and broadcast news reports on unemployment and labor struggles. While other representations are not as directly linked together, none of them appears in isolation. They are, instead, part of a complex web of representations, each reflecting and influencing the others. Image creators, storytellers, journalists—all those who create representations—work within the culture in which they live, and so the images and stories they tell help us understand how that culture explained its own experiences. At the same time, those who "consume" the representations incorporate the images and story lines into new ways of understanding their lives. Neither image creators nor audiences are passive or powerless; both make use of stories and images and bring their own interests to bear as they interpret what they see and hear and as they construct their own representations.

In understanding the relationship between image creators, audiences, and texts, it is important to remember that all of these elements exist within the context of real places and people. At times, it is difficult to define clearly the line between reality and representation, to know in any definite way how "accurate" a representation is or how directly it might influence the behavior of its audience. Yet it is also clear that reality and representation are closely linked. Each has the potential to shape the other. Representations are created in response to real events and experiences, and people are influenced not only by what they read, hear, and see but also by what they don't. Consequently, while we are focusing here on representations, we have tried to make clear how they connect and interact with the real experiences of working people in Youngstown.

We begin our discussion with the landscape of Youngstown, reading physical space as a kind of representation. Chapter 1 approaches the development of the local landscape chronologically, linking the development of place with important moments in local history. The physical space of this community was created by and reflects its history of work and conflict. In chapter 2, we focus on the representations that formed the constitutive narrative of Youngstown, about the relationship between the mills and the town, the meanings of work, and the importance of struggle. These stories and images were produced during the long heyday of the steel industry, from 1900 to the 1970s, and they define work as a source of individual and community identity, a meaningful activity that made Youngstown and its people unique. Chapter 3 focuses on Youngstown's role as a "poster child" for deindustrialization and a symbol of resistance to economic restructuring. While the loss of work challenged the constitutive narrative of Youngstown as an industrial city, nationally distributed stories about the shutdowns in Youngstown helped to create a constitutive narrative about the effects of deindustrialization for the nation. We also examine the changing meaning of work and the emerging conflict over memory. What would Youngstown mean without steelwork? Largely because answering that question was so difficult, the community lost its shared history and became an object of sympathy and ridicule. In chapter 4, we discuss how this loss contributed to a rise in crime and corruption and Youngstown's emerging image as a site of decay and failure. In the epilogue, we briefly consider Youngstown's future, arguing that to move ahead, the community must recuperate a more complete, critical understanding of its past.

In many ways, Youngstown's story is America's story. Youngstown offers a classic case of the rise of industrial America, the importance of economic and social struggle, and the human costs of economic restructuring. Work in America has changed dramatically in the so-called postindustrial era. Not only has industrial work become less dominant, but work itself has become increasingly contingent as more and more workers find themselves at the mercy of corporate interests. Amid these changes, Youngstown's story can help us understand not only how the meaning of work has changed but also why the changing meaning of work matters. A way of life has largely disappeared, but so too has people's faith in the value of their work, their sense of work as a key element in individual and communal identity, and their understanding of the relationship between work and community. As communities of memory built on shared work begin to fade, we are losing an important resource for the common good. Memory helps people understand their significance, and this in turn empowers future struggles against injustice and erasure. Understanding Youngstown can help us better appreciate the importance of memory. As Bruce Springsteen discussed with students in a Princeton University class on "Prophecy and the American Voice," one place "can embody the hopes and failures of the nation. It could be anyplace. . . . Like New Jersey."[8] Or Youngstown.

1

Reading the Landscape:

Conflict and the Production of Place

❖ ❖ ❖ ❖ ❖ ❖ ❖ ❖ ❖ ❖ ❖ ❖ ❖ ❖

The power of place—the power of ordinary urban landscapes to nurture citizens' public memory, to encompass shared time in the form of shared territory—remains untapped for most working people's neighborhoods in most American cities, and for most ethnic history and most women's history. The sense of civic identity that shared history can convey is missing. And even bitter experiences and fights communities have lost need to be remembered—so as not to diminish their importance.
—Dolores Hayden, The Power of Place:
Urban Landscapes as Public History

Northwest of downtown Youngstown, the Division Street Bridge crosses the Mahoning River. On a typical northeast Ohio winter day in January 1997, the sky is a steady light gray. Beside the gray bridge pocked with rust, in the flat plain of the river valley, stands the Jeannette Blast Furnace, a wide black tower with two sets of stacks lined up behind it, nine tall cylinders linked into one massive structure. Once, the "Jenny," as it was known locally, was the heart of the Brier Hill Works of Youngstown Sheet and Tube. Sheet and Tube and U.S. Steel employed almost ten thousand men and women on this land, creating new steel and operating rolling and processing mills. Today no more than thirty labor to prepare the Jenny for destruction. On an outside catwalk, a few figures in white suits are removing asbestos to make the pending explosion safe. On the ground beneath the bridge, a single man in a heavy denim jacket and a large welding mask aims a blowtorch at a large cylinder of rusty brown steel, an unidentifiable remnant of the old furnace, cutting it into pieces. The pungent smell of burning metal rises from the acetylene torch, a faint reminder of the elemental odors of sulfur and coal that once hung over the valley.

The pieces will be sent across the road to North Star Steel, which occupies a building passed down from the old Brier Hill Works, a cavernous black structure that was one of the newer parts of the plant when it was closed in 1979. In an ironic act of industrial cannibalism, the high-grade steel of the Jenny will feed the electric furnace of North Star's minimill, which melts steel scrap and reforms it as new steel pipe. Local efforts to preserve the furnace failed because of lack of funding, but the Jenny has again become valuable, not for the steel it could produce but for the steel of which it was formed. Within a few months, the Jenny would disappear from the landscape entirely.

Up the hill east of the Jenny is Brier Hill, where some of the workers' houses and a few small bars and grocery stores remain from the years when the neighborhood was full of Italian immigrants, bricklayers, and mill laborers, many of whom worked at the Jenny. Through the trees, you can glimpse a bit of St. Anthony's Catholic Church and its now empty school building, where a frieze set into the brick shows St. Joseph with his hand resting on the shoulder of a man shoveling coal into a blast furnace. Farther up the hill in one direction and down the hill and to the south in the other direction are two public housing developments, where the now predominantly black population of Brier Hill lives close by the few Italian-American families that have remained in the old neighborhood.

While the valley where the Brier Hill Works once stood remains an empty, brown field, the hills on either side of the river and other sections of the valley are beginning to recover from the city's long history of industrial pollution. More trees and weeds grow here now,

Jeanntte Blast Furnace, John Russo, 1996

The Jenny site after the furnace was torn down, John Russo, 1997

and the long, empty valley of the Mahoning River is becoming a meadow, open space erasing the memory of the huge steel mills that once filled the low land along the river. The string of plants ran for almost twenty-five miles, from the still-operating WCI plant in Warren, through Girard and McDonald, past the North Star complex, and down through the empty fields that once held U.S. Steel's Ohio Works, Republic Steel, and the largest mill in the area, the Campbell Works of Youngstown Sheet and Tube, all the way to Lowellville. In much of the valley, the only visible reminders of the steel industry are the railroad tracks running alongside the river. Once they were in constant use, bringing raw materials to the mills and carrying finished steel to market, but now cars run only occasionally to bring slag and other steelmaking by-products to be reprocessed into sinter to feed

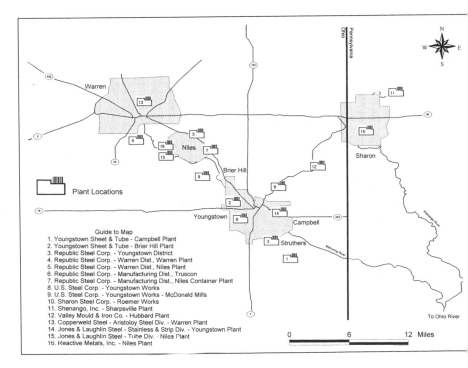

Guide to Map
1. Youngstown Sheet & Tube - Campbell Plant
2. Youngstown Sheet & Tube - Brier Hill Plant
3. Republic Steel Corp. - Youngstown District
4. Republic Steel Corp. - Warren Dist., Warren Plant
5. Republic Steel Corp. - Warren Dist., Niles Plant
6. Republic Steel Corp. - Manufacturing Dist., Truscon
7. Republic Steel Corp. - Manufacturing Dist., Niles Container Plant
8. U.S. Steel Corp. - Youngstown Works
9. U.S. Steel Corp. - Youngstown Works - McDonald Mills
10. Sharon Steel Corp. - Roemer Works
11. Shenango, Inc. - Sharpsville Plant
12. Valley Mould & Iron Co. - Hubbard Plant
13. Copperweld Steel - Aristoloy Steel Div. - Warren Plant
14. Jones & Laughlin Steel - Stainless & Strip Div. - Youngstown Plant
15. Jones & Laughlin Steel - Tube Div. - Niles Plant
16. Reactive Metals, Inc. - Niles Plant

Youngstown steelmakers, Dean Chance, 2001

furnaces at steel plants in Cleveland and Warren. A city that was once full of train whistles, the roar of blast furnaces, and the clanking sounds of moving railcars is now relatively quiet.

Most of the traffic today runs on the highway, over several bridges built since the 1960s. These newer bridges replaced old ones that linked downtown and workers' neighborhoods like Brier Hill, bridges that once carried thousands of men on foot and streetcar to and from work and that carried families southwest to Idora Park, the city's now-abandoned amusement park, or to Mill Creek Park, a long oasis of green that divides the deteriorating, largely African-American south side from the mostly white, working-class neighborhoods of the west side. The newer highway bridges skirt downtown and skim over the old mill sites, leading drivers to the suburbs and the growing commercial strips in Boardman to the south and Niles to the northwest.

Looking southeast from the Division Street Bridge, you can see downtown Youngstown, whose old buildings, most built before 1930 by prominent American architects, form a skyscraper museum. At one end of the downtown area stands the city's newest landmark, the prefabricated fortress of the county jail, one of four prisons built in the Youngstown-Warren area in the past decade. Uphill, several blocks north of the jail stands the huge football stadium of Youngstown State University, now the most prominent, visible piece of architecture in the area. The stadium's towering west stands are topped by a newly built luxury suite donated by the DeBartolo family, one of two local families that built fortunes by developing shopping malls in suburbs all over the country. The tinted two-story windows of the DeBartolo suite face back to the west, overlooking decaying neighborhoods where steelworkers and their families once lived, over the large complex of the Parkview Mental Health Clinic, to the cluster of buildings that make up St. Elizabeth's Health Center. South and east of the stadium sprawl the buildings and parking lots of the university, now the city's largest employer. On the far side of campus from the stadium is a corridor of cultural icons: the Butler Institute of American Art, the Arms Museum run by the Mahoning Valley Historical Society, the university's McDonough Museum of Art, and the main public library.

Butler Institute of American Art, Carl Leet, 2001

Many of these buildings were erected in the first decades of the century, just before and after the first major steelworkers' strike in 1916. They offered refined, elite cultural alternatives to Idora Park's ballroom and the city's many bars. The process of constructing cultural monuments culminated in Youngstown just a few years before the county jail was built, with the "steel museum." The Youngstown Historical Center for Industry and Labor puts steelmaking and steelworkers on display for the education and entertainment of the public, in a building designed by prominent architect Michael Graves to imitate the shape and feel of a steel mill.

LANDSCAPE AS REPRESENTATION

The view from the Division Street Bridge contains both Youngstown's history as a steel town and its less clearly defined present. Like any landscape, Youngstown has been constructed through the interactions between people and the environment as part of a process of economic and social struggle. We settle in places where the land offers useful resources, and we immediately begin to transform the land into a landscape.[1] Over time, working together and against each other, we divide and transform land, build structures, abandon our own buildings, tear them down, and rebuild. Throughout the process, our efforts to make a living, to position ourselves, and to define our communities influence the way we construct and reconstruct the landscape.

One way of thinking about a landscape is to view it as a representation, a text that can be read, much like a novel or a painting. Landscapes are created collaboratively and often combatively by those who live in them, and they are never complete, never static. Just as we use approaches from literary studies to analyze a novel or from art history to interpret a painting, we use ideas from cultural geography to interpret how people's ideas and experiences, especially the struggles between individuals and groups, are represented in the landscape. This book focuses on how representations of work and the loss of work reflect and influence the identities of Youngstown as a community and the people who live here. One of the most important representations of work and its loss in Youngstown is the landscape itself, which has changed dramatically over the past two hundred years. By reading the history of that landscape, we can identify some of the central themes and tensions in Youngstown's history—themes and tensions that reflect the experiences of American workers and their communities nationwide.

As cultural geographer Don Mitchell has suggested, where there is work, there is social organization. And the social organization of work is full of conflict and power relations. Landscapes are formed as individuals and groups struggle for control over property, over work, and, often, over each other.[2] The centrality of the steel industry in Youngstown helped ensure that labor relations and class divisions in the mills were mirrored in the community, through the usually unofficial division of neighborhoods according to class, race, and ethnicity; the location of domestic, commercial, and monumental architecture; the paths used first by streetcars and later by highways; and the organization of public spaces such as Mill Creek Park.

But the relationship between conflict and landscape is reciprocal. Landscapes not only are constructed by economic and social conflict, but also reinforce such divisions of power. The sheer size of the steel mills, as well as their central location, reminded workers of the power of the steel company and of their own smallness, even as it persuaded them that they were part of a grand and significant operation. The hilltop locations and the whiteness of the city's cultural monuments—the main public library, the Butler Institute of American Art, Stambaugh Auditorium—suggested a clear contrast between the grime and soot of the mills and the refinement and purity of the elite, many of whose homes stood grandly beside these institutions. Workers, many of whom were Southern European immigrants and African Americans, were invited to aspire to the heights of high culture, but the buildings and their positions also reminded them that they did not belong.

Landscapes are always changing, and these changes, too, are constructed by and reinforce cultural struggles. When the community must decide where to locate a new school building or what to do with an abandoned amusement park (two topics of public debate in 1990s Youngstown), residents, business owners, politicians, and others struggle to influence the decision. In Youngstown, for example, several groups have organized and fought to save historic sites. Others associate such sites with loss and urge that old structures be torn down. Still others view these sites as spaces for possible redevelopment. While some emphasize the importance of the past, others focus on opportunities for future growth, and the debate suggests a tension between memory and erasure. Often, these public discussions reenact old struggles between divided neighborhoods, people from different classes and ethnic groups, and local political groups. The reconstructed landscape will emerge out of the struggle between these different groups, though the struggle itself may be hidden as the landscape changes.

In reading any landscape, we must look not only at what is there, but also at what is hidden, the places where the winners of past struggles have gained control. In some cases, and this is especially true in Youngstown, new versions of the landscape have erased the past. When the Jenny was torn down in 1997, one piece of Youngstown's history was erased, continuing the process of removing most of the old steel mill buildings from the valley. Other elements of the landscape are similarly hidden, including features that are tucked into out-of-the-way places, such as the row houses built for immigrant and African-American workers that are hidden from most people's awareness in a section of town that gets little traffic. If we want to understand the landscape we see from the Division Street Bridge today, we must be aware of what is absent or hidden as well as the features that we can see.

Perhaps more than any other kind of representation, landscape is, as Dolores Hayden notes, a "storehouse" for memory. For people who have lived in a place for a long time, the landscape carries individual and communal memories. We recall events that occurred in specific places, or who lived in the house on the corner, or the route we traveled daily to go to work. When landscapes change, those memories are displaced—not fully erased, but also not as fully present as they once were. Place is a central aspect of identity, a source for defining ourselves, in part because places contain memories, and memories help us to construct our sense of self. When the places that define us change, we ourselves change, and this is as true for communities as it is for individuals. Landscapes contain shared memories, landmarks that hold significance for many members of the community, places where people come together and neighborhoods that include some and exclude others. When physical spaces change, other kinds of representations may become more important. Bruce Springsteen's description of the "beautiful sky of soot and clay" in his song about Youngstown stands in for the memories of those who lived close to the mill, for whom a heavy layer of soot on the front porch every morning was a sign of prosperity. Local artist Bryn Zellers's sculptures using gears and tools remind steelworkers of their labor, helping to preserve and reconstruct memories that have been erased from the landscape.

While these new forms of representation repackage and revise the past, and may be elevated into official versions of place (as in museum displays about the history of the steel industry in Youngstown), they may not fully encompass popular memory. It is important, however, that we consider both these artistic and official versions of the story and the stories of those who lived in the community. As George Revill notes in his analysis of community studies, a careful reading of the landscape of a specific place can help us understand "the processes that create a sense of stability from a contested terrain in which versions of place and notions of identity are supported by different groups and individuals with varying powers to articulate their positions."[3] While landscape does not always reveal the experiences of the working class overtly, it is the representation with which workers and their families have the most intimate, day-to-day contact. If we want to understand the meaning of place and the meaning of work in this place, we must work from the ground up, the landscape of everyday life in Youngstown. A brief historical tour of five moments in Youngstown's history reveals how its landscape has been shaped by conflict.

1844

In 1844, on David Tod's Brier Hill estate, a rich vein of black coal was discovered that would soon transform the Mahoning Valley. The river valley had a few coal mines and a few charcoal and coking furnaces, but most of the land was still the private homestead of one of the most prominent members of one of Youngstown's landowning families. Tod served in the state senate for several years, and in 1861 he would be elected governor. Along with being a politician and owner of several small coal mines, Tod was one of the founders of the Akron Manufacturing Company, which produced "iron, steel, nails, stoves, pig iron, and castings of all kinds."[4] It seems fitting, then, that his house sat on the hill, looking out over his property and the Mahoning River valley.

Youngstown was still a small village in the early 1840s, surrounded by large estates owned by the Tods, the Wicks, the Stambaughs, and a few other families. Most of these families had come from New England and the mid-Atlantic states, some as early as the first decade of the century.[5] Because bog iron, limestone, and wood were plentiful in the Mahoning Valley, mining, charcoal, and iron production had been mainstays of the local economy since the early 1800s, when the Heaton brothers built the Hopewell Furnace at Yellow Creek. By the 1840s, deforestation began to deplete wood supplies and threaten the early pig iron production. But in 1844, the discovery at Brier Hill of a rich vein of dark, compressed coal would initiate a process of industrialization that would transform this fairly quiet valley into one of the most productive iron and steelmaking regions of the world.

"Brier Hill black" coal made possible a dramatic expansion of Youngstown's iron industry. Because it burned hotter than ordinary coal, it could be used without a separate coking process in a blast furnace. Blast furnaces soon became standard features of the Youngstown landscape: between 1846 and 1872, eleven furnaces would be built in Youngstown and another ten in surrounding areas, starting with the Eagle Furnace just south of Brier Hill. Most of the furnaces were located along the Mahoning River, since water was used in the process of creating the "blast" of a furnace and because the river provided access to the Pennsylvania and Ohio Canal, which connected Youngstown's growing iron industry with the Beaver and Ohio Rivers to the southeast and the Ohio and Erie Canal and Lake Erie to the northwest. As part of this growth, David Tod moved the Akron Manufacturing plant to Brier Hill in 1859, and the company was renamed the Brier Hill Iron Company.

Natural resources like coal, ore, wood, and the Mahoning River explain much of Youngstown's history. Youngstown had been founded in the early 1800s by John Young, who purchased more than fifteen thousand acres from the Connecticut Land Company in 1797, and soon thereafter he mapped out a grid plan with a central square downtown that is still evident two centuries later. Young selected the Mahoning Valley site in part because it appeared to offer good prospects as farmland. Native Americans in the area had burned out a large section of trees in the valley to make room for their own cornfields. Other natural resources suggested other opportunities for economic development, including salt and timber.

Natural resources do not tell the whole story. Rather, individuals claimed control over the land and its resources, and their desires for economic gain had a long-term influence on Youngstown's history. The Tod family was one of several whose purchases of farms from Young and other early settlers allowed them to become industrialists and, largely because of their economic prominence, leading figures in the local community. By the end of the century, they and their fellow industrialists would control several large Youngstown-based corporations, and their mansions, a country club, and significant civic buildings would mark their presence on the hills above the Mahoning River valley, the highest points of the landscape both physically and culturally.

Of course, theirs are not the only marks on the landscape. They built the iron and steel industry on a foundation of labor provided by thousands of immigrants, mostly from Wales, Germany, and Ireland. When Tod and other estate owners started large-scale coal mining and iron-making businesses on their property, they established small villages on their estates, giving over part of their land to provide housing for their workers. By 1874, a large portion of Tod's Brier Hill estate had been developed into housing and industrial areas. A map of the area also shows two schools, a Catholic church, and a Jewish cemetery.[6] Among the most prominent markers of the presence of the immigrant workers were their churches; by the 1860s, Youngstown had German Protestant, German Reformed, German Catholic, Welsh Methodist, Welsh Baptist, and other ethnic churches, most located just north of downtown Youngstown. This central location would have made the churches accessible for workers all around the Youngstown area, and it suggests that these early immigrant groups had not yet established their own neighborhoods. They lived near where they worked, often on property made available by the coal mine and furnace owners.

While the landscape may not yet have been divided sharply, divisions were developing around labor issues. Almost from the beginning, labor disputes involved battles not just between workers and owners but also among workers over the issue of who "owned" the work. Local historian Howard Aley traces organized labor in the Mahoning Valley back to the 1830s and records the first meeting of the Mechanics of Youngstown in 1843.[7] The first strikes hit in 1865, and again in 1869, when fifteen hundred coal miners were off the job for four months. Despite losses during these initial strikes, the miners struck again in 1873. This series of strikes represented an important first wave of labor-management conflict, a class-based division that remains significant in Youngstown today. The *Mahoning Vindicator* opposed the strike, arguing that the problem was "indolent miners who, having no families to support, prefer, under cover of a strike, to loaf away months in whisky saloons"[8] and "evil counselors of the miners—counselors who levy upon the miner for bounty upon which to live as lobbyists, etc., at Columbus and elsewhere."[9] A "Letter from an Operator" in the *Miner and Manufacturer*, the newspaper of the miners' union, suggested other sources of division. The letter describes a meeting between miners and operators, where the workers asked for information on the coal market. The writer argues that workers have no business knowing about the market or the value of their work: "They must take what we have a mind to give for it." He goes on to suggest that if owners want to control the miners, the workers and their children must be denied education. This is followed by a paragraph illustrating how difficult it is for a miner to support a family on forty dollars a month, and it ends with the comment that "We don't keep our poor houses at this figure. We must do something for them."[10]

One result of this, as the 1873 strike illustrates, was a growing sense of solidarity among workers. Coal miners in the Mahoning Valley were supported by miners throughout the state. The *Miner and Manufacturer* reported that the Grand Lodge of the Miners' and Laborers' Benevolent Association agreed to support the Youngstown strike by suspending work at coal mines across the state. On the same page, though, the paper printed a short note directed to the coal miners of the nearby Shenango Valley, reminding them that the Youngstown miners had provided financial aid and a supportive work stoppage when the Shenango miners had struck the previous year: "Now all the Ohio Miners ask is that the Shenango Miners will extend to them the same support that they received at our hands last summer."[11] Solidarity was apparently being built at this point, but it was not yet a given.

Yet this burgeoning sense of worker solidarity did not extend to scabs or to nonwhite workers. The *Miner and Manufacturer* noted approvingly that the Pennsylvania Senate was considering a bill to "[make] it a criminal offense to import or employ Chinamen in that state."[12] When the coal mine operators threatened to bring black workers in as scabs during the strike, the usually antilabor *Mahoning Vindicator* commented that "We wish such a step could be averted. We want neither negroes nor Chinese."[13] The *Miner and Manufacturer* suggested that the black workers would not be content to become "the slaves of Northern coal kings. . . . The negro is tired of slavery and . . . he will soon be as ready to resist oppression as the best miner in the land." The argument was made, however, not in support of the black workers but against them. The paper goes on to note that the companies could "do justice by their employees . . . as easily . . . with white as black miners" and "if they intend to oppress and enslave labor, the blackmen will soon show their ivory."[14] Thus, as Youngstown began a long period of dynamic growth, a foundation of conflict based on class and race was being built alongside the iron furnaces, industrialists' mansions, and modest workers' homes.

With the development of coal and iron production, Youngstown's population grew dramatically, doubling between 1870 and 1880 alone. One-third of the city's residents were recent immigrants, most of whom lived within easy walking distance of the mills. In Brier Hill and other immigrant neighborhoods, workers and their families were crowded in small, often badly built houses on inexpensive land alongside storefront bars, gaming establishments, and brothels. Conditions were deplorable, both in the mill and in workers' neighborhoods.

While business and religious leaders reviled the immigrants' "immoral" behavior and openly feared community and labor organizing, they also supported charitable efforts and the development of urban spaces that would improve the workers' quality of life. Youngstown's first city planner, Volney Rogers, understood the link between poor living conditions and strained labor relations. As his biographer Bridgett M. Williams writes:

> Tired employees, disheartened by low wages and fired by trade union propaganda would be prone, [Rogers] thought, to acts of aggression against employers. Without alternative recreation, disgruntled workers would turn to drink; or perhaps vent their aggressions against families. For so many people to be confined into such a small area of the city and do nothing to alleviate tensions and suffering seemed unconscionable.[15]

Rogers did do something. He helped develop a trolley system to provide transportation so workers could live farther away from work. Even more important, he created an intricate park system, including the twelve-mile-long, 450-acre Mill Creek Park, designed by Frederick Law Olmstead, who also designed New York's Central Park, which was built for much the same reason. While one end of the park overlooked the smoky mills and noisy railway lines, not far away visitors could find pristine, bucolic vistas and ramble through apparently untamed woods.

At the end of the century, while elite leaders, most of them Protestants, were developing the park and transportation systems, immigrant communities were working to establish their own presence on the local landscape. As more eastern and southern European immigrants arrived, workers' neighborhoods began to build their own mostly Catholic churches. At the same time, however, immigrants claimed a central position by building ethnic Catholic churches around the corner from First Presbyterian Church and St. John's Episcopal Church near downtown. The location of St. Columba's Cathedral just a few blocks from well-established Protestant churches helped the Catholic community define itself as central, and its network of ethnic Catholic churches indicated the immigrants' refusal to quietly fade into the cultural landscape.

In the sixty years after "Brier Hill black" coal was discovered, Youngstown had been transformed, from a community of small-scale industries, farms, and shops to an industrial city dominated by steel mills, settled by immigrant workers with strong national identities as well as a strong feeling of opposition to capitalists. The population had grown quickly through the end of the century, reaching more than forty-four thousand by 1900, and the landscape was reshaped. Estates turned into villages, and the valley began to fill with industrial structures.[16] Black smoke and railway lines became standard features. Class and race conflicts had made relatively little mark upon the landscape, but by the first decades of the next century, such conflict would become a central force shaping the local landscape.[17]

1918

On September 20, 1918, the Jeannette Blast Furnace was "blown in," lit by Mary Jeannette Thomas, daughter of the president of the Brier Hill Steel Company, for whom it was named. A front page photograph in the *Youngstown Telegram* the next day showed a little girl in a white dress, surrounded by steel company executives and a few workers, reaching to light the furnace with a small torch.[18] The Jeannette was one of the later structures built during almost twenty years of massive development of the local steel industry. Tied in part to World War I but also to the growth of the auto and construction industries, the American steel industry had increased its production dramatically. In Youngstown, the most obvious sign of growth appeared in the now almost unbroken line of mill buildings running along the river through the middle of town. The Brier Hill Steel Company had consolidated its holdings by buying up several neighboring mills, including the Youngstown Steel Company and the Thomas Steel Company, in 1912, but it was a latecomer in the development of large steelmaking operations. The National Steel Company (which merged with Carnegie Steel in 1903 and later became part of U.S. Steel) had built the Ohio Works soon after the turn of the century; Brown, Bonnell, and Company had sold its main mill just south of downtown to the New Jersey–based Republic Steel Company in 1899; and Youngstown Sheet and

Tube, incorporated in 1900, opened the valley's largest plant, later dubbed the Campbell Works, southeast of downtown between East Youngstown and Struthers. By 1918, Youngstown was one of the largest steel-producing areas of the country, second only to Pittsburgh. In 1927, it was the largest, and the Mahoning Valley became known as the Ruhr Valley of America.

The mill buildings were massive structures, tall and dark, with smokestacks and furnace towers rising above long, warehouse-like rolling and finishing mills. Plant compounds were large, including numerous buildings, so that each company occupied a long stretch of valley land. The mills were easily the most prominent feature of the local landscape, simply because of their size, but they also claimed attention through the black soot that darkened daytime skies and the bright fires that lit the sky at night.

The mills' dominance could be seen in other features of the landscape, too. Housing and commercial areas as well as transportation patterns were established based on the location of the mills and their workers. Downtown was flourishing in the teens and twenties, and residential and recreational areas had been developed in all directions, aided by streetcar lines first opened in the 1870s. Several bridges and easements had been constructed to facilitate movement between the lowest elevations in the valley, occupied by the mills and the downtown commercial district, and residential areas, which were filling the hills on all sides.

Industrial growth required population growth. The city's population grew dramatically between 1900 and 1930, as Italians, Slovaks, Hungarians, and Greeks arrived to work in the mills. In 1920, 25.6 percent of the population of Youngstown, more than 33,000 people, were foreign-born or the children of immigrants, giving Youngstown one of the highest percentages of foreign-born, unnaturalized residents in the entire country. During World War I and right after, African Americans joined the stream of incoming workers, many brought in by the steel companies as supplemental labor during the war and as scabs during two major strikes. The African-American population in Youngstown grew by 250 percent between 1910 and 1920, though the total number was only 6,662, while the city as a whole increased by 40 percent to more than 132,000.[19] The influx of both immigrants and blacks into the community and the mills would contribute to the rise of nativism, xenophobia, and the emergence of the Ku Klux Klan in Youngstown politics in the 1920s.

Many of the immigrants found housing in Brier Hill, which had long been an entry point for newcomers. Others moved into the Steel Street area to the west of the Ohio Works, and still others swelled the population of the small village of East Youngstown, which by 1915 had ten thousand residents, almost all of them immigrants.[20] New arrivals often boarded with families that had been in the area a few years longer, a practice that was discouraged by the steel companies and seen by middle-class critics as disruptive to family life. But as in other areas, a large portion of Youngstown's new residents were men who either were single or had left their families in Europe. Boarding met both their basic physical needs and their need to establish connections with their countrymen in this strange new place.

Brier Hill had been established as a workers' neighborhood in the 1860s, when the area was going through its first wave of industrial growth. According to historic preservationist Rebecca Rogers, much of the housing stock in the south section of Brier Hill dated to before 1874, and some of it was even older than that. On the north side of Brier Hill, buildings dated to around 1900, and another section to the east was developed around 1910. It was one of the first areas outside of downtown Youngstown to be linked to the city center by streetcar in 1875; horsecars had run the route even earlier. The area had been occupied originally by Welsh, Irish, and German miners and ironworkers, then Poles and Hungarians moved in, and finally Slovaks and Italians.[21] The neighborhood's churches—St. Casimir's Catholic Church, St. Rocco's Episcopal Church, and St. Anthony's Roman Catholic Church, all built before 1910—show the presence of these ethnic groups. By 1918, many families in the area were taking in boarders, but the neighborhood was one of the more established in the Youngstown area.

In contrast, East Youngstown was a rough, undeveloped area, with more saloons than grocery stores and no churches at all. The area was

Youngstown, Ohio, Population Characteristics, 1890–2000

	Total Population	% Change	Foreign-born	% of Total Population	African Americans	% of Total Population
1890	33,220	115.2				
1900	44,885	35.	112,207	27.2	915	2.0
1910	79,066	76.2	24,860	31.4	1,936	2.4
1920	132,358	67.4	33,834	25.6	6,662	5.0
1930	170,002	28.4	32,938	19.4	14,552	8.6
1940	167,720	–1.3	26,671	15.9	14,615	8.7
1950	168,330	0.4	21,410	12.7	21,459	12.7
1960	166,689	–1.0	16,851	10.1	31,677	19.0
1970	140,909	–15.5	9,126	6.5	35,285	25.0
1980	115,511	–18.0	6,636	5.7	38,478	33.3
1990	95,732	–17.1	2,879	3.0	36,423	38.0
2000	82,026	–14.3			35,937	43.8

Source: U.S. Census of Population.

Note: Foreign-born numbers for 1980 are an estimate.

populated almost entirely by recent arrivals, unskilled laborers, many from eastern and central Europe (Lithuanians, Poles, Serbs, Italians). Most worked at the nearby Youngstown Sheet and Tube and Republic Iron and Steel plants, where working conditions were barbaric. Most employees worked twelve to fourteen hours per day for a yearly starvation wage of $440.[22] Living conditions were equally bad. As John A. Fitch noted in an article in the *Survey* in 1916, workers' housing was crowded, dirty, and unsanitary:

> As East Youngstown is a village of more recent origin, one need not be surprised, perhaps, at the lack of sewers and running water. . . . But the mud of the unpaved streets of that desolated [sic] village—mud nearly hub deep, a clinging, all-pervasive mud that plasters itself on shoes and trouser-legs, distributes itself over sidewalks, up from steps and across thresholds, a tell-tale record of a town's perambulations—seems somehow to be symbolic of the community's civic development and its regard for human values.[23]

When the workers at both Youngstown Sheet and Tube and Republic Iron and Steel went on strike in January 1916, East Youngstown proved to be a powder keg. Headlines in the *Youngstown Vindicator* suggest the tensions that were building. On January 6, one headline reported that two strikers had threatened a local merchant, another noted the arrival of an American Federation of Labor organizer, and a third stated that the sheriff had been called to the plant as strikers began to gather. The January 7 *Vindicator* bears a large banner headline: "Strike Spreads and Mob Rule Reigns in Village."[24] Reports on the escalation of the strike into a riot vary; some report that company police guarding the north entrance to the plant fired the first shot into the crowd of strikers, while others claim that the company police fired in response to a shot from a striker. Whatever the initial act, the strike quickly turned violent. By the time it was over, four blocks of East Youngstown had burned to the ground, eight strikers had been killed and twelve wounded, and more than one hundred were injured.[25]

State troopers were called in on January 8, and the sheriff asked the mayor of East Youngstown to close local saloons.

Local newspapers blamed the riots on foreigners, suggesting that the strikers were spurred on by Bolshevik instigators. Writing a few years later, Joseph Butler Jr., one of the founders of Youngstown Sheet and Tube who would later establish the Butler Institute of American Art, described the East Youngstown strike as "a drunken orgy among workmen of foreign birth."[26] However, a grand jury investigation of the strike reported early in March 1916 that they could not find any evidence that "any foreign government was responsible for the riot." Rather, the report argues,

> the men assembled in the riotous mob, already greatly under the influence of liquor and filled with a deep dissatisfaction at the conditions existing as between them and their employers in the steel industries, were appealed to and inflamed by the feeling of loyalty for their foreign governments, which governments they considered would be injured by the manufacture and sale of the munitions of war then being made by the industries with which the men were employed, although the evidence against such agitators has to date not been sufficiently direct as to warrant indictments against them.[27]

More important, the report goes on to indict the steel companies and executives, noting that the companies had acted with "an absolute disregard . . . either of the rights of, or justice to, the laboring class, or of the public generally."[28] In other words, the strike and riot were caused by the mistreatment of workers by the steel companies. Not surprisingly, the grand jury was made up of middle- and working-class men, a grocery store operator, a blacksmith, a carpenter, a farmer, and others. Nor is it surprising that the indictment was overturned by a state judge just a few weeks later, who argued that "it is no crime to fix wages and labor is not a commodity."[29] That year, the *American Labor Year Book* called the East Youngstown strike "one of the most dramatic that the country has known" because of the "destruction of so much property, the remarkable solidarity of unorganized workers, and the indictment of company officials as responsible for the result of low wages and unendurable conditions."[30] The immediate result was an increase in wages, but the strike also contributed to the rise of what is often termed "welfare capitalism" and the "American plan," meaning greater attention to quality of life and a call for new forms of worker-management cooperation. In Youngstown as elsewhere, this led to developments such as worker housing, company newspapers, company-sponsored sports teams, and other leisure activities.

As with the 1873 coal miners' strike, however, the 1916 East Youngstown strike highlights the intersections between class conflict and issues of race and ethnicity. The division between workers and companies remains a steady feature of Youngstown's political landscape. In a community dominated by recent immigrants, another division emerged between "native" Americans, which by this time would include the descendants of the German, Welsh, and Irish immigrants of the mid-1800s, and the recent arrivals, who were seen almost uniformly as undisciplined, immoral, and a threat to a stable American society. The force of this view can be seen in two ways.

First, native-born American workers in Youngstown often saw labor organizing as a foreign-born movement. Consequently, throughout the Youngstown region including parts of western Pennsylvania, steel companies made effective use of the antagonism of usually separate groups—native-born workers, xenophobic and antiunion groups, and black strikebreakers—in defeating union organizing efforts. For example, in nearby New Castle, Pennsylvania, during the 1919 steel strike, union activities and parades were attacked by crowds including the American Legion, who asserted that union organizing was a threat to the companies and national institutions.[31]

Second, the Ku Klux Klan gained power and visibility in the Youngstown area in the 1920s by emphasizing the protection of Protestant values and American democracy, rather than through the white supremacy arguments for which they are most known today. When the Klan became actively involved in the 1923 city elections, critics argued that this would further divide the community. But the group gained popularity among middle-class whites and won a majority on the city council because it offered a response to the perceived power of the large immigrant population, most of whom were Catholics.[32]

The Catholic immigrants the Klan targeted didn't accept this opposition without a struggle, however. According to local historian William Jenkins, Irish and Italian immigrants worked together to fight the Klan, though the Italians were more aggressive and more inclined to violence. Italian immigrants in Lowellville, Niles, and Brier Hill were involved in bootlegging, gambling, and other illegal activities during the 1910s and 1920s. In addition to its illicit activities, however, the mob protected the immigrant community by defending its ownership of certain jobs outside of the mills and providing support for families during times of economic hardship, such as the Depression. The mob also acted as a kind of community police force, defending the immigrant community against the Klan and its supporters. Jenkins cites a series of confrontations in Niles, a few miles northwest of Youngstown, involving a group of Italians who were "noted for their bootlegging and gambling" and the local Klan, who were supported by the Mayor and city council of Niles.[33] During a particularly tense standoff, an Italian group led by Jim, Joe, and Leo "Shine" Jennings (the Anglicized version of the original family name DeGennaro) barricaded the streets of Niles to keep Klan members from holding a promised rally. A number of individuals on both sides were injured and killed, including two Klan leaders who, according to Jennings family lore, were murdered by the Jennings brothers and their associates.[34] Against a background of injustice, prejudice, and conflict, many in immigrant communities saw the mob and its corruption as providing a measure of fairness.[35]

Conflicts based on class, ethnicity, and race marked the local landscape in significant ways. Youngstown became a highly balkanized city, divided between "natives" and recent arrivals but also along lines of race and ethnicity that kept newcomers separate from each other. Several elements contributed to these divisions, including community and family ties that immigrants brought with them, the valuable support networks they formed with others from the same country or region, the development of ethnic churches and social clubs, and the practice of assigning jobs based on race and ethnicity. New arrivals usually stayed initially with families from the same area who had come over earlier, and the newcomer would be brought into the mill by a more experienced countryman. The practice of hiring by personal connections continued with the second generation as fathers and uncles brought young men into the plant, replicating existing ethnic patterns. Sam Donnorummo, a Brier Hill resident, reported that one of his relatives got him his first job at Sheet and Tube.[36] African-American James Davis was assigned the same job, at the same pay, that his father had, and he recalls that only three departments in the entire mill would even consider hiring black workers.[37]

But the practice wasn't simply a matter of workers following lines of personal connection to their jobs. The companies also recognized the value of keeping the various nationalities separated, since wariness about different people and language barriers could help keep workers from organizing to seek better wages or working conditions. White workers dominated the skilled jobs in mill-shaping areas, while nearly all African-American workers were found in the grimy jobs in the coke plants and blast furnaces. Jobs were further segregated by ethnicity. While not uniform, Irish were usually found in transportation, Italians in masonry, Slovaks and Hungarians in the open hearth, native-born Americans and English in supervision, and African Americans in general labor gangs.

This balkanization within the plants was echoed by balkanization in the community as different groups settled into fairly well-defined ethnic neighborhoods. In Brier Hill, St. Anthony's Italian Catholic church was built before the largest wave of Italian immigration, and its presence drew many arriving Italians to settle in that neighborhood. While some of the German, Welsh, and Irish families that had settled there earlier remained, and African Americans began to move in just to the east, Brier Hill defined itself as the center of Youngstown's Italian community. But Brier Hill was not exclusively Italian. Davis, who grew up there in the 1920s, describes Brier Hill as "the melting pot that never melted." The area was divided into sections along ethnic lines, and Davis remembers fights between children from the different areas. "There were very strong ethnic ties and considerations there," he says, but "the one thing we basically shared, everybody black and white, was the poverty." Others remember more harmonious neighborhoods, though almost always with a strong sense of ethnicity. East side resident John "Denny" Fitzgerald insists that everyone in his Irish and Italian neighborhood got along well, because they "just didn't have the animosity that you have today with people always trying to get ahead,"[38] and Oras Vines remembers having no problems as the only African-American child in a Struthers neighborhood populated by a mix of ethnicities—Irish, Slovak, Polish, and Romanian.[39] But some of that community harmony was facilitated by careful maintenance of ethnic identities through churches, civic groups, and informal networks. Campbell resident Edward Stonework Jr. notes that each ethnic group in the area had its own restaurants and bars, a practice that created a "harmonious situation."[40]

In some public areas, however, people from different ethnic groups came together more easily. At Idora Park, the amusement park located at the end of the Park and Falls Street Railway line, Youngstown's ethnic communities came together but also asserted their ethnic and racial identities. Idora's rides, midway, ballroom, games, and picnic areas offered a family-oriented alternative to bars and clubs, and in the park and on the streetcars that brought people to the park, people from different backgrounds mixed easily. At the same time, Idora Park sponsored events that reinforced ethnic and racial categories. African Americans could use Idora's swimming pool and ballroom only at designated times. Idora also sponsored ethnic festivals featuring exhibitions of national dances and costumes, religious services, and ethnic foods.[41] These festivals commodified group identity, defining it as something to be celebrated and displayed in a commercial setting, rather than in free public spaces such as churches and neighborhoods.

One of the most significant ways that divisions and conflicts were inscribed on the landscape was through the Youngstown Sheet and

Tube Company's development of worker housing. In part as a response to the 1916 strike, which some attributed to the instability of East Youngstown and the workers' continuing allegiance to their home countries, Youngstown Sheet and Tube embarked on an ambitious plan to build homes and townhouses for its workers. While other companies had provided some worker housing, as U.S. Steel did in McDonald and Youngstown, Sheet and Tube developed a large-scale program that had several significant outcomes. Youngstown Sheet and Tube formed the Buckeye Land Company in 1917, which built three tracts of houses in Struthers and an area of townhouses as rental properties in East Youngstown (which was renamed Campbell in 1923 after the president of Youngstown Sheet and Tube). The plan had two purposes. First, having adequate worker housing would help the company secure government contracts. In September 1918, the federal government announced that it would assign war contracts only to those communities that had sufficient worker housing, and because of development programs by Youngstown Sheet and Tube, Carnegie Steel, Republic Rubber, and others, Youngstown was included on the list of communities with adequate housing.[42] Second, the company housing program was designed to help Youngstown Sheet and Tube gain control over its workers. Through the Buckeye Land Company, Youngstown Sheet and Tube would encourage its workers to buy houses, therefore creating a more stable, reliable, docile workforce. The combination of having a fairly significant debt and having the mortgage held by the employer would deter workers from joining unions or striking. The housing was, as local historian Donna DeBlasio points out, well constructed and modern, and both mortgage rates and rents were reasonable.[43] Yet despite their neat, benign appearance and the real benefits to workers of having affordable access to high-quality housing, these buildings are the most concrete, enduring representation of worker-management conflict on the Youngstown landscape. Most of the Buckeye buildings still exist, while the mill is almost entirely gone.

In addition to the investment of home owning, company housing allowed Youngstown Sheet and Tube a way of controlling workers'

For Rent—In Campbell

A few houses at low **rates**, for white employees, as follows:

2 Rooms and Bath, Upstairs,	$11.00 per Month
2 Rooms and Bath, Downstairs	$13.50 per Month
3 Rooms and Bath, 2 floors	$16.00 per Month
4 Rooms and Bath, 2 floors	$18.50 per Month

Newly painted inside, Clean and Comfortable. Easy walking distance to North Gate of Campbell Works. Hot and cold water, sewer, gas and electricity available.

Rental Agents Office on the property at No. 40 Chambers Street.

?

Where would your family live Mr. **Employee,** if you were to suddenly die of pneumonia or by automobile accident? The Buckeye Land Company **pays the premiums for 10 years** on the Life Insurance for the unpaid balance which goes with the sale of each Buckeye House. This is worth your investigation. **For your family's sake, give them this protection.** Mail us this coupon for further information.

Name ....
Check No. ....
Address ....

THE BUCKEYE LAND CO.

Advertisement for the Buckeye Land Company, Youngstown Sheet and Tube Bulletin, *15 February 1930* interactions with each other. By designating different housing for different workers, the company helped to keep members of various ethnic and class groups separate, creating an additional obstacle to successful worker organizing. Youngstown Sheet and Tube's worker housing was divided into four plats, whose names and locations emphasized class and race differences between workers: Loveland for "skilled workmen, foremen, and superintendents"; Overlook for American-born "high grade employees"; Highview for "worthy" foreign-born workers; and Blackburn, a rental area for recent immigrants and African Americans.[44] The Blackburn plat in East Youngstown, the only one of the four plats located downwind from the massive Campbell works, provided two areas of concrete slab townhouses for recent immigrants and African Americans, though each group was assigned a separate housing area. The others were built in Struthers, south and west of the plant. Thus, newcomers who had not yet proven their loyalty and blacks who were regularly used as strikebreakers during disputes were kept separate from the more "valuable" white skilled workers.

Company housing, especially the Highview plat, was also a tool for encouraging Americanization. "Foreign-born employes [*sic*] who have made themselves valuable employes [*sic*] in the mill and are worthy of living under better conditions than many other convenient locations now afford" were invited to consider buying a home in Highview.[45] As the language here indicates, the company saw Highview as a reward for those foreign-born workers who were interested in becoming "good Americans." Other ads for the Highview plat emphasized the "American-like conditions" it offered for those "who want to live under good, clean, healthy conditions, where their children can grow up as Americans."[46] This push for Americanization was not unique to Youngstown Sheet and Tube, of course, nor was company housing the only tool employed. Americanization was a community-wide effort involving English courses at the YMCA and the newly created Youngstown International Institute, settlement houses, and regular public commentaries in the newspapers and by politicians. But Youngstown Sheet and Tube's Buckeye Land Company construction of worker housing inscribed conflicts over Americanization as well as class conflict on the residential landscape of Youngstown.

1942

The year 1942 was a pivotal one for steelworkers and the residents of Brier Hill. With the Depression over, the evening skies above the Jenny were again red and its great stacks belched the "black gold" (soot) that daily dusted the Brier Hill landscape. At the height of World War II, Youngstown's steel mills were producing at full capacity, and the Great Depression had become a lingering memory. A major victory for organized labor provided another reason for celebration: five years after the "Little Steel" strike, the National Labor Relations Board (NLRB) found the steel companies guilty of unfair practices during the strike. The "Little Steel" companies (Youngstown Sheet and Tube, Republic, Inland, and Bethlehem) were forced to recognize the Steel Workers Organizing Committee (SWOC) as the bargaining representative of its employees. Brier Hill steelworkers, together with their counterparts at the Campbell Works and Republic, could look ahead hopefully to a new era of industrial unionism that promised a level of prosperity and security unknown to steelworkers and their families and that would again change the landscape of the Youngstown area. To be sure, the residents of Brier Hill had much to celebrate in 1942, even as they sent their men and women to war.

The NLRB ruling was the culmination of a long period of labor unrest that had reached its zenith during the "Little Steel" strike in 1937. As a result, organizers and striking steelworkers who had been fired were reinstated with back pay, and Youngstown Sheet and Tube and Republic entered into collective bargaining with the SWOC. The acceptance of unionism and a negotiated agreement did not end the labor and social conflict in Youngstown, however. Rather, it institutionalized conflicts that had developed over the previous fifty years, solidifying a pattern of class conflict that would remain even as the landscape of Youngstown shifted dramatically.

By the 1930s, Youngstown had become the prototypical industrial city. Fueled by the growth of the steel industry, Youngstown's multiracial and ethnic population reached its peak in the early 1930s. In the late 1920s, the city's economic success could be seen all across the local landscape, in the smoke-filled skies over the busy steel mills, the high rate of home ownership (48 percent in 1929), and a thriving downtown business district full of fancy movie theaters and busy department stores.[47] The community's civic pride was displayed in its public library, art museum, and two large, elaborate public auditoriums, as well as in the success of a local "community chest" fund-raising drive. All this pointed to a bright future for the city. But things changed when the Depression hit the steel industry.

Youngstown was among the hardest hit of America's industrial cities, with unemployment at 23.1 percent, second to only Denver. Earlier class tensions surfaced with renewed force during the 1930s, starting with demonstrations for more public support. Communists from Ohio, Pennsylvania, and West Virginia descended on Youngstown on Memorial Day 1931. As Youngstown's mayor, Joseph Heffernan, described it in an article in the *Atlantic Monthly,* the protesters gathered "to emphasize their class struggle. Among the large foreign-born and colored population, they thought they would have a fertile field for revolutionary doctrine, and they counted upon being able to work more effectively when these groups were conscious that they had no real part in the patriotic celebration." The demonstration ended in a riot with over two hundred arrested.[48]

Demonstrations continued throughout the Depression, eventually focusing around union organizing efforts at the local steel mills. While workers had shown their capacity for militant activity in 1916 and 1919, the large employment pool of immigrants, jurisdictional rivalries among unions, and the local ownership of the mills inhibited the development of labor unions in Youngstown. But as local ownership consolidated and some mills were taken over by national companies, and as union activism nationwide challenged practices such as company unions and corporate paternalism, steelworkers in Youngstown flocked to trade unions, setting off a key struggle with the captains of industry. After years of rejecting unions, "Big Steel" mills in Youngstown, U.S. Steel's Ohio and McDonald Works, were quickly organized, but the "Little Steel" companies, including Republic and Youngstown Sheet and Tube, resisted, leading to the famous "Little Steel" strike of 1937. While the most dramatic and publicized episodes of "Little Steel" took place in South Chicago, the "most important theatre of the strike was in Youngstown, Warren and Niles where Republic and Youngstown Sheet and Tube had their chief operations" and where thirty-two thousand workers joined the strike.[49]

Republic and Youngstown Sheet and Tube were virulently antiunion. Their chief executives, Thomas Girdler and Frank Purnell, were proponents of what is called the "Mohawk Valley formula." Perhaps the most systematic method developed to defeat union organizing and strikes, the formula called for employers to label union leaders as agitators; develop propaganda networks in the community to belittle union demands; mobilize "citizen committees" and stage mass meetings supporting employers; organize community police and legal machinery against imaginary union violence; build and help arm a large police force composed of local, state, and company police and vigilantes; develop puppet "employees' associations"; and stage well-publicized back-to-work movements and large marches to dramatize plant reopenings and to suggest the moral superiority of nonstriking workers. The Mohawk Valley formula was most effectively used in the "Little Steel" strike, especially in the Youngstown-Warren area.[50] Such practices added to the already tense relations between the working class and the elite.

In Youngstown, the antiunion actions of Republic Steel and Youngstown Sheet and Tube went even further. Both companies hired extra plant guards and company police and stockpiled munitions. Landing strips were constructed inside the plant gates in order to continue to supply operations during the strike. The companies helped orchestrate the activities of employer associations, civic and public interest groups, and local government officials. Youngstown's city council granted the mayor emergency powers, and the county sheriff hired additional deputies taken from the ranks of antiunion mill employees. On June 19, 1937, at the Stop Five gate outside of Republic Steel, a riot erupted between company police and strikers and their families. Two strikers were killed and twenty-three others were wounded in the melee. Ohio governor Martin L. Davey called in the National Guard, who began to harass steelworkers or anyone sympathetic to SWOC organizing. With the mills effectively militarized and community support for the workers undermined, employees began to return to work.[51]

But while Republic Steel and Youngstown Sheet and Tube won in the short run, the 1942 NLRB ruling put the move to unionism back on track. The companies were forced to sign bargaining agreements and reinstate union members fired during the strike. Equally important, a separate government investigation publicized the companies' actions during the strike, reinforcing long-standing patterns of labor-management conflict. In addition, because of the investigation and the NLRB ruling, workers felt for the first time that the government was on the side of workers instead of employers. The balance of power between labor and management shifted just slightly in favor of workers.

In the postwar era, disputes over wages, hours, and working conditions meant that strikes and labor conflict became ritualized and institutionalized. While workers gained better wage and benefit packages, and a complex network of negotiated job rights developed covering a wide range of workplace activities, the repeated strikes also meant frequent periods of unemployment.[52] Among the postwar labor disputes, the steel strike of 1952 would become particularly important for Youngstown because it was the first time the president of the United States seized a major portion of an American industry in peacetime, which led to a historic confrontation over the constitutional question of the separation of powers: *Youngstown Sheet and Tube v. Sawyer.* Truman argued that steel companies had engaged in a "conspiracy against the public interest," and as a result the state could take over the mills. This connection between the community interest and the seizure of the mills was imprinted on the consciousness of Youngstown steelworkers. It would resurface in the 1970s when the community faced widespread shutdowns and infused efforts to prevent mill closings and seek community ownership of the mills under the principle of eminent domain.[53]

Yet even while strikes created uneven patterns of employment, Jack Metzgar argues in *Striking Steel: Solidarity Remembered* that the union struggles of the 1950s also brought remarkable gains in workplace rights and improvements in the standard of living.[54] Good labor contracts helped workers afford to move to the suburbs and begin the process of buying an apparently middle-class lifestyle. Because such a large proportion of Youngstown's working class worked in the steel industry, these changes had an especially powerful effect on the area, reconfiguring the physical landscape of Youngstown and its imaginative landscape of work and conflict. Although some scholars argue that the success of unions in the 1940s and 1950s led, ironically, to a decline in working-class identity, with consumption replacing production as the basis of class definition, Youngstown's history suggests a more complicated reading.[55] While strong support for the strikes of the period suggests a high level of working-class solidarity, racial and ethnic divisions meant that postwar gains affected workers differently. In part because of discrimination in government loan programs, but also because they already held higher-paid jobs in the mills, whites were able to move to the suburbs. For African Americans, meanwhile, improved wages meant that more families could buy homes in the city, providing the foundation for black businesses and a thriving middle-class community.

Brier Hill had long since become a predominantly Italian steelworkers' neighborhood, but soon its residents began to look to the suburbs. They moved to the west side of Youngstown, to Austintown, to Boardman, and to Girard. Suburban migration began in the 1940s, causing the city's population to drop while the metropolitan area continued to grow. As whites moved out, more African Americans moved in, a population shift reinforced by the development of two public housing developments bordering the Brier Hill area. The trend would escalate in the 1960s. In 1960, almost 65 percent of those living in Brier Hill were white, about half of them foreign-born, and most of those from Italy. Ten years later, almost three thousand of those residents had left, and the neighborhood was now 63 percent African-American and Hispanic. Meanwhile, the suburbs were growing rapidly. In Boardman, for example, between 1949 and 1954, more than two thousand homes were constructed for seven thousand new residents, and $33 million was spent on new business construction.[56]

While residents often describe these moves as simple choices, the expression of a desire for a nicer, newer, cleaner neighborhood, larger forces contributed to the shift. As in other places, suburbanization was fueled in part by racism, which had long been reinforced by hiring practices in the mills that separated workers according to both race and ethnicity. These divisions were enforced by labor and company officials, the seniority provisions in the collective bargaining agreement, and underlying solidarity around whiteness.

As Youngstown's African-American population grew, and as Puerto Ricans began to arrive in the early 1950s, white families fled to the new suburbs, revising some patterns of ethnic neighborhoods.[57] In his study of steelworkers in Youngstown, Robert Bruno documents the shift toward ethnic diversity and away from racial diversity: "premiddle income wages [had] produced more racially integrated neighborhoods than ethnically mixed ones. But as collective bargaining began to raise wages, steelworkers moved away from the mills and found themselves living next door to families of different ethnicity."[58] As neighborhoods became more ethnically mixed, churches became the most important centers of ethnic life in Youngstown. Many families that lived in the suburbs drove into the city, to Brier Hill and other areas, to attend Italian, Polish, Hungarian, Irish, and other ethnic churches and clubs. While ethnic working-class enclaves broke down, once racially integrated neighborhoods became more segregated. The process was supported by lending and real estate practices, which kept black home buyers from even looking at homes in the new suburbs, much less being approved for home loans.

Even as the community divided along racial lines, some spaces continued to function as points of intersection. In the workplace, some African Americans began to agitate for access to better jobs, challenging company practices such as the use of tests to bar black workers from some positions. Eventually such agitation led to a major lawsuit against both the steel companies and the United Steel Workers of America. The testimony of African-American workers helped persuade the court to issue a consent decree that would aid women and minorities in getting hired and promoted. In leisure spaces, too, when whites and blacks came together, tensions sometimes escalated. At Idora Park, for example, groups of African-American and white teenagers clashed. In 1967, one such scuffle escalated into riot after two young men "reportedly goaded a large crowd by shouting 'Black Power!' and 'Kill the Police!'"[59]

The suburban expansion of the Youngstown landscape was further reinforced by changes in transportation patterns, especially the development of the I-680 beltway in the 1960s, which was part of a larger urban renewal effort. Together with two other highway sections built during the period, I-680 forms a rough circle around downtown Youngstown, with spokes connecting to the Ohio Turnpike to the south and west. The $90 million project was part of the national interstate highway development program, strongly supported by local government, especially city engineer, later mayor, J. Philip Richley. The I-680 project destroyed several old neighborhoods in Youngstown, and many working-class residents were relocated. For some, relocation offered an opportunity to sell homes with declining property values and move to "finer living quarters" in the suburbs.[60] But others preferred to stay and protect their neighborhoods. As Richley notes, "We dispossessed an awful lot of people between the urban renewal program and the expressway system. We probably relocated about a thousand families during the fifties and sixties, and it was a very, very difficult job." While he acknowledges that relocation is a "complete psychological and physical upheaval," he also cites the development of I-680 as his proudest achievement. As he saw it, the expressway system provided mobility so people could relocate and allowed for commercial and residential development. I-680 gave "consumers choices about where to live, work and where . . . to send [their] children to school." Richley felt that this was his most important accomplishment. Put differently, the chief engineer and mayor of Youngstown felt his greatest achievement in office was helping people leave the city. The promised residential and commercial development resulting from the construction of I-680 never occurred in the city, but the suburbs boomed.

The highway project effectively cut downtown Youngstown off from much day-to-day traffic, directing drivers and, more important, shoppers to the new strip malls being built by two rising local families, the DeBartolos and the Cafaros. In 1951, the DeBartolo Corporation opened its first shopping center, Boardman Plaza, south of Youngstown, offering a department store, an ice cream parlor, and the area's largest grocery store as well as a twelve-hundred-car parking lot. The first Cafaro mall was built a few years later in Niles, northeast of Youngstown. Nationally, as historian Lizabeth Cohen notes, residential movement to the suburbs combined with the decline of downtowns created an opportunity for developers to "reimagine community life with their private projects at its heart."[61] While some pattern of movement from older neighborhoods to newer ones had existed earlier in the century, Youngstown saw a dramatic shift in the 1950s and 1960s as increasing numbers of residents and businesses moved away from the city center. Even the steel companies took part in suburbanization, even though the mills remained in the city. In 1956, Youngstown Sheet and Tube moved its corporate operations to a fifty-two-acre site near Boardman Plaza. As consumption and commerce were increasingly associated with these developing "edge cities," Youngstown's central business district declined.

As workers and commerce moved out of the central part of the city, the shape of Youngstown's landscape changed, but the underlying conflicts inherited from the community's past did not dissipate. The new suburban neighborhoods and sparkling new shopping malls might have looked like conflict-free zones, new spaces with yet-to-be-determined meanings, but sometimes what looks new rests quite solidly on old foundations. Such was the case with Youngstown's developing suburbs. As residents of Brier Hill and other urban working-class neighborhoods left the city, they didn't necessarily leave their working-class lives behind. In some cases, new neighborhoods reconstructed old patterns. Fred and Josephine Ross, for example, moved from Brier Hill to a new housing development on the west side in 1966, but their new neighbors included a number of steelworkers and other working-class families from Brier Hill.[62] While patterns of ethnicity may have shifted, the new suburban neighborhoods often replicated the working-class sensibilities of the urban areas left behind. As Bruno notes, workers had developed a strong sense of class conflict, and moving to a new home or buying a boat didn't erase that sensibility.

The division between workers and more affluent classes was also reconstructed in suburban housing. As white steelworkers and other

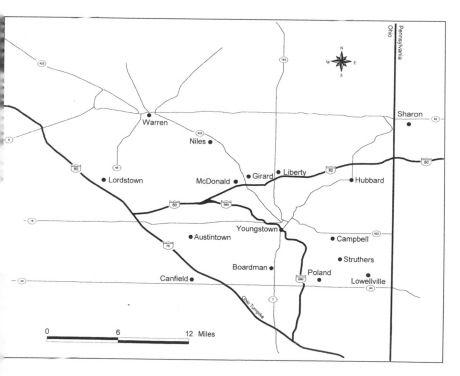

The Youngstown-Warren Area, Dean Chance, 2001

industrial laborers were settling in Austintown and Boardman, more affluent families headed for Poland and Canfield, and most of the families of the local "iron barons," as John Ingham calls them, left Youngstown altogether by the 1950s, moving to Cleveland and the east coast.[63] Some areas of Liberty and Boardman saw more upscale development, while Austintown and the satellite communities of Girard, Niles, and Hubbard remained steadfastly working class.

Class and race conflicts were rooted in the history of the steel industry, but other conflicts with more complicated roots also survived in the changing Youngstown landscape, evidenced by the city's high crime rate. Where local organized crime in the 1920s and 1930s had protected the interests of immigrants against the Ku Klux Klan, by the 1950s separate factions of the local mob had merged with crime families from Chicago and New York and were now battling each other for control of illegal activities. In 1963, a *Saturday Evening Post* cover story dubbed Youngstown "Crime Town, USA," describing seventy-five car bombings, known locally as "Youngstown tune-ups," and eleven killings. Youngstown became a mob battlefield largely because of its location midway between New York and Chicago. The rackets in Youngstown were very profitable. "The bug" (numbers), barbut (dice), bookmaking, and the operation of "cheap shots" (after-hours liquor, gambling, and prostitution establishments) had long flourished in Youngstown, especially in ethnic communities such as Brier Hill, Campbell, Struthers, and McDonald. By the early 1960s, these activities began to appear in Austintown and other suburbs. Like class and race conflicts, organized crime patterns also emerged in the new edge cities.

So embedded was organized crime that the *Saturday Evening Post* argued that "the Youngstown area exemplifies the truism that rackets cannot survive without two basic conditions—the sanction of police and politicians and an apathetic public. Here those conditions have combined to produce a breakdown of the democratic process." No doubt, local politicians and police were under the influence of organized crime. But so pervasive was the "climate of corruption" in what the FBI called "Murdertown" that most citizens, including bankers and church officials, viewed it "with cynical indifference." Despite systematic efforts by the FBI to rid the area of corruption, little was accomplished. After all, an FBI agent confided, "the racketeers and the crooked politicians have no other way to exist. It's a simple question of economics."[64]

The territorial fights among crime families in Youngstown were mirrored in the legitimate business sector. Local steel companies tried to protect both product and labor markets from competition from new industries. Harry Meshel, a former Ohio Senate leader from Youngstown, argued that in the 1950s, "a small tightly linked elite" used friendly politicians, banks, and even labor unions to actively undermine economic development and diversification.[65] For example, throughout the 1950s and 1960s, the steel industry fought to exclude the growth of the aluminum industry in Youngstown by making land acquisition difficult and creating a hostile climate for business. Consequently, while other regions with similar infestations of organized crime saw increases in production, construction, and economic diversification in the 1950s, Youngstown stagnated economically as a result of monopolistic practices by local business elites. This economic stagnation would be intensified by yet another strike—not a labor strike, but a capital strike.

1977

On September 19, 1977, Youngstown Sheet and Tube announced the closing of the Campbell Works. Within the next five years, Youngstown Sheet and Tube would close the Brier Hill Works, U.S. Steel would shut down both the Ohio and the McDonald Works, and Republic Steel closed its Youngstown Works. The Ohio Bureau of Employment Services estimated that fifty thousand jobs were lost in basic steel and related industries. Estimates suggest that the working class of Youngstown lost $1.3 billion in manufacturing wages annually, unemployment reached 24.9 percent in 1983, and the community saw an unprecedented number of personal bankruptcies and foreclosures.[66] Since the 1950s, economics textbook publishers had seen the term "depression" as anachronistic, arguing that the smaller recessions of the 1970s were not significant enough to merit such a label. But they introduced the term "regional depression" to describe what happened in Youngstown. The shutdowns brought many changes to Youngstown's landscape, though in some cases, it simply continued a trend that had developed during the 1960s as the community abandoned its city core and the working class turned to other kinds of work.

While "Black Monday" in September 1977 stands out as the major historical marker of deindustrialization in Youngstown, the steel industry had begun to decline years before. Following the series of strikes in the 1940s and 1950s, Youngstown mills were consistently the last to restart production, owing largely to their landlocked position. As the economics, technology, and scale of steel production changed, it became more essential to locate facilities near large bodies of water to reduce transportation costs.[67] That is, the geographic location that had once been Youngstown's advantage was now an obstacle to reinvestment. In the 1950s and 1960s, U.S. steelmakers began to disinvest in their steel operations and diversify into other industries. As a result they did not invest significantly in new steel technologies and lost their productivity leadership.[68] Rather, they tried to protect their steel interests by fighting unfair trading practices of foreign steel companies.

In Youngstown, despite repeated pleas from steelworkers, companies did not upgrade the old mills. By 1969, when Youngstown Sheet and Tube was taken over by Lykes Corporation, all of the local mills were owned by outside corporations, none of which were committed to reinvestment. Rather, they seemed content to run the old mills into decay and disrepair, until they simply could not compete on a global scale. Youngstown Sheet and Tube had been a local company with deep roots in the Mahoning Valley, and its headquarters remained in the area even though it had steelmaking and mining facilities elsewhere. Lykes Corporation was a highly leveraged conglomerate with headquarters outside of Youngstown and no commitment to or history with the local community. Lykes saw Youngstown Sheet and Tube as a means to increase cash flow and provide steel for its primary interest in shipbuilding. Despite promises to modernize its Youngstown operations, the company focused its modernization efforts on the Indiana Harbor Works in East Chicago, Illinois. The Campbell Works and Brier Hill were never upgraded. The capital strike was on.

The valley landscape reflected seventy years of steelmaking. While pollution control devices had been introduced, the earth, air, and water surrounding the mills had long been polluted from years of dumping the by-products of steelmaking. Inside the plant, workers faced an increasingly dangerous environment as a result of breakdown of the aging equipment. While preventive maintenance did occur, it was merely a holding action as steelworkers were frequently forced to "cannibalize" parts from one area of a plant to keep other areas functioning. As breakdowns increased, productivity dropped and provided Lykes with another convenient excuse for the eventual plant closing. To make matters worse, Lykes asked steelworkers in the 1970s to join the company in opposition to mandates by the Environmental Protection Agency (EPA) to clean up the mills. With the threat of taking money away from modernization and shutdowns looming, the steelworkers felt they had no other choice but to "make book" with the company. In retrospect, the steelworkers' loyalty to the company was reduced to economic blackmail.

Community response to the mill closings reflects important aspects of Youngstown's history. The city's churches, many the focal point for the area's ethnic communities, and the most militant members of the local labor community almost immediately began to organize. Church and labor leaders organized the Ecumenical Coalition of the Mahoning Valley. With assistance from Attorney Staughton Lynd and Gar Alperovitz, director of the National Center for Economic Alternatives, the coalition established local and national research networks, organized community support, explored alternative employee ownership plans, developed legislative agendas, and engaged in direct action that included the occupation of Youngstown Sheet and Tube administrative buildings and U.S. Steel headquarters in Pittsburgh.[69] As Scott Camp argues in a study comparing the responses to shutdowns in Youngstown and Johnstown, Pennsylvania, Youngstown was more militant because it had a stronger history of independent unionism, more activist local clergy, and a more diverse local steel industry, with several large companies rather than just one.[70]

Overall, the Ecumenical Coalition was viewed natonally as a remarkable example of community organizing against deindustrialization, but it received only moderate support from the local community and little support from local or national institutions, including banks and the steelworkers union. While the Ecumenical Coalition's plans to buy the Campbell Works and then the Brier Hill Works did not succeed, the group did draw national and international attention to plant closings. They challenged the notion that shutdowns were part of a natural economic order, and they reminded the nation of the social and moral dimensions of deindustrialization. Further, in part because of the coalition's efforts, Congress eventually passed plant closing legislation to ensure workers adequate warning of shutdowns. In other communities throughout the Rust Belt, local government organizations, guided by the Youngstown example, enlisted the principle of eminent domain, the right of the local community to claim ownership of private property for community uses, to claim abandoned industrial sites for a variety of community and economic development projects.

While this spirited response to the shutdowns invigorated some in the community, the overall effect of the steel mill closings on the Youngstown landscape was devastating. Those who could left or retired, while others tried to retrain or to start their own businesses. Still others became itinerant construction workers.[71] While some made successful transitions, most former steelworkers experienced either forced retirement, intermittent employment, or unemployment. In fact, unemployment in Youngstown was over 10 percent throughout the 1980s and reached depression levels in 1982 and 1983. Even when unemployment rates dropped to 12 percent in the mid-1980s, much of the decrease could be accounted for by people who had given up looking for work or who had left the area.

Job loss had a direct impact on the landscape. Whether workers remained unemployed or found new jobs that paid less, the mill closings led to significant declines in personal income, and as a result bankruptcies doubled between 1979 and 1980 to almost two thousand claims. Youngstown continued to have high bankruptcy rates well into the 1990s, due to a combination of high unemployment rates and the lower pay offered for the jobs that were available. Unable to keep up with mortgage payments, many lost their homes.[72] As more and more houses stood empty and the real estate market declined, property values dropped precipitously. This represented another type of economic loss, since working-class people often had most of their assets invested in their houses. Arson increased dramatically, averaging two a day for much of the 1980s. The fires associated with arson had replaced the fires that were associated with the mills. Other dilapidated houses were torn down, leaving city blocks ravaged. As a result, a large portion of Youngstown's housing stock was destroyed, leaving the city dotted with empty lots. Near the city core, Youngstown State University tore down abandoned homes to create new parking lots, which were needed as enrollment increased because of government loan programs that made it possible for some ex-steelworkers and their children to enter the university. In a town that had once boasted the highest home ownership rate in the United States, the beautiful residential landscape of urban Youngstown was reduced to small districts that were, as some put it, "still worth saving."

Most of the abandoned property was in the city, in residential neighborhoods that had been populated mostly by African Americans.[73] As whites sought other employment starting in the 1960s, and especially after the 1974 consent decree forcing both the steel companies and the unions to enhance opportunities for nonwhite workers, African Americans began moving into higher-paid jobs in the mills, and Youngstown's black community became even stronger economically. Nonetheless, African-American workers were still likely to have

Youngstown-Warren MSA, Annual Average Civilian Labor Force Estimates (since 1970[a])

	Labor Force[b]	Employment	Unemployment	Unemployment Rate[c]
1970[d]	218,600	205,000	13,600	6.2
1971	225,100	207,100	18,000	8.0
1972	226,900	212,100	14,800	6.5
1973	232,500	221,800	10,800	4.6
1974	236,700	223,700	13,000	5.5
1975	236,700	209,800	26,900	11.4
1976	234,200	210,500	23,700	10.1
1977	234,000	215,000	19,000	8.1
1978	235,200	217,500	17,700	7.5
1979	237,100	219,900	17,100	7.2
1980	238,900	210,500	28,400	11.9
1981	234,000	205,700	28,200	12.1
1982	237,000	190,300	46,600	19.7
1983	225,600	188,100	37,500	16.6
1984[e]	222,200	195,900	26,300	11.8
1985	221,300	196,300	25,000	11.3
1986	223,700	200,000	23,700	10.6
1987	221,600	200,000	21,600	9.7
1988	221,300	204,900	16,400	7.4
1989	223,200	208,400	14,900	6.7
1990[f]	277,700	257,500	20,100	7.3
1991	278,400	258,000	20,400	7.3
1992	284,400	256,900	27,500	9.7
1993	280,500	256,900	23,700	8.4
1994	28,300	260,700	22,300	7.9
1995	284,500	266,600	17,900	6.3
1996	283,100	265,200	17,900	6.3
1997	286,000	269,300	16,700	5.8
1998	283,500	266,600	16,900	5.9
1999	282,100	266,600	15,500	5.5
2000	278,300	262,600	14,800	5.3

[a]Defined as Columbiana, Mahoning, and Trumbull Counties. Before 1990, defined as Mahoning and Trumbull Counties. These estimates, prepared in cooperation with the Bureau of Labor Statistics and U.S. Department of Labor are by place of residence and revised to 2000 benchmarks.

[b]Employment and unemployment may not add exactly to labor force, due to rounding.

[c]Rate derived from unrounded estimates.

[d]1970 through 1983 data based on 1970 Census residence factors.

[e]1984 through 1989 data based on 1980 Census residence factors.

[f]1990 and later data based on 1990 Census residence factors.

less money saved, smaller pensions, and less home equity, and were more dependent on the steel industry, so they suffered disproportionately when the mills closed. In the long run, this would intensify racial divisions in the Youngstown area, which by the end of the century would be among the most segregated communities in the country.

The landscape was also changed by the social and psychological costs of the shutdowns. Youngstown's primary community mental health center, Parkview Counseling Center, saw a threefold increase in its caseload in the 1980s, with significant increases in depression, child and spouse abuse, drug and alcohol abuse, divorces, and suicide. Even the caseworkers struggled with the emotional aftershocks of the shutdowns. Unable to deal with the increased caseloads, many became frustrated and isolated from friends and peers, and nobody took care of the caretakers.[74] As demand for services grew, Parkview Counseling Center built a new facility in the early 1990s. The new center is part of a growing health care corridor that stands where many old houses were demolished in the 1980s.

The disappearance of the aging hulks of the steel mills themselves was the most important transformation of Youngstown's landscape. A few mill buildings were sold off. With the aid of a ten-year tax abatement, North Star Steel, a subsidiary of Cargill, the world's largest agribusiness, bought part of the Brier Hill Works and built an electric furnace to produce pipe. In other cases, community leaders tried to turn former mill sites into industrial parks. For example, the CASTLO project (named for the three small towns—Campbell, Struthers, and Lowellville—bordering the old Youngstown Sheet and Tube Campbell Works) refurbished part of the Campbell Works and turned it into an industrial park. But twenty-five years later, CASTLO remained empty except for a tire reprocessing plant and several other small businesses. Most of the mill buildings, especially those near the center of Youngstown, were torn down by the mid-1980s. U.S. Steel's Ohio Works, for example, was torn down to avoid paying property taxes. Unable to attract new business, U.S. Steel Real Estate, a subsidiary of USX (formerly U.S. Steel), allowed those areas to lay fallow for over a decade before selling them to the city for one dollar. By the end of the

1980s, the Jeannette Blast Furnace stood as almost the only reminder of what Youngstown had once been.

But the landscape was also changed during this period by other industries. Many steelworkers and their families had turned to other work years before the shutdowns, especially in the expanding local auto industry. In the 1960s, General Motors built a new assembly plant in a rural area northwest of Youngstown. At its height, GM's Lordstown complex employed over twelve thousand people. For the working class in Youngstown, Lordstown was a powerful alternative to the aging, unsafe, and dirty work in the mills. The technologically advanced manufacturing operations at Lordstown provided a clean, ergonomically designed work environment with excellent pay and benefits. With Lordstown, nine hundred separate companies within a sixty-mile radius supplying parts and services to Lordstown, and a burgeoning transportation system supporting the GM complex, the automobile industry became an economic replacement for the steel industry and forever changed the landscape of the Mahoning Valley.

With the development of Lordstown, thousands of industrial jobs followed white working-class housing and commercial development to the city's outskirts. When combined with the mill closings, this suggests a dramatic shift in geographic representations of work. Even though Lordstown and its associated plants became one of three dominant employers in the Mahoning Valley, and even though the auto plant is every bit as large as a steel mill, it does not occupy a central place in the local landscape. Quite the opposite. Its rural location decentralized work in Youngstown, making it almost invisible from the perspective of city residents. Few workers live within walking distance of the Lordstown plant, a point reinforced by the huge parking lots that can be seen from the Ohio Turnpike as one drives past the complex. The movement of the community's main site of industrial labor to the outskirts of the city affects many aspects of community life, from traffic patterns and the city's tax base to people's day-to-day consciousness of work. When the mills dominated the center of town, no one could ignore their importance, but the beige hulk of the assembly plant

GM Lordstown Plant, Joseph Rudinec, 2001

simply doesn't look as massive or as forbidding as the towers lit by smoke and fire or the half-mile-long, black "sheds" of a steel mill. While GM plays a significant role in the area's economy, it doesn't dominate people's ways of thinking about work in the same way the steel mills did.

This more modest geographic demeanor might suggest significant changes in ideas about work, but despite changes in the landscape, some of the conflicts related to work remained the same. More than sixteen thousand people from Ohio, West Virginia, and Pennsylvania applied for work at Lordstown when it opened in 1966. The new workforce at Lordstown was younger, better educated, and less experienced with trade unions than the workers in other auto assembly plants. These characteristics were considered necessary to keep pace on what was to be the world's fastest and most technologically advanced assembly line. But the new workforce were also the sons and daughters of the region's steelworkers, miners, and rubber and pottery workers with a militant trade union tradition. Further, these workers were not immune from the social and cultural attitudes of the 1960s, characterized by the motto Question Authority. As one autoworker, Ed York, put it, "At nineteen I felt immortal. When I returned to GM after the war, I felt I had done everything. I had a half a million Vietnamese trying to kill me and I survived. What could management do to me?"[75]

If GM thought the new landscape of work or the development of new suburban neighborhoods had erased the community's history of labor-management conflict, it was soon proven wrong. The company brought in its "get tough" General Motors Assembly Division (GMAD) to organize production of the Vega. GMAD attempted to establish absolute authority over production through job reductions, layoffs, elimination of shop rules, speedups, and individual harassment, but the new workforce engaged in what was called "spontaneous insubordination"—creating strategic bottlenecks and conducting industrial sabotage. When GMAD pushed harder by adding overtime and denying emergency breaks and access to union representatives, working conditions became intolerable and workers went on strike. While the strike itself was unremarkable, the media coverage was not. Workers were described as representatives of a rebellious generation and as victims of the "blue collar blues." "Lordstown Syndrome" became synonymous with the alienation and discontent that supposedly came when better educated workers experienced a boring, repetitive, fragmented, and highly rationalized production process.[76] Yet to the many workers from the Youngstown area, it was merely the continuation of labor struggles of past generations.

Other local companies also discovered that the new landscape did not erase the division between workers and managers. Major strikes and shopfloor struggles occurred at GM's Packard Electric, where the workforce of more than 14,500 was dominated by women. Packard Electric was seen as godsend for single women with children, because of the high wages and benefits, which were won through a series of in-plant labor disputes and wildcats. So disruptive to GM were these job actions that in 1974 the president of Packard Electric announced that the company would no longer build new facilities in the Youngstown-Warren area. Turning to workers with a less conflict-oriented history, Packard Electric has since become the largest employer in the Maquiladora section of Mexico, and by 2000, the Mahoning Valley workforce had been systematically downsized to just 7,000 workers.[77]

Nor was labor conflict limited to the manufacturing sector. In fact, Youngstown was the site of some of the country's first nurses' and teachers' strikes, the longest strike in the publishing industry against the *Youngstown Vindicator* in 1962, and the first union of college and university faculty in the state of Ohio. These events indicate that the "us versus them" sensibility was not limited to the steel industry, and, perhaps most important, they illustrate the close web of connections within the labor community in the Youngstown area. For example, when the *Vindicator* attempted to publish during the newspaper strike, the local AFL-CIO, headed by Al Shipka, came to the support of the strikers. This hardened the resolve of the strikers and resulted in periodic outbreaks of violence, including the torching of *Vindicator* delivery trucks. As the strike continued, the Newspaper Guild, together with Shipka and some investors, established a competing paper, the *Steel Valley News*, staffed by striking employees. The local labor community organized a boycott of the *Vindicator* and its advertisers and urged community members to frequent those who advertised in the *Steel Valley News*. When Youngstown State University (YSU) faculty began to organize almost a decade later, Shipka's son, Tom, a young philosophy professor, played a leading role. Because state laws forbid faculty to organize or strike, the newly developed YSU chapter of the Ohio Education Association launched a signature campaign to put community pressure on the board of trustees to allow a union election. Seven thousand signatures were collected throughout the community, four thousand of them from the workers at Lordstown. After six months and considerable resistance, the board of trustees consented to have an election, and 90 percent of the faculty voted in favor of unionization. The community's investment in trade unionism encompassed not only the traditional working class but also professors, some of whom were locals, sons and daughters of steelworkers. Some had even worked in the mills themselves during summer vacations.[78] Clearly, although the geography had changed, Youngstown's landscape of conflict remained.

1997

In January 1997, after a prolonged but small-scale preservation drive failed, the Jeannette Blast Furnace was torn down. Even before explosions brought down the stacks, workers wielding blowtorches began tearing apart sections of the Jenny, cutting the furnace's high-grade steel into pieces small enough to cart under the Division Street Bridge to the North Star scrap mill. By August, when the sixth annual Brier Hill Italian Fest drew thousands to the intersection of Poplar and Calvin for three days of eating, drinking, dancing, and visiting with old friends, the landscape of Brier Hill had changed dramatically. No longer could Italian Fest revelers look down the hill to the Jenny's brown towers, physical reminders of their fathers' and grandfathers' years of toil as steelworkers. Now, the Italian Fest celebrated Brier Hill boys who had made good, becoming doctors, lawyers, politicians, and successful businessmen.

But a few elements of the steel industry remained on the community's landscape, both in physical structures and, more important, in a lasting legacy of labor conflict. While many in the valley saw the steel industry and its union activism as part of a distant past, two important labor disputes occurred in the 1990s at WCI Steel and RMI Titanium in Warren, companies that had formerly been owned by Republic and U.S. Steel. WCI Steel represented the last vestiges of the region's old steel industry: it operated in a section of Republic Steel's Warren Works that included what had been, in 1939, the largest blast furnace in the world and was now the last remaining blast furnace in the area. Its workforce included many former steelworkers from

Youngstown Sheet and Tube, U.S. Steel, and Republic. To update the plant, the United Steelworkers of America (USWA) negotiated a concessionary labor agreement that featured greatly reduced wages, benefits, and staffing. By 1995, however, WCI had paid for its capital improvements and had become the second most productive steel facility in the United States. But when steelworkers asked to unify their fragmented pension program, the company refused and a two-month strike ensued. During the strike, USWA members showed that they had not forgotten the militancy inherited from previous generations of steelworkers. When the company threatened to sell the highly profitable plant, steelworkers warned that they would destroy the blast furnace. The company tried to continue operations and hired a security firm known for provocation, and in the resulting violence a picketer was run over by a convicted felon who was acting as a security guard. The strike lasted three months and ended largely on the steelworkers' terms.

The story was similar at RMI Titanium, another remnant of the local steel industry that became profitable in the 1990s because of significant concessions by workers. As at WCI, a contentious, sometimes violent strike ensued, and eventually a temporary injunction closed the plant. The strike lasted six months before an agreement was reached that secured comprehensive pensions for RMI employees. Steelworkers at both WCI Steel and RMI insisted that they were fighting not just for themselves but in memory of past struggles of local steelworkers who had fought to improve working conditions and to save the Youngstown mills. Despite the devastating impact of the steel mill closings, many workers in Youngstown had not lost the will to seek social and economic justice through any means available to them.

This commitment to labor activism carried over to other local industries. Workers at GM's Lordstown plant were involved in four wildcat strikes over subcontracting issues and in support of a discharged shop chairman and autoworkers at other U.S. sites. They also helped end a two-month Teamster strike at the Superior Beverage Company, which had been trying to break the union for over a decade. Superior had heard stories of successful union busting from representatives of West Coast Industrial Relations and mistakenly believed that West Coast's tactics could work in Youngstown. But Superior underestimated the commitment of Youngstown workers to labor justice. The strike ended when three thousand autoworkers held a 3:00 A.M. "rally" in support of the Teamsters, where they overturned several trucks and security cars. When the company was threatened with more "rallies," Superior asked the Ohio governor to send the National Guard to protect the property. When the governor refused, the strike was settled. Ten years after local workers had tried peacefully to claim their right of eminent domain, the Superior strike demonstrated that there were other ways for workers to claim ownership of work and space.

As the last rusty mill buildings fell, and as old houses continued to be destroyed by fire and demolition crews, Youngstown once again had important "natural resources" to offer would-be investors: empty land and unemployed men and women. Among the first industries to take advantage of these resources were distribution facilities. Several moved into the Salt Springs Road Industrial Park, lured by significant tax abatements, low building costs, and a large pool of workers willing to work for low wages. Like the Lordstown plant, the warehouses created a very different landscape than the one created by the steel industry. Instead of towering stacks and blast furnaces that might last seventy years, the modern buildings were little more than aluminum boxes, anonymous and insubstantial. As construction workers suggested, these buildings would last about as long as their tax abatement. And their small parking lots showed that they provided relatively few jobs.

Youngstown soon became home to another kind of warehouse: prisons. Between 1992 and 1997, four new prisons were built in the Mahoning Valley: the maximum security Ohio State Penitentiary in Youngstown, Trumbull Correctional Institution, the low and minimum security Federal Correctional Institution in Elkton, and the private, medium security Northeast Ohio Correctional Center, developed on the north side of Youngstown by the Corrections Corporation of America (CCA). The four new prisons employed sixteen hundred workers, provided a $67 million payroll and $720,000 in taxes, and generated an additional $200 million in economic activity in the Mahoning Valley. This amounted to over 7 percent of the area's total economic growth in the 1990s. As the *Vindicator* headline touting the prison economy ironically suggested, "Steel bars are still part of big business in the region."[79]

Like the auto plant and the distribution facilities, the prisons create a very different kind of landscape than the steel mills they replaced. Instead of furnace stacks, guard towers are now the tallest structures. Instead of open hearth fires lighting the night sky, floodlights now illuminate prison yards. Yet these new structures also occupy much less central locations on the landscape; most are located away from heavily trafficked areas, with a significant buffer separating them from residential neighborhoods. Except for the Mahoning County Jail downtown, the other prisons are relegated to a ring around the city, some within city limits and others a few miles outside. The prisons function much like the hidden worker housing Don Mitchell studied in *The Lie of the Land*; they change the local landscape in important, troubling ways, yet their presence is largely obscured. Local residents know they exist, and many turned out for public tours of the supermax facility before it opened. Yet for most, these new security fortresses don't change the visible landscape. For many, this invisibility must be comforting. No community wants to be identified as a penal colony.

But the community's troubles are highlighted by the very visible county jail, the only one of the new facilities to occupy a central location in the local landscape. Standing near the Youngstown Historical Center for Industry and Labor, the opulent old Powers Auditorium, the bus station, and the still-struggling downtown business district, the jail has become the most prominent feature of the downtown landscape. As the Jenny's stacks had represented Youngstown's prosperous if conflicted past, the twelve-story jail ominously suggests the community's future. On the one hand, the new jail reminds residents of the high crime rate, tied largely to the failure of the local economy. On the other hand, the jail does not always operate at full capacity because the community does not generate enough tax revenue to cover payroll. In October 1999, several hundred prisoners were given early release from the jail because it could not meet federal standards for staffing and occupancy within its limited budget.

As prisons became the growth industry in Youngstown, residents

Mahoning County Jail, Carl Leet, 2001

worried about how they would affect the community's reputation and its quality of life. The high density of prisons in and near Youngstown might be read as evidence that criminals somehow belonged here. Certainly, prisons offered steady work but also some unusual concerns about working conditions, and not simply in terms of safety. As the city still struggled for economic recovery, some of the local prisons and jails would likely house a few ex-steelworkers, and all were likely to hire some. As one United Steelworkers representative commented, the new prisons would have "steelworkers guarding steelworkers."[80] But most of the public concern focused not on who would work at the prisons, nor on how many locals would end out in them, but on how they would be run. While the Prison Forum led by community activists Alice and Staughton Lynd worried about the treatment of prisoners in the maximum security facility on the east side, others were concerned—rightly, it turned out—about the kinds of prisoners being imported from Washington, D.C., for the CCA prison on the north side.

The prison economy highlighted a new kind of conflict in the Youngstown area, a battle between those who see bringing jobs to the Mahoning Valley as the first priority and those who resist the idea of reinforcing Youngstown's reputation as "Crime Town, USA." The very notion of turning to prisons as a source of economic development is problematic. As urban policy expert David Rusk said about Youngstown when he visited in 1995, "I've never been in an urban community before where jails and prisons are treated as a growth industry."[81] Public hearings on the private CCA prison split the community between those who were desperate for work, many from the east side of Youngstown, and residents of the more prosperous areas of the upper north side and Liberty, who worried about how a prison built in their neighborhood would affect safety and property values. The debate echoed the long-standing division between the working class and more well-off citizens that began in the nineteenth century.

The CCA promised to bring new jobs, stimulate business for local vendors, and provide adequate security for the medium security prison. Prison supporters and CCA won out, but controversy continued when the prison opened in 1997. Local press and politicians touted the hundreds of new jobs at the prison, but problems were soon evident. Public officials were refused entrance to inspect the facility, several inmates were assaulted and murdered, and finally in July 1998, six prisoners (five of them convicted murderers) escaped at midday. Their escape through a prison fence went undetected by prison officials, who were alerted to the incident by other inmates. As the warning sirens sounded and word spread, residents in comfortable north side and Liberty neighborhoods, who had felt fairly protected from the city's high crime rate, felt that their worries were proven correct. Although the escapees were caught easily, community fears remained, validating the worst fears of those who opposed prison development.

An investigation following the escape showed several problems at the for-profit prison. While the prison had been billed as a medium security facility, it had instead become a dumping ground for some of Washington's most hardened criminals. And prison security, which residents had been promised would be more than adequate, proved inept and insufficient. Some suspected that the lax security was related to the low wages paid to prison guards, who may have been bribed to smuggle wire cutters into the facility. The incident drew national press attention, including stories on National Public Radio, *Dateline,* and *Sixty Minutes,* as well as a storm of proposals for changes in local and state legislation to provide stricter regulation of private prisons.[82] But conflict and controversy continued. After apologizing to the community, improving security, and paying local police over $1 million in overtime associated with the jailbreak, the CCA entered into an agreement with Youngstown's U.S. congressional representative James Traficant for his support of proposals to build two more prisons in the region, including one on the site of the old Campbell Works. Public outcry was swift against more new prisons. As Youngstown mayor George McKelvey suggested cynically, the area could do better if it were to become the home to a nuclear waste dump or landfill, ideas that had once been proposed as new developments for the old mill sites.[83] But even as many community members warned that the Mahoning Valley was becoming a penal colony, others still insisted that the area needed the jobs the prisons would bring.

Crime fears reignited another set of conflicts between the city and the surrounding suburbs. While Youngstown has long had a reputation for organized crime, the economic chaos in the Mahoning Valley contributed to the perception that the city was dangerous and crime-ridden. Between 1980 and 2000, Youngstown often led the nation in the per capita murder rate. Although most of the crime was considered "drug related" and largely in black neighborhoods, African Americans attributed much of the problem to the disproportionate impact of the mill closings on black families and the lack of economic opportunity for urban youth. By the early 1990s, many white residents of the suburbs and the west side refused to come downtown, and newcomers were warned not to buy houses on the north side, which some saw as in decline. The split between the city and its suburbs, and within the city between the west side and the rest of the city, were highlighted in a series of protests by residents in some "better" areas against proposals to build low-income housing in Austintown, a west side project to develop a support center for single mothers trying to get off welfare, and continuing school board discussions about whether to build a new central high school, which would bring together white, black, and Hispanic students from the now largely segregated neighborhood schools. When YSU's Urban Studies Center and the *Vindicator* invited urban analyst David Rusk to visit Youngstown and offer advice on area development, his most urgent suggestion was that the city and its suburbs needed to work together for economic development and to balance "disparities in terms of segregation, housing, and income."[84] While the city had supported suburban development through funding of the I-680 bypass project in the late 1960s and early 1970s, the suburbs now refused to follow Rusk's advice. The Mahoning Valley had grown increasingly divided, largely along lines of class and race that paralleled the dividing lines between the city and surrounding townships.

Yet despite perceptions, a large portion of crime in Youngstown was not, in fact, random acts of violence but organized crime, including a few murders and an extensive pattern of bribery and corruption among the city's political leaders. As the population and prosperity of the region faded with the mill closings, participation in local gambling operations decreased, and mob leaders became increasingly involved in efforts to control public works projects, county courts, and area politics. In 1999, a twenty-year investigation by the FBI resulted in a long series of indictments. Testimony from Lenny Strollo, an area mob leader, and a number of his associates revealed bribes of elected officials, rigged public works contracts, tight connections with local law enforcement and the area's water board, and case fixing in local courts. Such testimony led to convictions of the local sheriff, county prosecutor, county engineer, and aides for Congressman Traficant. While few residents were really surprised to learn that organized crime was closely involved in so many aspects of the community, these revelations contributed to the failure of several tax levies in the 1990s to support improvements in education, parks, mental health, and economic development. Often, citizens feared that new taxes would just line the pockets of organized crime figures in the Mahoning Valley.

From 1844 when "Brier Hill black" coal was first found on David Tod's homestead, to 1918 when the Jeannette Blast Furnace was "blown in," to 1997 when the last symbol of Youngstown's steelmaking history was torn down, the few acres where the Brier Hill Works once operated have been at the center of a shifting landscape. By the end of the twentieth century, that landscape had been shaped and reshaped through the history of work and the loss of work and its culture defined by a history of conflict over class and race, over ownership and conditions of work, the use of space, and shifting community identity.

Approaching the landscape as a representation of the community's history of conflict helps to uncover some of the points of tension that can get lost when landscapes are defined as naturally evolving spaces that are simply the backdrop against which history occurs. As our overview suggests, this approach highlights the role of class and race conflict on the development of housing, the way new landscapes of consumption arise not simply because of U.S. economic expansion but also out of racism, or the way a landscape of prisons and warehouses illustrates the community's struggle to redefine itself. Reading the landscape through this lens also reminds us to look for what the landscape itself hides. The persistence of conflict even as work moves and the landscape is reshaped reminds us that the relations of labor and the production of space are constructed on the foundation of history. The culture of a community may survive even as space changes. Landscape and history together tell much of the complicated story of a place.

Like any representation, the landscape tells us only part of the story of this place. To more fully understand the meaning of work and the loss of work in Youngstown, we must also examine other representations. To grasp why the loss of the Jeannette Blast Furnace matters in Youngstown, read newspaper accounts of the closing of the Brier Hill Works, listen to Bruce Springsteen crooning about "my sweet Jenny," look at paintings of the mills in neighborhood bars, and watch films that explain how steel is made and why the citizens of "Steel Town, U.S.A." are so proud of their hometown. All of these representations interact with landscape and history to form a cultural milieu. Together, they shape people's understanding of their experiences and help to form a "community of memory" that defines the meaning of place both now and in the future.

2

Steel Town

In Youngstown, we make steel.
We make steel and we talk steel.
—from a 1945 war bond film, Steel Town

Like the landscape, representations of work in Youngstown were produced through and contributed to the central conflicts of the community, especially conflicts rooted in class and race. While the steel production process established a structure that fostered conflict, in day-to-day experience, people understand their lives through their interaction with representations. Within and between representations, multiple and often contradictory ideas about the value and struggle of work emerged. In Youngstown, where the shared work of steelmaking was so central, ideas about the relationship between work and place helped to form the community's identity and gave individuals a sense of themselves. Despite the conflicts that we see in many of the representations that shaped Youngstown's identity as "Steel Town, U.S.A.," that image lasted for almost a century. If we are to understand the significance of what was lost here, we must begin by understanding the complex but deeply valued meaning of work and place that formed the backdrop against which deindustrialization was staged.

This chapter examines a wide range of stories and images about work in Youngstown, most of them created by and directed to people within the local community. In public venues ranging from the local newspaper to the walls of a union hall and in the memories of workers, these representations helped to construct the complex community of memory that viewed steelwork as almost synonymous with Youngstown. Working in the mill was at once the only option and the best option. Steelwork might involve workers in a battle with local police and mill managers, but it might just as likely involve them in a large, united effort to win a war in Europe or to create important new buildings or bridges. At times, both the steel mill and the steelworker become emblems of goodness, productivity, power, and community spirit, while other images focus on struggle, whether that struggle was simply the hard work of making steel or the more human battles over the control and conditions of labor.

While Youngstown went through many changes during the century when steelmaking fueled the area's economy and defined its identity on the national landscape, some central patterns persisted. First, images of steel mills emphasized the significance and even the beauty of steelmaking, yet as they glorified the technology and enterprise of steelmaking, they also erased the role of steelworkers. Second, images of work suggest complex and contradictory meanings. Work might represent virtue, pride, and a sense of belonging to a significant project that was much larger than the individual, but it might also mean danger and hard physical labor. Third, class conflict and labor-management struggles often took center stage in images of work, linking work and conflict in powerful ways. In all three kinds of representations, though, a single image may suggest multiple, contradictory readings. These different readings helped to create multiple communities of memory that would ultimately conflict as Youngstown tried to redefine itself later in the century.

CAPITAL OF AN INDUSTRIAL EMPIRE

Youngstown was identified as "Steel Town, U.S.A." for most of the twentieth century. A promotional book published by the chamber of commerce in 1933 describes Youngstown as the "capital of an industrial empire" without much exaggeration.[1] A book of drawings of Youngstown scenes, published in 1934, opens by describing how everywhere one looks, one "is reminded that here the dynamic and vitalizing source of all things is steel."[2] A 1940s postcard offers "Greetings from Youngstown, Ohio—Steel City, USA." A locally produced textbook in 1950 devotes a whole chapter to the importance of steel in people's daily lives, explaining that "the steel industry . . . account[s] for more than 90% of business activity of the Youngstown area."[3] Until the mills closed, and long after, Youngstown was known as "steel town."

While this identification gave Youngstown a clear identity and emphasized the community's shared dependence on the steel industry, images that emphasized the steel mills also suggest a key element of conflict in the community. On the one hand, these images represent steelmaking as a significant and even aesthetically attractive process. Steel mill images often highlight the dramatic fires of the blast furnace and open hearth, as well as the massive size and central position of the mills within the community. Yet, as chapter 1 showed, the power of the mills shaped not only the physical landscape but also important social divisions, and these are not seen in most images that focus on the mills. The mill operates as a unifying image, one that glorifies the technological wonder and impressive power of steelmaking but does not acknowledge the hard work or class and race divisions that were also part of the industry. As this chapter shows, one of the most important themes in representations of work is the tension between steelwork as a community enterprise, something that united the people of the Mahoning Valley across divisions of class and race, and steelwork as the object of a continuing battle between workers and the elite as well as among workers themselves.

We can begin to understand the usefulness of representing work by showing images of steel mills by looking at several promotional books, which almost always emphasize the abstract idea of steelmaking rather than images of steelworkers. First, such images allowed the community to present itself—both to its own residents and to potential new business owners or investors—as a unified, settled, middle-class community. As historian Stephen V. Ward argues, industrial communities typically presented themselves to prospective new businesses as progressive and cultured, with harmonious social relations and a docile but energetic workforce.[4] Promotional books and brochures often linked Youngstown's steel industry with the quality of community and family life. A 1913 chamber of commerce book promoted the city as a location for business by using numerous photos and drawings of steel mills along with images of downtown office buildings, the marble-covered lobby of a local bank, the bright lights of the city's business district at night, and photos of churches and local residential neighborhoods. Steel is clearly presented as a central part of what makes Youngstown a thriving community. The book also showed images of residential areas, including clusters of workers' housing, small apartment buildings, modest brick tudors, and the mansions of the upper class, suggesting to prospective business leaders that the city offered both an ample and a stable workforce and pleasant neighborhoods for themselves and their managerial staff.[5]

In many cases, though, texts downplayed the steel mills to emphasize the quality of community life. While the introductory text of the 1934 collection *Youngstown in Pen and Pencil* described the city as "continually overcast with the discharge of the furnaces" that "cast a rosy murkiness over the horizon" even during the daytime, only four of the book's fifty-seven illustrations pictured steel mills.[6] Most of the book presented prettier pictures of civic buildings, churches, schools, upper-class homes, and scenes from Mill Creek Park.[7] Many of the drawings show downtown skyscrapers, most built during the late 1920s and early 1930s, some designed by prominent American architects. Such images present Youngstown as modern and prosperous, a city dominated by banks and corporate offices. Even the few mill

Truscon Steel, Youngstown in Pen and Pencil, *Nicholas U. Comito, 1934*

drawings suggest sleek modernity: simple line drawings show smoke-free blast furnaces amid clean-looking industrial buildings. The sky looks clear, and a few men walk beneath modern-looking structures. An image of Truscon Steel (which later became part of Republic Steel) shows the inside of the mill as an open, light space with neat rows of rollers tended by a few workers. These images of Youngstown as a lovely, clean, largely middle- and upper-class community, with beautiful homes and refined cultural institutions, completely erase the largely immigrant working class and, with it, any suggestion of social turmoil, the economic struggles of the Depression, or even the everyday smoke of the mills. This erasure is all the more significant when we recall that the book was published during a time when Youngstown had among the highest unemployment rates in the country and as major labor struggles were brewing in Youngstown. Only a decade earlier, the Ku Klux Klan had risen to power locally by touting the danger of the area's large immigrant population. The creators and audience for these texts were most likely members of the elite (or aspiring elite), who might have appreciated an image of Youngstown that centered on them and that tied the community's prosperity and its civic achievements to them, rather than to the labor that created the wealth.

A similar idea is presented, though with less emphasis on the community's elite, in a promotional brochure from the early 1930s. The main headline in the foldout brochure reads "Youngstown: The City of Homes," and it appears opposite a large photo of a small child standing in a grassy field. A few smaller photos below show houses, churches, and other municipal buildings, and another large image shows a waterfall in Mill Creek Park. Like promotional materials dating back to the 1880s, this brochure depicts Youngstown as a good place to live, with business opportunity just one reason for companies to consider moving to town. Along with this emphasis on the quality of community life in Youngstown, the brochure paints a picture of the steel mills as a fascinating and beautiful part of the city's landscape. While the brochure shows no photos of steel mills, beneath the "City of Homes" headline, the text describes how

> strangers, riding through Youngstown at night, are startled and thrilled by a terrifying spectacle. Flames suddenly leap to the sky, throwing the outlines of the city into relief. As they watch, spellbound, the train thunders past miles of mills where

YOUNGSTOWN
• • *the City of Homes*

STRANGERS, riding through Youngstown at night, are startled and thrilled by a terrifying spectacle. Flames suddenly leap to the sky, throwing the outlines of the city into relief. As they watch, spellbound, the train thunders past miles of mills where thousands of men are turning out thousands of tons of steel. For the skyward leaping flames are the familiar nightly symbol of the city's activity. Youngstown is one of the great steel centers of the world.

But Youngstown is not only famous for steel ... it is noted as the City of Homes. It is fifth in the whole United States in home ownership. Over 47 percent of its citizens are masters of their own castle.

There are two reasons for this. One is that this city pays out more wages per annum than any other equal area in the world. Men come here with their families to find well paid employment. They prosper. Soon they are able to purchase a home of their own.

The other reason is a more intangible one. It is found in the mental attitude that people get who settle here ... a reason that involves living conditions, health, happiness, the children's future and a love of the town they are living in.

As you read this folder we think you will see why Youngstown is called the City of Homes. You will see why, in addition to their ability to finance a home of their own, such a high percentage of the citizens of this town have decided to link their future with that of the community.

"Youngstown: The City of Homes," c. 1931, Mahoning Valley Historical Society, Arms Family Museum of Local History, Youngstown, Ohio

thousands of men are turning out thousands of tons of steel. For the skyward leaping flames are the familiar nightly symbol of the city's activity. Youngstown is one of the great steel centers of the world.

The text then links the mills with home ownership, explaining that workers come to Youngstown because "this city pays out more wages per annum than any other equal area in the world. Men come here with their families to find well paid employment. They prosper. Soon they are able to purchase a home of their own."[8] It is worth remembering, though, that Youngstown's high rate of home ownership was carefully nurtured by the steel mills, largely as a response to labor unrest during the 1910s, and was seen in part as a way of controlling workers. By emphasizing home ownership and workers who were devoted to their families, this brochure defines Youngstown as a stable community, a safe place to live and conduct a business.

Other texts of the time remind us, however, that many native-born middle- and upper-class citizens saw the working-class immigrants as a problem to be managed. In December 1930, *Town Talk,* a local magazine aimed at the community's elite, featured a story praising the members of the Youngstown Federation of Women's Clubs for their involvement in Americanization efforts. The club's department of American citizenship provided naturalization classes for immigrant women, in an effort to "create able citizens" and ensure the stability of immigrant families. It was essential, the report argued, for immigrant mothers to "become conversant with American laws and customs and that right speedily."[9] Together, these two texts suggest that defining Youngstown as a steel town created a challenge for promoters. To prosper as a steel town, Youngstown needed a large labor force, and that meant a significant number of recent immigrants. But to attract new businesses, the community needed to present itself as a stable place, which was increasingly important in the 1930s as labor unrest became more visible. The tension between being able to offer a large labor force and ensuring the docility of labor-management relations emerges in these promotional images.

It is ironic, then, that at the end of the 1930s, immediately after some of the most violent labor conflicts in Youngstown's history, promotional images put even more emphasis on the drama and beauty of the mills. Of course, those images still appeared together with others that emphasized the city's civic and economic strength. Like *Youngstown in Pen and Pencil,* a set of about a dozen postcards from 1939 focuses on the area's churches, office buildings, the public library, and other civic buildings. But the series also features three steel mill images. The postcard set was published as a folder, with a cover image of a large steel mill building with its distinctive raised roofline and a fiery interior shot, split by the banner headline offering "Greetings from Youngstown, Ohio." Two of the postcards in the series offered colorful pictures of steel mills: "Night View of Republic Steel Corporation" and "General View of Youngstown Sheet and Tube Company, Night View, Campbell Works." In each postcard, the large, black mill structure sits alongside the tree-lined river, with bright

"*Night View of Republic Steel Corporation, Youngstown, Ohio*,"
Youngstown, Ohio: City of Steel Mills and Parks, *1939, Lake County (Ill.)*
Discovery Museum, Curt Teich Postcard Archives

orange bursts of fire and small, clear trails of smoke funneling into
dark skies. In one, the city lights fill the background, while the background of the other suggests green hills. Both present the mill as fitting
easily into the landscape, as if it had grown there. The nighttime set-
tings also emphasize the beauty of the mills, especially the brightness
of flames and the warm glow of heat from inside the mill buildings.
The images portray the mills as both impressive and attractive, but
like the earlier collection that focuses on Youngstown's elite sites, the
postcards offer no sense of what steelwork was like nor any acknowl-
edgment of the people doing the labor.[10] The point, after all, was to
promote the city by highlighting its most visually impressive locations.

The distorted vision of Youngstown's landscape offered in the
postcards is made clearer when we look at photographs of Youngstown, which as early as 1905 show the mills not as isolated or pretty
but as integrated into the landscape and overshadowing the city with
smoke. For example, a 1905 photo, part of the Detroit Publishing
Company collection, shows the view from the south side of the

"Panoramic View of Youngstown, Ohio," Panoramic Photographs Collection, Prints and Photographs Division, Library of Congress

Mahoning River, looking toward the city. A cluster of mill buildings fills the middle of the image, but the background is completely obscured by smoke.[11] Similarly, a 1908 panoramic shot looking toward downtown Youngstown from the Market Street Bridge shows a lineup of mill buildings stretching almost the whole width of the photo, with city buildings in the middle ground, and churches and residential areas fading into the smoke in the background.[12] The mill is central in nearly every photo of Youngstown from this period, and the black-and-white images emphasize the mills' smoke and soot rather than their more beautiful fires.

Smoke and soot represented the city's productivity. Indeed, workers and their families often commented that they liked to see a thick layer of soot on the windowsill or front porch, because that meant that the mills were running full tilt. But for more elite residents, smoke and soot also undermined the quality of residential life. It was seen as a health hazard during some periods, but often simply as an aesthetic problem. Elite Youngstowners might take pride in the dramatic view of the mills at night, but they didn't necessarily appreciate the smoky skies or the smell of steelmaking. At various times, local groups organized to try to address environmental issues related to the mills. During the 1920s, perhaps in response to one such community orga-

nizing effort, the Youngstown Sheet and Tube Company sponsored a series of cartoons designed to deflect responsibility from the steel companies to consumers. The cartoons focused on how citizens might clear the city's skies by burning "smokeless fuel" instead of coal. One cartoon shows "Mrs. Youngstown" and a visitor standing in Mill Creek Park, looking down over the city, which is blanketed with smoke. The visitor, representing the vision of Youngstown as a refined and cultured community, comments that with "so many things to be proud of—I can't understand why, with all the natural beauty, fine homes, your beautiful business buildings, you permit your city to be so smoky and dirty." "Mrs. Youngstown" replies that "we used to think that in order to enjoy prosperity, we must have smoke and dirt— but we've learned different—we're going to get together and clean up." Yet like *Youngstown in Pen and Pencil,* the cartoon pictures only homes, public buildings, and the central business district, not steel mills. Other cartoons in the series make clear that the mills were exempt from this public discussion because, as a business owner comments in one cartoon, "I can't run my business without making smoke!" Of course, the series was produced by Youngstown Sheet and Tube, which had a vested interest in deflecting public discussion about smoke from the mills to home owners.[13]

Most steel mill images focused on the mill as an object of admiration to be seen from a distance, from the outside, rather than a place of work. This was true even when texts acknowledged the work in-

"Mill Creek Park," Web Brown, Youngstown Sheet and Tube Company Audiovisual Archives, Youngstown Historical Center for Industry and Labor, Ohio Historical Society

volved in making steel. A 1950 schoolbook about Youngstown, sponsored by the Industrial Information Institute, a group dedicated to promoting local industry, uses the beauty of the mills as a unifying theme, something that holds the Youngstown community together. In *Working Together We Serve the World,* author Howard C. Aley explains that Youngstown was known for "the brightness of the sky over our heads. The brilliant glow of our steel mills brightens our skies on even the darkest nights. The beautiful orange-red glow of molten metal seen as we pass near the great steel mills is a sight that is never forgotten."[14] Like the postcard images, this description emphasizes the beauty of Youngstown's steel mills, though Aley goes on to briefly acknowledge the "thousands and thousands of workmen, our friends and neighbors, busy . . . helping supply the world's growing needs for iron and steel."[15] The visual appeal of the mills is connected here with workers and the significance of steelwork, though with little attention to the details of the work. Students are invited to see the mills as major elements in the local landscape, part of what makes Youngstown both beautiful and important, but they are also positioned as outside observers, appreciating the mill and its workers for what they produce. Indeed, the primary emphasis of the book was not on Youngstown as a community, nor on the work that dominated the community's economy, but on the products Youngstown's steel mills made possible. Youngstown "serves the world," the book argues, by providing steel for consumer goods.

This focus on consumerism fits with 1950s American culture, as suburbanization created greater demand for automobiles, new appliances, and other items using steel. Portraying Youngstown's steel industry in terms of consumerism encouraged readers to see themselves not as producers but as purchasers, and thus to identify not as members of the working class but as middle-class suburbanites. The shift is made most clearly in a slender folio published in commemoration of Ohio's sesquicentennial, *Youngstown, 1953.* The book offered a cover drawing of the city, with Republic Steel as a relatively small but central element near the bottom of the picture, towered over by the Home Savings and Loan Building. The book included interior and exterior views of several steel mills, and the text makes clear the key role of the steel industry in the community's history and prosperity. But steel is also connected with family life, which is depicted in an image that combines steelmaking with consumption. A two-page drawing shows a stereotypical nuclear family—mom in frilly apron and high heels, dad in a casual shirt and pants, and a boy and girl holding hands—all looking intently at a montage of steelmaking images. A large ladle pours molten steel, a blast furnace and stacks rise in the center and to the right, while small, gray cartoon images across the bottom of the page, in the white strip created by the spilling metal, show various bars and beams, machinery, furniture, and other objects presumably made of steel. No caption appears with the illustration, but none is needed. Steel is at the center of the community, at the center of the family, impressive but also very practical.[16] Positioning the family as observers of this spectacle of productivity suggests that they are the beneficiaries rather than the producers of the bounty of the

Centerfold, Youngstown Grows with Ohio, *Youngstown Sesquicentennial Committee, 1953*

steel industry. The image shows no workers involved in the process of making either the steel or the goods that use steel. Work is erased in favor of consumption.

Promotional materials from the steel companies in the postwar period also decentered or erased work. Company calendars, booklets, and promotional films produced by several area steel companies included images of their mills, both inside and out, and images of mines and freighters, emphasizing the integrated efficiency of the business. Often, these images highlight technology, showcasing gleaming machinery and the huge scale of the operation, even when the images include workers. Representations created by the Youngstown Sheet and Tube Company were especially prone to this focus on technology. A 1950 commemorative book, *Fifty Years in Steel,* and a 1961 promotional film, *Letter to Youngstown,* both emphasize effective management and development of the mills, with little attention given to workers.[17] Given the history of labor tensions during the 1950s, when Youngstown steelworkers went on strike almost every other year, the company's focus on its technology can be read as a means of directing attention away from workers and toward the capital that was controlled by the corporation.

The most interesting example, though, appears in a series of calendars published by the company, apparently for its workers. Each page of the 1949 version features a hand-colored photograph of a mill or mine scene, many focusing on newer facilities. The back of each page provides a history of "our company," giving details about the development of various operations, mergers and acquisitions, changes in corporate leadership, and other business issues, with no attention to major strikes or labor developments. The most interesting feature of the calendars, though, is the quote that appears on the front of each page, under the photo. The January page quotes from the Bible, "To rejoice in his labor; this is the gift of God." A later quote from Grover Cleveland reminds workers that "Honor lies in honest toil." Such quotations, all from well-known sources, offer authoritative messages touting the value of work. In what may have been an effort to appear labor friendly, the calendar even quotes labor leader Samuel Gompers:

Youngstown Sheet and Tube Company calendar, 1949, Mahoning Valley Historical Society, Arms Museum, Youngstown, Ohio

"Show me that product of human endeavor in the making of which the workingman has had no share, and I will show you something that society can well dispense with." A similar pattern appears in the 1953 calendar, but now the quotes have no attributions to famous people. They are presented as aphorisms, yet they also appear to come from the disembodied voice of the company, urging workers to value their honor over their wages. "You cannot give people a higher standard of living; they must produce it," reads one. Another urges readers to "Get all you can for the money you spend; give all you can for the money you earn." A third appeals to nationalism and Cold War sentiments by suggesting that "Communism is not economic—the issue is the preservation of the freedom of man as a living soul." Both the 1949 and 1953 calendars seem to invite workers to see themselves and their labor as part of the large, significant enterprise of the steel company. They are exhorted to work hard, not for the sake of what they get, but because hard work is an abstract good, closely tied with freedom and virtue. While no direct references suggest a contrasting option, it is important to remember that the 1950s was a period of great union strength, and steelworkers may well have felt that the union and their working-class communities were their primary affiliations. Images that focus on the mill and its machinery, combined with the quotes below, seem to suggest a different way of seeing the world. By the early 1960s, any commentary on work disappears from the calendars. Technology takes center stage, as each calendar page features a color photo of machinery, with workers almost always appearing as small figures, easily dominated by the more powerful technology of the mill. The implied argument has become a silent one, constructed visually. It may be that Youngstown Sheet and Tube believed that union affiliation was weakening, or perhaps it had simply given up on trying to define the meaning of work for its employees.[18]

The significance of Youngstown Sheet and Tube's use of mill and technology images to define work in terms of its relation to the company becomes clearer when we note that other companies took a more worker-centered approach in their promotional efforts. Promotional materials created by Republic Steel and Sharon Steel in the 1960s present images of happy and knowledgeable workers using up-to-date equipment and their own expertise. Republic's promotional film, *Men Who Make Steel*, positions workers at the center of the company's business, opening with a statement about how the "men who make steel" provide many necessary items for other Americans and beginning each segment with a reference to "the men" who work in various aspects of steelmaking.[19] A 1968 booklet promoting the Sharon Steel Corporation featured illustrations by Norman Rockwell, one of the most recognized American artists of the twentieth century. Each image represents a different part of the steelmaking process, but each also focuses on one worker, who occupies the foreground of the painting, either smiling proudly at the viewer or intent on his work. The machinery occupies the middle ground, significant and visually interesting but not as central as the workers. The booklet's title—*The Men and Machines of Modern Steelmaking*—also suggests the importance of workers and their control of technology.[20] These contrasting approaches suggest a tension within the community about the relationship between workers and the steel corporations, especially as American culture grew to see technology as a source of efficiency but also a potential threat to human interactions and fulfillment. Putting images of workers at the heart of their promotional images does not necessarily mean that Republic Steel and Sharon Steel valued their workers more highly. They may simply have understood the promotional value of representing the steel industry as a human enterprise, not just a technological one.

Steel companies were not the only creators of images of steel mills, nor were they the only ones to grapple with the problem of defining the relationship between the companies, the community, and the workers. Youngstown native Kenneth Patchen's poems contrast sharply with the images produced by civic promoters and steel companies, suggesting that steelworkers may have had a more complicated, darker view of the mill. Patchen draws on his childhood memories to create an image that reminds us of the difficulty of living amid the smoke and grime of a mill town. In "May I Ask You a Question, Mr. Youngstown Sheet and Tube?" (1943) he describes the "Mean

The Men and Machines of Modern Steelmaking, *Norman Rockwell, 1968, Sharon Steel Corporation*

grimy houses, shades drawn / Against the yellow-brown smoke / That blows in / Every minute of every day. And / Every minute of every night." Smoke pervaded daily life, not simply by shaping the rhythms of life or defining local identity, but in taste and smell: "To bake a cake or have a baby, / With the taste of tar in your mouth. To wash clothes / or fix supper, / With the taste of tar in your mouth. Ah, but the grand funerals. . . . "[21] The final lines of the poem highlight the close connection between the working-class life Patchen describes and the steel mills: "Rain dripping down from a rusty eavespout / Into the gray-fat cinders of the millyard . . . / The dayshift goes on in four minutes."[22] The poem moves from home to tavern to millyard, highlighting different scenes of community life from those shown in promotional brochures, but also emphasizing how important the mill was in the lives of Youngstown's working class.

Patchen's "Family Portrait" similarly notes the connection between the mill and the family, though with a very different tone than we saw in the promotional booklets. The opening images of this 1949 prose poem focus on the mill: "Great tarry wings splatter grayly up out of the blinding glare of the open-hearth furnaces. In the millyard the statue of some old bastard with a craggy grin is turning shit-colored above the bowed heads of the night shift that comes crunching in between the piles of slag." The reader follows the speaker's gaze, moving from the large, dark mill to the anonymous "night shift," before turning to the family itself, a movement that clearly positions this individual family among a larger extended community centered on the grimy, powerful mill. The mill's shadow remains as we turn to the father, whose back muscles "ripple like great ropes of greased steel. An awesome thing to see!"[23] The mill imagined here offers a very different kind of drama from that seen in the promotional materials, which emphasize the beauty of the fires rather than the resignation and exhaustion of those who tended those fires.

Local painters similarly suggest that the mill is not necessarily impressive and beautiful, but rather potentially frightening or confusing. In Martha McCloskey's 1936 painting, *Mills*, the viewer looks down as if from a nearby hillside on an unnamed steel mill, a dark, almost chaotic place, with many buildings crowded together and no people in sight. A cluster of smokestacks punctuates the lighter, cloud-filled sky. The image, painted mostly in black, deep purple, and brown, shows the mill as imposing, confusing, and uninviting.[24] Similarly, Albert Parella's undated *View from the Bridge* shows a covered bridge that looks as if it leads into a section of the mill that fills the background, possibly intended as an image of the Center Street Bridge, where the street ran between the Republic mill and the Campbell Works. Railroad tracks run into the murky space of the bridge. Open cargo bins full of reddish ore and a row of slag buckets stand to the left. The perspective positions the viewer on the bridge, giving what might be a worker's view of one part of the mill.[25] For both of these painters, working during the middle decades of the twentieth century, mills were central to the local landscape. Like Patchen, however, McCloskey and Parella present the mills darkly, as places that are confusing, grimy, and unpopulated.

Mill Entrance, *George Breckner, 1953, Butler Institute of American Art*

George Breckner's 1953 *Mill Entrance* also shows the mill as a confusing place, though here it does not seem so threatening. Using light grays and tans, Breckner offers a very clean-lined image, again from the perspective of someone about to enter the mill. Three furnace stacks rise in the background, while the foreground is dominated by the large, angled, flat surfaces of a bridge that doesn't quite fit together. The image seems precise because of its crisp lines and careful shadowing, and the mill stacks and buildings in the background appear solid and realistic. But the bridge seems to block entry, and the shapes behind it don't fit together to form a realistic sense of space. The result suggests obstruction and confusion.[26]

Such paintings serve a different purpose than the postcard images created during the 1940s, yet the contrast also suggests a tension between images that portrayed the steel industry as beautiful and impressive and those that offered a more skeptical, critical view. All of these paintings are included in the collection of the Butler Institute of American Art, where they were most likely seen primarily by middle-

and upper-class visitors, for whom the images may have confirmed a sense that the mills were foreign, possibly even frightening, places.

These paintings, like many of the promotional images, focus on the mill as a structure rather than as a place of work, and they show very few people. The focus in many images of the steel industry is on the mill and its machinery. Steel mills were a key part of the local economy and a defining element in the community's identity, yet images of Youngstown often downplay or prettify the mills, and they almost always downplay the role of workers. While Youngstown Sheet and Tube used high-minded quotes about work to persuade steelworkers to see themselves as part of a significant and valuable enterprise, and to put that enterprise above their own interests, Patchen's poems about working-class home life remind us that steelmaking was hot, dirty, often dangerous work. No wonder community leaders and steel company public relations departments emphasized images of the fiery drama of steelmaking rather than the grimy struggle of working life. In the larger discursive landscape of Youngstown, however, the workers were not forgotten.

MEN WHO MAKE STEEL

When Youngstown Sheet and Tube paired images of steelmaking machinery with quotes about the value of work and company histories that erased labor struggle, it offered a mixed message to its worker audience. While steelworkers often talk with pride about their work, we have to wonder how they responded to the company's insistence on the honor of steelwork, especially when part of the message suggested that workers "give all they can for the money you earn" and when the company history completely erased all of the major labor battles of the previous decades. When Republic Steel and Sharon Steel put images of steelworkers at the center of their promotional materials, they recognized the importance of work and workers. *Men Who Make Steel* and *The Men and Machines of Modern Steelmaking* valorize work, but they do so within the context of promoting the steel companies and downplaying any hint of worker solidarity. As these examples suggest, images of work and workers functioned in complicated ways. Work could be a source of identity and solidarity, but collective identity could also serve to minimize or heighten tensions between workers or conflicts related to labor organizing. Work could be seen as beneficial to body and spirit, yet such images could also serve to distract workers from concerns about safety or wages. Workers themselves were often valorized, either as experts or as men of virtue. The worker might represent individual success, or he might stand for the collective power of the union, and that image of the successful, powerful worker could be used in multiple ways—to defuse union activism or to spur workers on to greater union solidarity.

Being identified as a steelworker in Youngstown linked the individual with a larger collective body of workers or union members, and this collective identity almost always involved both class solidarity and class conflict. In some cases, as when white, skilled, native-born workers appropriated the identity of steelworker for themselves, excluding unskilled immigrants and African Americans, work defined collective identity in ways that emphasized conflicts among workers. At the same time, steelworker identity could erase individuality, making the individual worker anonymous. In becoming equated with his or her job, then, a steelworker might both gain and lose identity. The shared identity of workers suggested participation in the collective power of working-class solidarity, but questions also arose about who was eligible to be part of that solidarity and how the working class interacted with the rest of the community. Work defines who people are in these images, but work-based identities were also contested.

In an 1899 collection of poems, *Labor Lyrics and Other Poems,* Irish immigrant and Youngstown ironworker Michael McGovern defined himself as "the puddler poet." If his chosen label didn't make his work-based identity clear enough, his poems did. The opening poem of the book describes the beauty of the rolling mill, both from the outside and from the inside. The speaker sits on a hill, watching the "rays of

light / That from the furnace flow," but he also describes the plea-
sure of working in the mill: "We millmen, e'er fulfill / Our tasks
amidst the hum of joy." Identifying himself and his colleagues as "we
millmen," "puddlers," or "veteran toilers," McGovern based their
identity in their work. [27] That identity isn't simply a label, however.
Work defines the puddler's perspective on politics, the economy, and
the press. Moreover, this perspective is distinctly classed, separate
from and opposed to the perspective of "the idle rich," "plutocrat
rulers," and the "college dudes [who] are bosses."[28] The work men
do, in McGovern's eyes, defines their social position but also their
opinions, their behavior, and their identity.

Work defined the puddler's character, yet it also separated him
from other men. In "My Workingman," McGovern's female speaker
describes her virtuous worker lover, who is "true to native land,"
"brawny," "hardened well with toil," possessed of an "honest soul,"
and true to "labor's cause."[29] Yet as these lines hint, McGovern sometimes used the image of the individual worker to define a distinction
between union men and scabs, a division that ran along lines of race,
nationality, and skill. *Labor Lyrics* appeared during a period when
skilled workers, most of whom were native-born or northern European immigrants, were concerned about the increasing numbers of
unskilled eastern and southern European immigrants and African-
American migrants who seemed poised to transform the industry
and the meaning of work. He emphasizes this point in a series of
poems about labor conflict, setting "the toiling puddler" against the
"moneyed men" across the "dividing line" of "Wealth's oppressive
pow'r," yet he also clarifies how issues of race and skill divide workers when he contrasts "blacksheep" and "whitemen."[30] In this context, the individual whose virtues are extolled in "My Workingman"
is not simply a good man but a specific kind of good man: he represents white, native-born, unionized, skilled labor. He is at once a virtuous individual and a representative of a larger, but exclusive, group.

Carl Sandburg, a major twentieth-century American poet and labor
journalist whose writing often focused on working-class characters,
also examined the tension between individual and shared identity,

though without as strong a sense of class solidarity. In "Smoke and Steel," his collage-like 1920 poem about steelmaking, Sandburg suggests that the steel mills of "Pittsburg [*sic*], Youngstown, Gary—they make their steel with men."[31] He shows how the process of making steel erases individual differences, noting that "men change their shadow" when they work in the mills. Written during a period of expansive growth when unskilled immigrant workers dominated the steel industry, "Smoke and Steel" presents divisions of race and ethnicity as real but also changeable. He acknowledges the hostility of these divisions through his language, yet he also suggests that work blurs other aspects of identity. "A nigger, a wop, a bohunk changes," he writes, implying that differences of ethnicity are softened by the smoke of the mill as each individual becomes a steelworker. The image becomes much more graphic when Sandburg focuses on the dangers of steelwork: "Five men swim in a pot of red steel"; they are "kneaded into the bread of steel / . . . knocked into coils and anvils." The workers become part of the steel, both figuratively and literally, but they do not disappear entirely. "Look for them in the woven frame of a wireless station," Sandburg writes, implying that their presence may remain in the steel they make.[32] Steelworkers' identity is melted together, perhaps, but not entirely erased.

The tension between individual and collective identity emerges even when Sandburg refers to workers individually. He addresses one stanza to "you Steve with the dinner bucket" and quotes a series of workers' comments during their lunch break:

One of them said: "I like my job, the company is good to me. America is a wonderful country."
One: "Jesus, my bones ache; the company is a liar; this is a free country, like hell."
One: "I got a girl, a peach; we save up and go on a farm and raise pigs and be the boss ourselves."[33]

By naming "Steve" and referring to the various workers as "one," Sandburg emphasizes the different attitudes and concerns of the steelworkers, yet the repetition of "one" also downplays their individual identities. They are separate but not really differentiated.

In Sandburg's poems, unlike McGovern's *Labor Lyrics*, the erasure of individual identity crosses boundaries of race and ethnicity, but it does not translate into an organized sense of class consciousness or class struggle. While Sandburg acknowledges that workers have little power—they must "Do this or go hungry"[34]—and while he wrote the poem during the steel strikes of 1919 when he was working as a journalist reporting on labor issues, his images do not cast workers as a political group. As Philip R. Yannella notes in *The Other Carl Sandburg*, this poem celebrates the "worker-as-creator" and the importance of steel but does not imagine a "heroic working class about to rise up to take its just due."[35] For all of Sandburg's populist tendencies and his interest in working-class and immigrant lives, "Smoke and Steel" remains more a paean to the life force of steelworkers than a call for solidarity. His individual workers represent all workers, and they function as both individuals and representatives, but they do not move toward collective action. Steelwork creates a shared identity for workers but it does not, in Sandburg's vision, lead to collective consciousness.

Similarly, the idea that shared work creates shared identity but not class consciousness appears two decades later in a 1945 war bond film, *Steel Town*. Here, shared identity is defined on the level of community, implying that steelworkers and others in the Youngstown area share common interests and goals. This emphasis promoted the war effort by inviting viewers to see themselves as part of a larger enterprise, in this case not a steel company but a community, which was, in turn, part of a national effort. The film uses individual workers to emphasize the importance of community, moving back and forth between individual and communal identity. After the opening scene that focuses on Youngstown's central business district, the film shows a large group of men walking to and entering the mill. The camera follows the workers into the mill, and then the voice-over identifies some of them individually: "That's Johnny Chanco on the snort valve, controlling the blast. When things get too hot, he's got to think quick and move quicker." After a series of similar introductions, the film shows several scenes and voice-overs that emphasize family and community life. For example, we visit an Italian immigrant worker's home at Christmas, a scene that emphasizes his pride at being able to provide for a large family. A rehearsal of the community symphony, whose members are "steelworkers and their wives and daughters," positions workers as participants in high culture, downplaying stereotypical class divisions that might lead viewers to expect steelworkers to play popular music rather than concertos. This approach defines workers as similar to others in the community. In addition, a symphony is a collective endeavor, a group of people working together for a higher good. The voice-over explicitly links the collective effort of music making with the way steelwork is done, commenting that "steelworkers learn to do things together, like in the mill," again emphasizing the importance of community, which the film implies is necessary for the United States to win the war.[36] Collectivity here is not tied to class consciousness and certainly not to organized labor. Rather, the film calls for workers to feel patriotic and to see their labor as part of a national collective effort to win the war, an effort that protects their own families but that also draws Americans together across lines of difference. Looking at Youngstown's landscape years later, it is clear that appeals to patriotism had resonance. Every small community in the area has its own monument to local soldiers who died in America's wars.

This erasure of class difference through the commonality of work also appears in *Our Neighbors Tell Us about Their Work*, a 1949 publication that was part of the locally produced schoolbook series by Howard C. Aley. The book uses individual workers to represent different kinds of work but erases class differences, suggesting instead that all workers are essentially alike and all play an equal part in the community. Produced during the late 1940s and early 1950s, a period of significant growth in local unions but also of national worries about communism, the book reflects the probable desire of its sponsors to emphasize commonality rather than difference. Like the other books in the series, *Our Neighbors Tell Us about Their Work* presents an image of a peaceful, conflict-free community in which all workers are happy and everyone gets along. The book introduces the reader to a number of Youngstown workers: Mr. Melter (who works in the open hearth), Miss Banks (a teller at the local bank), Mr. Roller (who operates a rolling mill), and Mr. Strong (who works on the labor gang), among others. Just as "Steel Town" became Youngstown's nickname, here each character's work becomes his or her name. Each worker describes his or her job, always with a sense of pride and no mention of labor conflict or workplace dangers. As Mr. Melter points out, all the workers at the steel mill, from the laborers to the engineers, work together to make the steel that is formed into cars, buses, streetcars, and household goods, and all share a similar feeling of pride in their contribution to modern life.[37] Despite the emphasis on identifying different kinds of work, this shared pride suggests that all these different kinds of workers have a common mission and live together in harmony without any sense of class division. Lawyers, bankers, engineers, rolling mill operators, open hearth workers, and laborers all live on the same street, gather in each other's homes for dinner, and attend a Fourth of July picnic together. So while different kinds of work identify the different characters, all the workers represent "our community," a place that is, as Mr. Melter says, "one of the most important in the world" because of the steel it produces.[38] This image of workers as representative of a homogeneous, prosperous, contented community was important during the 1950s, when labor unrest was an almost constant feature of the local scene. The industry and educational leaders who formed the Industrial Information Institute and its Schools Advisory Committee may have hoped that this emphasis on community would help persuade the next generation of local workers to see themselves as part of one shared community in which workers and managers could "cooperate" rather than struggle over wages and working conditions.

Despite this public image of community equality and shared worker identity, oral histories suggest that workers were conscious of differences, both racial and ethnic differences among workers and class differences that separated workers from management and from some others in the larger community. While many white workers and some

African Americans describe the mill as comfortably integrated, with black and white workers cooperating on the job and sharing food and conversation during lunch breaks, others insist that divisions were clear and sometimes hostile. In a presentation reflecting on his experiences in the mill and the union, African-American union leader Arlette Gatewood noted, "Some of the more major problems were the washhouse, where you changed clothes and took a shower. If you were a scarfer or a chipper or a slagger, it was a very dirty, dusty job. In nine cases out of ten, you could not go home in the clothes that you worked in. . . . In many instances, all the blacks were on one side and all the whites were on the other. Or if it was integrated, there was maybe just a couple of black guys on one side." Yet Gatewood also points out that management helped to perpetuate segregation, to keep workers fighting among themselves. While problems also existed within the union, Gatewood acknowledges, the union eventually helped to alleviate racial divisions.[39] As Gatewood's recollections suggest, divisions among workers were, for some steelworkers at least, less important than divisions between workers and managers.

Workers' descriptions of their experiences in the mills show that they wanted to see themselves as "the same as everybody else," yet they also emphasize the conflicts that keep workers and managers at odds. Fred A. Fortunato worked at Republic Steel for many years, including during the period of the 1937 "Little Steel" strike. In explaining the importance of unions as part of an oral history interview, he offers a vision of "labor people" as "well-educated and sophisticated, the same as anybody else." He goes on, however, to describe the conflict between workers and management by pointing out that managers "preach" that they want to "get along with our people that work for us because they're the backbone of this company. But it isn't so. Even when I worked down there, when I worked in the plant, the foremen were forbidden to associate with the men on the outside." At the end of his interview, Fortunato calls for respect for labor unions, acknowledging that labor leaders and union members are seen as threatening but that they are, at heart, good Americans like "everybody else": "Labor organizations are not what the people think they are—a bunch of hoodlums. They are not. They are first class citizens and they're out there to win and gain the benefits for the individual to advance and come to be a good American and a good citizen."[40]

Representations of work did not define it only as a source of identity but also as a source of personal development, an activity that offered clear benefits or that demonstrated one's virtue. Especially during the 1910s and 1920s, good work was represented as a source of mental and physical health. Most of these representations appeared in local newspapers, both the *Vindicator* and the Youngstown Sheet and Tube Company's in-house paper, the *Bulletin*. In both cases, such publications represented advice being given to workers rather than workers' own reflections on their work experience. "A Prescription," an anonymous poem appearing in the January 1922 issue of the *Bulletin,* suggests work as the cure for all ills: "If you are poor—work / If you are rich—continue to work / If you are burdened with seemingly unfair responsibilities—work." Indeed, as the poem says near the end, "No matter what ails you—work."[41] Similarly, an article in the *Vindicator* promised that "The Right Kind of Work" was "the Very Best Aid to Well-Being." The article cited a report from a doctor at Johns Hopkins who claimed that "though you may have a poor wage, and small thanks for your labor, your muscles, your stomach, your intestines, your flesh and blood are given a richer reward in the way of vibrant health."[42] The language here suggests a practical work ethic, in which labor helps to create a strong mind and a strong body, making the individual a better, happier person. The details of work are left out, of course. These idealistic messages focus on the abstract idea of work rather than the concrete reality of mill life, and the problems of work are explicitly set aside. Given the dangers of steelwork, both the risks of injury and the long-term effects on workers' health, these early messages that equate work with vigor and contentment seem, at minimum, ironic. The publication of a poem such as "A Prescription" in the *Bulletin,* which also regularly ran reminders about safety precautions, seems negligent if not almost sinister.

Another common theme was the value of what workers produced, both the concrete, material goods and the more abstract production of what was usually termed "the American way of life." Work was valuable because it was productive, and workers were either productive because they were virtuous or virtuous because they were productive. In *Men Who Make Steel,* the opening voice-over tells us, "Wherever you live in this land, whatever you do for a living, you have reason to know and to respect the people who are passing here. You see, these are the men who make steel. They are 650,000 strong in America, and without them, your way of life never could have come into being."[43] As in the Aley textbook series, the message here is that steelworkers help to create American prosperity and virtue. It is significant that this image appeared most often in the 1940s and 1950s, during a period of growing prosperity for steelworkers and increasing attention to consumerism nationwide.

Productivity and virtue were explicitly linked in many texts. One apparently led to the other, though which came first wasn't always clear. Some images defined workers as naturally virtuous. Michael McGovern's early twentieth-century poem "My Workingman" describes the virtues of a steelworker who is as "true to native land" as he is to his sweetheart, equating patriotism with personal affection. His hands are rough, but his heart is good: "No act that bears the taint of wrong / His honest soul can soil."[44] But other representations suggest that work makes men better. As James J. Donnelly wrote in the *Bulletin* in 1921, "honest work enobles a man." But "honest work," he suggested, was labor that the worker valued for its own sake, not for the sake of the money earned.[45] Appearing just a few years after two major strikes over wages, one of which had precipitated a riot in which strikers burned down their own community, the suggestion that work makes men virtuous may be read as wishful thinking, or it may have been intended as an invitation to workers to live up to this supposed nobility.

A 1922 poem in the *Bulletin,* "Steel—America's National Cream," offered a remarkable blend of rhetoric and imagery to praise the virtue and significance of steelworkers and their product. The poem opens with monumental descriptions of the power of the mill: "where the smelters roar! / Where the fiery monsters gulp the ore; Where thundering furnaces rock the earth." It continues with almost sexual descriptions of liquid steel: "America's National Cream / Sputters and flows in a white-hot stream / Where half-naked men with ladles in hand / Hurry it off to its bed in the sand." The men who do this dramatic work are dedicated laborers. They "work and sweat and work again"; they "damn the man who will dare to shirk." Such men "love their work" because "they are part of everything they create."[46] Such poems represent workers as both skilled and virtuous, committed to the larger effort of making steel. They appear as demigods, powerful and important. These poems compliment workers while also encouraging them to see themselves as committed to a virtuous enterprise. On the one hand, read in the context of local concerns about unruly and lazy immigrant labor, they might appear as praise of white, native-born workers or as an effort to improve the image of all steelworkers, immigrant and native-born alike. On the other hand, given the context of publication in the company newspaper, they might be read as exhortations to workers to work hard and be loyal to the company, to care more about the work than about their wages.

Representations of the virtues of work were also directed at school-children, who were encouraged to view work as a form of service. In Aley's textbook *Working Together We Serve the World,* readers were told that local steelworkers "busy themselves in helping supply the world's growing needs for iron and steel." Students were encouraged to think about their future jobs as offering an "opportunity to help supply the wants and needs of our neighbors as well as of people far away." Not surprisingly, this emphasis on work as service to a larger good, consumption of products made with steel, also erased labor conflict. Because work exists to serve the world, not an economic necessity for either the company or the worker, labor conflict is described as a simple matter of oversupply: "Sometimes there were more workmen than were needed." But immigrants continued to arrive, creating conflict between workers: "Workmen felt forced to work for very low wages for they knew that there were many men without work outside the factories, who would readily take their jobs."[47]

As these examples show, service, productivity, virtue, and cooperation were often linked in images of work. The virtue of work came from its purity, the dedication of workers to an ideal of productive labor rather than to earning money or achieving self-fulfillment. At the same time, the text's description of labor troubles as a simple problem of oversupply, caused by too much immigration, ignored the strong labor tensions in 1950s Youngstown and cast blame for labor conflict on the community's large immigrant population. Many of the schoolchildren reading this book were themselves the children of immigrants, and many of their fathers participated in organizing the steelworkers' union in the 1930s, including the bitter and violent "Little Steel" strike of 1937. In some cases, children may have encountered this explanation of labor conflict during a period when their fathers were out on strike, since Youngstown steelworkers were involved in the nationwide strike wave of the 1950s. In both cases, the conflicts focused on wages and working conditions, not the labor supply. By defining work in terms of service, Aley, writing under the sponsorship of a steel industry group, could use the notion of work as a source of virtue to directly undermine any sense of the validity of workers' struggles.

Workers' own comments about labor conflict make clear that they did not always buy into the model of work as virtue or service, largely because of the way they were treated by the steel companies and by those in the community who were not sympathetic to their concerns. Fred A. Fortunato describes union men as "individuals that have been hurting so long that they want to get a piece of the pie." Dan Thomas explains that workers fought for unions because they were "looking for dignity." Augustine F. Izzo tells a story about one worker's explanation of the value of the union, which emphasized not improved wages or pensions, but the immense value of being listened to: "The reason I belong to the union and the reason I fought so hard to get one, is because . . . when the foreman or supervisor or whoever it may be comes out to chew me out for something, after he gets done, he's got to stand there and listen to my side of the story. . . . To me, that's worth more than money could buy."[48] Public statements about the value of work apparently didn't provide any real sense of respect to these workers. They felt that they deserved respect, but they didn't believe that they got it until the unions were formed.

Yet workers also created their own valorizing images of work, not in their contributions to the Sheet and Tube *Bulletin* and only rarely in letters to the editor of the *Vindicator,* but in their own spaces. In workers' bars, union halls, and homes, images of steel mills often adorn the walls. One of the most striking and powerful examples hangs in the meeting hall of the old USWA Local 1330. Local 1330 represented workers from U.S. Steel's Ohio Works and was one of the most powerful locals nationally. Victor Kosa's large 1944 painting, approximately ten feet high by twenty-five feet wide, includes three panels showing different parts of the steelmaking process. The left side panel, labeled *Tapping—Blast Furnace,* shows the outside of a working blast furnace. On the right side, we see an interior scene of three men *Pouring Ingots.* The larger middle panel shows the inside of a mill, with several men charging an open hearth furnace. While the painting uses dark tones, it also conveys a sense of light and heat. The style is similar to Works Progress Administration (WPA) murals, with workers' bodies outlined in dark strokes to emphasize their muscles and give a definite sense of action. Yet the workers also appear fully integrated into their setting. For steelworkers, especially perhaps for those who see the image today, twenty years after the mills closed, the image offers a clear reminder of what their work was like. "That's pretty darn close to the way the mill was," one retired steelworker commented.[49]

Among the most interesting of the workers' images are those that link labor and religion, which appear in Italian Catholic churches whose members were mostly steelworkers and their families. A bas relief frieze on the outside wall of St. Anthony's school building in Brier Hill, erected in the 1950s, suggests that God is with the workers in the guise of St. Joseph, who supports and blesses their labor. St. Joseph, the patron saint of workers, stands behind a worker with his hand resting on the man's shoulder as if to support and comfort him. The worker's significance is made clear by his size—more than

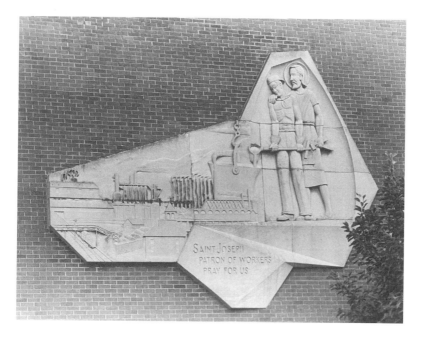

Frieze, Carl Leet, 2001, St. Anthony School Building

life-size, much larger than the mill, but smaller than the saint—and by his position, looking down on the mill both in the frieze itself and a few blocks downhill of the school. The image is comforting, showing the worker as an almost religious figure, both watched over from above and more important than the large enterprise where he toils. The image does not present work as a source for character building nor as a public service, but as a higher calling, almost an act of faith.

In addition, the St. Anthony frieze connects the virtue of labor with the virtue of family and community, albeit in a different way from the Aley books. Context and sponsorship make all the difference. St. Anthony's stands both literally and figuratively at the center of Brier Hill, the core of Italian immigrant community life. The frieze, like the school building that it adorns, was paid for to a large extent by donations from local workers who were also church members. Their willingness to support a parochial school for their largely

Americanized children and to include as part of the school an image that links labor and faith suggests that workers themselves were invested in the idea that their work was valuable and virtuous. The image shows respect for the men whose wages paid for the building and for their children's education in it, and for many of the children attending the school, it must have seemed like an image of their future. Ironically, many of those children later lost their jobs and in some cases their homes and families when the Brier Hill Works shut down.

A somewhat more active image linking labor with religion appears on the outside of another Italian Catholic church in the working-class neighborhood of Smokey Hollow. The parishioners of Our Lady of Mt. Carmel include many families that have moved up into the middle and even upper classes but who still return to the old neighborhood church. The flat metal piece, entitled "St. Joseph—A Spiritual Force of Labor," shows St. Joseph and the worker, a shirtless, muscular man, leaning toward a cross that is superimposed on a set of gears. The two figures appear to be working together: they face each other, both grasping a carpenter's square and reaching toward the cross. In the upper right-hand corner, a hand—presumably the hand of God—reaches down toward them. The image and its caption portray work as an activity inspired and aided by spirituality. Both Catholic church images suggest a similar message: work is a virtuous and spiritual activity, approved of and aided by God. Interestingly, the St. Anthony's image looks down on the local mill, suggesting comfort and support, while the Mt. Carmel image reaches up, suggesting the possibility of self-improvement, possibly even the reinvention of self, aided by God. The Mt. Carmel sculpture was donated by the William J. Cafaro family, whose upward mobility starting in the 1950s was built on shopping mall development. By the time the piece was installed in the 1960s, Cafaro had become a national developer, a symbol of success for the local Italian community.

Images linking work and spirituality also appear in the stained-glass windows of St. John's Episcopal Church, the church attended early in the century by many of the leading steel mill owners and managers in

St. Joseph—Spiritual Force of Labor, *Carl Leet, 2001,*
Our Lady of Mount Carmel Church

town. Dedicated in 1955, after most of the steel barons had sold their
mills or moved away and in the midst of a period of both union strength
and repeated strikes, the ten small, circular windows feature colorful
images of workers in various stages of the steelmaking process, including a miner, a sailor on a cargo ship, a worker at an open hearth, a strip
mill worker, and an engineer. Each image is accompanied by a quote
from the Bible. The window depicting an open hearth worker reads,
"God hath showed his voice, and the earth shall melt away." The image of the strip mill worker is accompanied by the line, "The voice of
the Lord is mighty in operation." Unlike the more working-class Catholic churches, where the images do not explicitly reference organized
labor, St. John's includes a window depicting the "cooperation between
those who labor and those who direct," an image of five men talking
around a table, with a caption that reads, "We took counsel together

*"We took counsel together and walked in the house of God as
friends," 1955, St. John's Episcopal Church*

and walked in the house of God as friends." Given the labor troubles
of the period, the message seems ironic.

While the windows themselves are intriguing, the texts explaining each window from the program of the 1955 dedication service are
even more interesting. They echo the Catholic images' suggestion that
God watches over workers, but they also emphasize "our gratitude
for those who must work dangerously" and offer political commentaries on the uses of natural resources. Some focus on "God's concern
for man in the job of making steel," while others use ideas from steelmaking as metaphors for spiritual life. A window showing a worker

removing a sample of molten steel for testing notes that "constant self-examination (individual and corporate) is likewise a regular discipline to guarantee the integrity of our Christianity." Images of work serve to aid the spiritual development of the parish here, while in the Catholic church images, spirituality serves as a support for labor.

The more elite perspective of the Episcopal church is reflected most clearly in the commentary on the image of labor negotiations. The commentary notes that "collective bargaining and all relationships among those who work together" should emphasize cooperation, a term that often functioned as a kind of code for suggestions that workers should go along with company demands. In many representations of the 1930s, 1940s, and 1950s, cooperation was offered as an alternative to conflict, a very real problem that most images carefully avoided mentioning directly. Similarly, the dedication text indirectly acknowledges other kinds of conflict in the community, noting that "a church like ours" can "provide a setting where people whatever their race, vocation or station in life" can come together. Acknowledging the conflicts of the community, the statement ends by suggesting, "In a tension-ridden society this window can serve as a multi-colored reminder that love and understanding are the weapons of a Christian building a better world." Moving away from the sense of work as virtuous, the Episcopal dedication service emphasizes a sense of stewardship, positioning parishioners as peacemakers, appreciators, and benefactors rather than as laborers.[50]

Throughout the century, though in different ways at different times, steelworkers were praised in public representations for their skill and expertise. We see this, in part, in Michael McGovern's identification of himself as the "puddler poet," a title that, during the era when tensions were building between craft workers and unskilled labor, laid claim to special skills, not simply hard work. A similar idea appears in a 1921 poem in the *Bulletin,* which expressed admiration for the skill and dedication of "The Boys of the Open Hearth." The poem describes how others have "watched them test the heat within" and "seen them dodge the charging crane."[51] Their bodies work hard, but they also use their brains. Such images were relatively rare, however, until the 1950s and 1960s, when images of steelwork begin to show workers as engineers and scientists. Republic Steel's promotional film *Men Who Make Steel* warns viewers that the old image of the steelworker shoveling coal into a furnace is "out-of-date": "Today, many of the men who make steel are more familiar with a slide rule than a shovel. They work with the tools of science and research." At first, the *Men Who Make Steel* seems to suggest that the real workers in the steel industry are the managers, the ones who do the planning. As a poem from the 1932 Youngstown Sheet and Tube *Bulletin* put it, "Back of It All" was "the thinker who thinks things through."[52] Yet the film goes on to show workers in many aspects of steelmaking, from the "skilled miners" who work with "modern tools" to men with the "experience and judgment" to properly operate a rolling mill to the "woman's touch" that handles the "quick, deft sorting of individual sheets." Steelworkers, the film suggests, bring "skills, experience, and enterprise" to the industry.[53] Such images might invite workers to identify themselves with the more educated, professional sectors of the company, and thus to be less committed to the union. At the same time, this approach separates the workers of the late 1950s and early 1960s from their supposedly less well-educated and more activist predecessors, and it allows steelworkers to view themselves as separate from (and better than) other workers who are not part of such an elite workforce.

Ironically, the idea of steelwork as skilled, expert labor sometimes meant that workers were erased from the scene. A 1962 Labor Day ad from a local bank praises Youngstown steelworkers as "one of the most capable, technically skilled labor forces anywhere." Yet unlike most other Labor Day ads, this one does not show an image of a worker. Rather, we see a large steel mill complex, in silhouette against a dramatic sunset, with the words "Well Done!" in white letters against the dark ground. The text reminds readers that "Youngstown's bright future, in great part, rests securely on the shoulders of the men and women who make up its labor force."[54] That powerful and important labor force is invisible, however. Youngstown Sheet and Tube's 1961 *Letter to Youngstown* emphasizes the high skill levels required in the technologically advanced process of modern steelmaking by showing almost no steelworkers. The few laborers shown in the film wear protective gear, including asbestos suits and headgear that make them look almost like robots. Most of the people whose faces we see are supervisors and researchers, wearing white lab coats and operating levers or dials rather than heavy equipment.[55] As with many of the images promoting Youngstown and its industry, these texts that define steelworking as a highly skilled, highly technical enterprise place structures and machines rather than people at the center of the image. Such images distance steelmaking from organized labor, both by erasing workers and by representing workers not as blue-collar industrial laborers but as trained professionals. In oral history interviews, workers who were in the steel mills during this period almost never describe their work in terms of technical expertise or even in terms of the mastery of machines. While the companies may have benefited from presenting themselves as leaders in technology and their industry as completely modern, workers may have recognized that such an approach diminished their importance.

Another strategy for managing conflict was to emphasize the strength of the worker, which suggested not just individual vitality but, more often, the power of the union. In many images, the figure of a single white man, usually depicted as very muscular and proud, stood for labor as a whole. Even before unions were organized, labor was often imagined as strong and powerful, sometimes as a genuine compliment but more often in the context of persuading workers to cooperate with management. Sometimes, "the worker" represented virtue and pride, while at other times he stood as a conflicted figure, representing collective power but also commitment to the community and cooperation, a message that appears most often during periods of labor-management conflict. This was especially true in advertisements and cartoons published in commemoration of Labor Day. Tensions surfaced clearly in these ads, often through a contradiction between visual images of labor as powerful and accompanying written texts that reminded workers that they should "cooperate" with management. Labor was presented in heroic terms, but that heroism was also turned inside out and used as an argument to encourage workers to accept their situation instead of fighting for better treatment.

A 1927 cartoon headlined "Bringing Home the 'Bacon'!" shows a brawny man hoisting a large box on one shoulder, with a sledgehammer in the other. He wears a henley-style work shirt, with the sleeves rolled high to emphasize his muscular arms. His overalls are rolled

"Bringing Home the Bacon!" Labor Day editorial cartoon, Youngstown Vindicator, *4 September 1927*

down, bunched at his waist, revealing his muscular chest. The image clearly suggests the strength of labor, and the word "labor" is written on his shoulder, just in case his identity wasn't clear. He occupies the center of the page, with a row of smokestacks and mill buildings in the background, positioning the worker at the center of industry and making him appear much larger than the mills. The box is labeled the "full dinner pail," referring to arguments being made in the local press calling for workers to cooperate with management, since the companies provided the "full dinner pail." The box overflows with packages and papers, many with labels reminding the viewer of the benefits American labor enjoyed during the boom years of the steel industry: "industrial independence," "highest wage standard in the world ($)," and "highest living standard." Yet the box also contains a page labeled "100% Americanism," which may have served as a call to patriotism but also a reminder that workers were not all alike.[56] In the 1920s, Youngstown had one of the highest percentages of foreign-born residents in the United States, and the majority of mill workers were not "100% American." The Ku Klux Klan had gained significant power in local politics early in the decade by emphasizing its anti-immigrant stance, a version of "100% Americanism." Moreover, a cartoon in the *Vindicator* would likely have been seen mostly by non-steelworkers and by native-born steelworkers rather than by immigrants. The cartoon may have helped remind white, native-born workers of the differences between themselves and the recent immigrants and African Americans who worked in the mills, many of whom were active in union organizing. By reminding white, native-born workers of the "100% Americanism" of steelworking and by using the figure of a strong white man, the cartoon may have encouraged them to view the immigrant-driven union efforts with suspicion or to associate the immigrants with Bolshevism. While the cartoon compliments workers by emphasizing their strength and their centrality in the local economy, it also raises tensions about workers' identities and reminds them that mill owners control their paychecks and their "dinner pails."

This pattern continued in the 1930s. In a 1935 advertisement sponsored by the "public spirited citizens of the Youngstown district," the powerful figure of the worker is positioned amid the buildings and smokestacks of the mills with the city's skyscrapers in the background. Again, the worker towers over the buildings, creating the illusion that labor was more powerful and more central than the mills or business, while the written text emphasizes "mutual esteem and understanding" and labor's "willingness and fairness . . . to co-operate with employers."[57] A similar ad the following year, sponsored by fifty-two local and national businesses (including the Youngstown Typographical Union, Sears and Roebuck, local drugstores, and even a local dentist), used yet another muscular white man, this time in a tight-fitting, muscle-revealing T-shirt, with one hand in a fist at his waist and the other holding firm to a large grapple hook, framed within a gearlike three-fourths circle, smiling proudly. The text of this ad is less contradictory, but like the others it emphasizes the benefits and recognition that were available to American labor. It reminds readers that labor deserves the public's "homage," because "the laboring man is the strength of this land, and the hope of the nation lies in the strength of labor."[58]

Another strategy used the image of the individual worker to emphasize individual effort and success, in an ad that represented the American dream as attainable but only through individual effort, not through collective labor struggle. A 1936 ad, sponsored by twenty-two local civic clubs and business organizations, including the Youngstown Association of Insurance Agents and the Youngstown Garden Club, shows a construction worker standing on a steel beam, waving down at a businessman driving a convertible. The headline reads, "I knew *him* when he pushed a wheelbarrow." The text notes that "a big percentage of the higher-ups in American industry today started at the very bottom of the ladder." The image and the text together remind workers that those who have enough "ambition and skill" will be able to "scale the heights," because in America, "opportunity cares not from whence you came nor to what class or creed you belong." Workers are responsible for their own prosperity, the ad suggests, but opportunities to advance on the basis of individual effort are "made possible by the good will among all classes—the spirit of 'live and let live.' It can be preserved only by maintaining harmonious relations among all citizens." Again, the individual figures represent larger groups of workers, but they also emphasize a division between workers, pitting the interests of those who seek labor solidarity against the interests of those who aspire to "scale the heights" on the basis of individual "ambition and skill." During the largest organizing drive in steelmaking history, and amid popular appeals to socialistic ideals, the "public spirited citizens of Youngstown" urged steelworkers to view themselves as individuals, not members of the working class.[59]

In the years leading up to the 1937 "Little Steel" strike, such messages seem designed to erase the unequal power relations in the mills, to appease workers, and to persuade them to participate fully in company-run workers' organizations rather than the developing unions. The strength of the figure of the individual worker suggests that labor already has all the power it needs, and cooperation suggests a negotiation among equals, an image that ignores the conflicts of interest and outright battles that were emerging at the time. Public statements that insist forcefully that "everything is all right," by praising the willingness of both labor and management to "talk over common matters"[60] or by telling workers that they are already powerful, often highlight gaps and points of tension. This is especially true when such messages are sponsored by those who already hold power or by groups affiliated with them.

Advertisements, cartoons, and columns in the local newspaper proclaiming the importance and *power* of labor may, at first glance, suggest a sense of mutual respect and harmony between workers and owners, and some workers may have bought into the image. In an oral history recorded in 1981, Grover Mace remembered his role in one strike as a go-between. As Mace tells it, he persuaded the general foreman to remove the armed guards from the mill by reminding him that "the whole majority of the men working in there are good men . . . that you could depend on and trust." He concluded, much as the ads suggest, that the mill ought to operate like a community: "We ought to be in the mill like we are in the neighborhood; love one another, help one another."[61] On the other hand, steelworker Archie Nelson recalled that "there was quite a bit of respect and cooperation, there for a period of time," but he immediately points out that "there's a lot of propaganda involved in that."[62] The ideal of mutual respect and peace clearly appealed to workers as well as management, but if such harmony really existed, no ad urging cooperation or flattering workers would be necessary.

As Nelson's comment suggests, many steelworkers recognized the intent of the ads, and for some, they functioned more to spur opposition than to elicit cooperation. Not only did workers continue their organizing efforts, leading to one of the most important strikes in the history of the steel industry, they also offered their own images of the power of labor, making clear the difference between the imaginary power of the muscular figure of the *Vindicator* ads and cartoons and the transformative power of collective action. *Steel Labor*, the weekly newspaper published by the Steel Workers Organizing Committee (SWOC) beginning in 1936, offered its own view of "How a Steel Worker Views the Meaning of CIO" (Congress of Industrial Organizations). The cartoon shows a large group of men, most wearing caps and safety goggles, all smiling, mostly white but with one black face among the crowd. They are gathered under the CIO flag, and the benefits of the union are spelled out on either side of the flag: "To insure a stable prosperity with humane working hours and living wages," "more time for hobbies and recreation," "active industrial representation," and, most interestingly, "moral ascension." This collective image suggests a very different vision of the meaning of worker power, based not on individual strength or cooperation but on solidarity and clear goals for improving workers' lives. The cartoonist, E. W. Hudson, a steelworker from Glenwood, Illinois, explained that it represented his "wishes for the success of the unionization campaign."[63]

When labor organizers used the single man image, the message offered was quite different from that of the *Vindicator* ads and cartoons. In its 1936 Labor Day issue, *Steel Labor* ran a front-page drawing of

TO INSURE A STABLE PROSPERITY

WITH HUMANE WORKING HOURS AND LIVING WAGES

MORAL ASCENSION

MORE TIME FOR HOBBIES AND RECREATION

ACTIVE INDUSTRIAL REPRESENTATION

"How a Steel Worker Views the Meaning of CIO," E. W. Hudson, Steel Labor, *6 March 1937, United Steelworkers of America*

the usual muscular white man, in this case holding up an anvil in one hand and a pickax and a set of safety goggles in the other. His short-sleeved, open-necked shirt shows his strong arms and shoulders, and his face bears a look of serious determination. Instead of a mill in the background, this man stands in a field. To his left, two figures rise from the ground, both nude, as if to echo the creation of Adam. One reaches an arm toward the worker, who towers above him, while the other shields his eyes, as if the scene were too bright. The caption explains that "Organized Labor Sets a New Light and Meaning to the Life of Mankind."[64] The worker icon here represents power, but instead of a text urging workers to cooperate, the image and caption urge workers to become part of the new power of the union. The caption also promises change, a "new light and meaning" that will, it seems, lead to a new kind of man. This image is as idealistic as those suggesting cooperation, but the idealism is based not on the strength of labor but on the promise it offers workers for a better world.

"Organized Labor Sets a New Light and Meaning to the Life of Mankind," Steel Labor, *5 September 1936, United Steelworkers of America*

In December 1936, a full-page ad in *Steel Labor* used the same image of the brawny man holding the grapple hook that had appeared in the *Vindicator* ad placed by small businesses in September of that year. In *Steel Labor*, the man stands before an oversize banner that reads "WE are on our way." The text emphasizes the success of the organizing drive, explaining to steelworkers, mill bosses, and local businessmen that they should accept and support the new union. Here, SWOC appropriated the idea that labor was powerful, offering the strength of labor to leverage greater support for the organizing effort from both steelworkers and their communities. Instead of suggesting that workers should cooperate with management, the *Steel Labor* ad reminds "Mr. Business Man" that the union's strength might affect his business. A union worker will make more—and thus spend more—money. But the local businessman is also given a warning that he should remember that the union is winning this struggle and that he should "act accordingly."[65] The warning uses the image of labor as powerful to seek aid for labor's cause, in contrast to the other ads that use the image to persuade workers that labor is already powerful enough. It is important to note that the audience for *Steel Labor* almost certainly included many more steelworkers than businessmen, and the intent of the message may well have been to persuade potential union members of the benefits of unionization and the power that they could wield through collective action.

In the 1940s, after the United Steelworkers union had been officially recognized, the uses of the steelworker icon changed, and the supposed power of labor disappeared from public imagery. In 1946, Republic Steel ran an ad featuring the head and shoulders of a white male worker, but the figure of the worker was no longer a brawny hulk. Now, he looked like an ordinary guy, and the image even suggests that he is surprised to learn that he is valuable. The worker looks straight at the viewer, gesturing with his thumb to his chest, and the headline (in the worker's voice) asks, "You mean *I'm* Worth $6,000?" The ad responds,

> Yes, sir. . . . That six thousand dollars is the money that Republic stockholders and bondholders invested before you

Advertisement promoting union membership, Steel Labor, *19 December 1936,*
United Steelworkers of America

> could have a job at Republic Steel. That six thousand dollars
> furnishes you with a place to work, tools and equipment to
> work *with,* the raw materials for making steel and steel prod-
> ucts, and all the other things that make it possible for you to
> hold down a good job. Six thousand dollars just to provide one
> job for one man![66]

The ad seems aimed both at workers, who are reminded that someone else owns the means of production and that they have jobs because someone else "makes it possible," and at investors, who are
reminded that their money provides jobs and paychecks to grateful
workers. After all, the ad says, without such investments, there would
be "no community of Republic families to help make Youngstown a
bigger, better, more prosperous city." Ironically, once organized labor
gained some measure of real power, the steel companies were less
likely to represent the worker as a powerful figure. Here, he is presented as a dependent, not on the union but on the company and its
investors. He is invited not to cooperate but to be grateful and, we
can assume, not to ask for anything more than the six thousand dollars that has already been invested.

The icon of the individual worker, always a white man, continued
to appear in Labor Day ads and cartoons throughout the 1950s, and

it continued to both flatter workers and tell them how to think. As in the 1927 ad, the connection between labor and American patriotism often took center stage. A 1953 ad calls the American worker "Mr. American" and insists that he is "100% sold on the American free way of life, because he has seen it work." The admiration, we're told, is mutual: "All America" knows that "America has grown great and grown strong" because of "the American working man."[67] In a 1956 ad from the Hall Painting Company, a proud worker wearing a painter's cap stands with his hands on his hips, looking down on the world he has helped to build—a city full of skyscrapers, industrial buildings, ships, and an airplane. The caption salutes "American labor—now, as always—builders of a better world." But most important, the ad concludes, "the united efforts of loyal workers and foresighted management" have produced "America's greatest product—FREEDOM FOR ALL!"[68] During the red scare of the 1950s, this emphasis on Americanism might have served to assuage concerns that unions were sympathetic to communist ideas, yet it also reminds workers that "the American way" serves them well. The tension is illustrated well in a 1958 editorial cartoon from the *Vindicator*, showing the usual worker icon looming above office buildings and industrial scenes. The caption suggests that "we pay just tribute to the workingman's vital contribution to the rich cornucopia of American life," but it goes on to warn of turmoil within "the House of Labor," citing a quote from Ulysses Grant: "Labor disgraces no man; unfortunately, you occasionally find men disgrace labor."[69]

One image stands out from this collection, offering similar images and messages but with an important variation. A 1949 Labor Day cartoon in the *Vindicator* shows a figure very similar to the one pictured in 1927: a well-muscled, shirtless white man, holding a sledgehammer, standing over an anvil, with smoke and steam rising behind him from the line of mill buildings over which he looms. The headline reminds readers to "Count our Blessings," which are shown in the list held by the worker. While many items on the list are the same as in 1927—high wages, prosperity, high standard of living—others are new and unusual: "strong unions," "recognition," "protection of rights," and the "right to organize."[70] While the worker icon was often used to critique or challenge labor solidarity, for at least one brief moment the image of the strong worker embraced the idea that strong unions might also be worth celebrating.

IT'S WAR IN YOUNGSTOWN

As many of the representations of steel mills and workers suggest, labor conflict was a key element of ideas about work in the Youngstown area. Images that emphasize harmony and virtue offered positive images of work, yet they also helped to deflect or control conflict. Images of work as an unqualified good and workers as content and powerful indirectly told the audience, many of whom would have been workers and their family members, that whatever struggles or conflicts they encountered in their working lives were unimportant or should be smoothed over. But conflict was not always hidden, and images created by workers and those who sympathized with their cause regularly use struggle and even warfare as central themes.

Images of the dangers of steelwork clearly convey the difficulty and struggle of that labor. While Sandburg's image of "five men swim[ming] in a pot of red steel" highlights the dangers of millwork quite graphically,[71] Kenneth Patchen's poems offer a more thoughtful, personal comment on the struggles of mill workers. In "Anna Karenina and the Love-Sick River" (1943), Patchen describes his father being brought home after he "got hurt / Very badly in the mill." The focus isn't on the accident or even on his father, but on the unspoken attitude of resignation demonstrated when the father is carried into the house. "The point is this," Patchen tells us: "During the quarter of a century / My father spent in the mills, never once / Did he come from work through the front door; / And the men who brought him home that day / Took the trouble to lug him in by the kitchen. / This is one of the most beautiful things I know about." Yet the speaker cannot explain its beauty. "I'm afraid you've got me there," he says.[72]

While the image of always coming in through the back door might suggest familiarity, it also positions the father as somehow lesser, too dirty to come through the front door, and thus, perhaps, not quite worthy. A few years later, in "The Orange Bears," Patchen again looks at the injuries, physical and psychic, suffered by steel mill workers. The orange bears of the poem are steelworkers, who had had "Their paws smashed in the rolls, their backs / Seared by hot slag, their soft trusting / Bellies kicked in, their tongues ripped / Out." But their struggle wasn't only a matter of physical injury. The orange bears have also been beaten down emotionally: "their coats all stunk up with soft coal / And the National Guard coming over / From Wheeling to stand in front of the millgates / With drawn bayonets jeering at the strikers?" The poem closes with this comment: "A hell of a fat chance my orange bears had!"[73]

As "The Orange Bears" suggests, the dangers and difficulties of steelwork were never fully removed from labor struggles. At heart, though, labor conflict meant a continuing battle between workers and the mill owners and their representatives. The fight often concerned wages, working conditions, and the right to organize, but the conflict extended to workers' political and social independence. For example, in the election of 1900, managers tried to influence workers' votes by reminding workers that the steel companies "filled the dinner pail." Workers responded sarcastically, mocking management and pointing out that their labor, not managers' benevolence, is what really filled the dinner pail. The conflict is highlighted in a pair of "dinner pail" poems, written by Michael McGovern, that ran in the *Vindicator* in September 1900. He first offers a manager's version, in which the mill owners remind workers "those who get from us their feed / To us should e'er be true." The poem goes on to compliment the workers, noting, "There are no fighting men on earth / With you can now compare. / . . . But don't forget, it lies with us / To fill the 'Dinner pail.'" McGovern explains that this "savors of a lecture of a master to his slaves," and he offers an alternative version, "the answer of a free American citizen workman to the autocrat who grew wealthy on labor's products." In "The Workingman on the 'Dinner pail,'" he asks, "Are workmen's aspirations but / For food, for drink and sleep?" He then suggests that God must be offended when workers are "told that damning tale / That 'We (who never toil or spin) / Control your 'Dinner pail.'" As McGovern points out in a letter introducing another poem on this theme, management's arguments "insult the intelligence of the plundered working man, and are but giving him a crumb from the great table of industry on which his labor has piled up the good things of this world."[74] Another *Vindicator* column that month reported on conversations with workers who were offended by the dinner pail argument, largely because it suggested that all they cared about was food. One worker is quoted as saying that he also cared about his children's schooling. He complains that he can only afford to buy his children the cast-off books of children from the "avenue." "Mill men," the columnist notes, "are no different from the men that work at every kind of labor, we all have our little buckets when at work and we want them full of good healthy food, but that is not all we want."[75]

The theme of social conflict between classes resurfaces in a 1918 poem in the *Youngstown Vindicator,* written by a steelworker from nearby Warren. Oswald Greig's "The Dinner-Pail Brigade" describes the split, charging "the capitalists" with stealing from workers because "There's not a millionare who a red cent ever made, / But by the blood and life sweat of the Dinner-Pail Brigade." He highlights the worker's lowly social status, his lack of education and power—"Every one's my master; I'm nothing but a slave"—but he goes on to call for solidarity, urging fellow workers to "Get into line, fall into step; there's millions in your masses."[76]

Yet while many representations called for solidarity among workers, others suggested important differences and cast some workers as more deserving than others. These images pitted strikebreakers against unionized workers, often in ways that simultaneously emphasized divisions of race and ethnicity. Thus, McGovern begins one of his poems by describing the "ruler of the mills" as a taskmaster who "squeezed" work from laborers like juice out of lemons, an image that locates conflict about labor along lines of class. Yet a few lines later, he turns his attention to the company's practice of hiring strikebreakers to replace union men, describing the strikebreakers as "blacksheep" and the union men as "whitemen."[77] A number of his poems use this language to distinguish the good workingman from the strikebreaker, suggesting a division drawn along racial lines, though the division might not be between white and black as we see those races today. At the turn of the century, when these poems were written, those racial lines might well have marked divisions between native-born men of German or English descent and recent Italian or Slovak immigrants, who were viewed as members of another, darker race. While exactly whom McGovern meant when he referred to the "blacksheep" may not be clear, his argument against the use of strikebreakers and his judgment of both the company and the scabs was quite clear.

A similar argument emerges two decades later in a *Vindicator* report of comments by several AFL leaders, including Samuel Gompers, denouncing immigration as a threat to American labor. In the article, Gompers and others are quoted as describing recent immigrants as "undesirable, criminal, illiterate, defective, and pauper aliens." As a former grand chief of the Railway Conductors' union points out, organized labor was "interested in the exclusion of Chinese coolies during the eighties, and of Japanese in 1907," so the anti-immigrant sentiments of the 1920s should be seen as consistent with conservative AFL labor politics.[78] Labor's anti-immigrant stance, like McGovern's references to "blacksheep" and "whitemen," suggests that work was viewed as the rightful property of white, native-born men. The article appeared during the period when the Ku Klux Klan was gaining power in Youngstown, and it seems to echo the concerns of KKK supporters, who feared the economic competition offered by immigrants.

Most of the representations of work as a source of conflict focus on strikes, of course, though these images often involve other conflicts, among workers and between workers and various authorities—mill guards, local police, or the National Guard. Local and national news stories as well as several visual images of strikes show work-related struggles and occasional physical battles, though how the conflict is described and who is deemed responsible shift over time and according to the perspective of the publication in which they appeared. Images of earlier strikes, especially the 1916, 1919, and 1937 steel strikes, present work-related conflict as intense and complex, pitting workers against management, guards, each other, and America itself.

Before the 1916 strike, local newspapers noted recent profit reports from the steel companies and urged them to share their profits with the workers. Reports described the organizing efforts of several AFL representatives who had come to town during the weeks prior to the strike, noting their use of multilingual organizers to reach out to the many recent immigrants in the community. These preliminary reports regularly noted the AFL organizers' warnings to the workers to "avoid lawlessness" and violence, suggesting that some in the community were worried about what labor unrest would bring. The local press also added to that concern, however, offering a vision of union organizers as outside troublemakers. The *Youngstown Telegram* ran an editorial three days before the strike, commenting on the recently announced profits and a profit-sharing plan by the local mills. The editorial notes that "the majority of workers want justice, peace and comfort and not turmoil." The problem, the paper warns, is "itinerant agitators who profit on labor disturbances and are always ready to rush to the place where there is a possibility of creating strife. By choice they are thugs, loafers and grafters off the earnings of honest men. They are murderers if necessary. They do not want honest unionism, better wages or peaceable adjustment of wage differences. They thrive only on lawlessness." The solution offered, however, was not panic nor aggressive action by the companies but "for the employer to play the game squarely with his employes and he can do this by sharing with his employes [*sic*] when unusual profits come his way." While the overt message was that the steel companies should treat their workers well, the passage also creates an image of organized labor as led by "thugs, loafers and grafters."[79] This approach anticipated the strategies developed by James H. Rand, president of Remington Rand, who outlined a list of antiunion tactics in 1936, which he dubbed the "Mohawk Valley formula." While other elements of the formula would be used extensively in

Youngstown labor politics in later strikes, the *Telegram*'s descriptions of union organizers enacted the first plank as early as 1916: "When a strike looms, brand the leaders as 'agitators.'"[80] After thousands of Sheet and Tube workers walked off their jobs and as the strike grew more tense, the emphasis and tone changed. News reports noted that strikers had stockpiled bricks, bottles, and rocks, and the *Telegram* described battles between strikers and other workers who attempted to cross the picket lines.

When the strike turned into a riot, reporting became increasingly incendiary and increasingly focused on the strikers' immigrant status. While national newspapers described the rioters simply as "East Youngstown Steel Workers,"[81] local papers described them as foreigners. The *Vindicator*'s banner headline announced that "Mob Rule Reigns in Village," and a smaller heading reported that "Loot Is Found on Foreigners: About Thirty Suspicious Characters Are Arrested by Local Police."[82] The *Telegram* was more sympathetic, or perhaps paternalistic, toward the rioters. In one story, the *Telegram* quoted East Youngstown residents who insisted that the worst of the rioting was caused by outsiders, "professional looters," not local residents (who were friends or family members of the owners of local businesses that were destroyed) and not the foreign anarchists or instigators that the *Vindicator* suspected. The *Telegram*'s editorial on the strike placed the blame for the riot on the good citizens of Youngstown, who had ignored the poor and immoral living conditions of its neighbor community: "When strangers from strange lands are brought in here to contribute by their labor to the advancement of American industry and the upbuilding of American wealth and are permitted to live in such surroundings as those of East Youngstown, the blame for lawlessness lies upon the community that does nothing to prevent it."[83] At the same time, however, the *Telegram* emphasized the devastation of the riot, featuring large photos of the crowds gathered at the gates of Youngstown Sheet and Tube before the riot and the burned-out buildings and desolate streets of the community afterward. Local news coverage sensationalized the riot, yet it also defined labor struggle as a matter of national identity and morality. Immigrant steelworkers were cast as wayward children in need of better "care" from the larger community or as dangerous agitators, while the steel companies and even the AFL organizers were presented as thoughtful, cautious, and well meaning.

Ethnic and racial divisions played an even more central role in reporting on the 1919 steel strike, as the *Telegram* and the *Vindicator* both printed a number of reports and articles, some of them reprints from other papers, that defined the strikers as un-American radicals who were barring "good" American workers from their rightful work. A column in the *Telegram,* reprinted from *Harvey's Weekly,* praised Judge Elbert Gary, president of the U.S. Steel Company, for "fighting the battle of the country's industrial salvation" against the "foreign element on whom the outside union agitators had exercised an unsettling influence." Gary's argument, the column noted, was based on the "bedrock proposition of sound Americanism that a man has a right to work for whom he pleases and on such terms as he and his employer can agree upon as satisfactory."[84] Along similar lines, a cartoon in the *Vindicator* showed a large figure holding a sign labeling him as "Foreign Labor Element" wielding a club over a small man who scratches his head and comments, "This guy can't understand our questions, let alone our ideals," while another on the same page showed the frustrated figure of "Bolshevism" expressing dismay that labor and capital were meeting together to work out their differences.[85] On the same day, the *Telegram* ran an editorial describing the signs in steel mills "printed in five languages," while some of the workmen "who have resided here many years are still aliens and unable to speak English." The editorial ends by warning that a "swarm of agitators" was "waiting to invade this country, not with intent to work but with intent to ruin it."[86] Such images made clear that the labor problems of the day were caused by "the foreign element," and they may have contributed to the native-born versus immigrant splits that led to KKK dominance of local politics just a few years later.

While local newspapers fomented suspicion of recent immigrants and cast labor struggles as battles over ethnic identity and who controlled the right to work, national reporting, especially from the leftist press, took a different approach. The *New Republic* ran a three-page story on the Youngstown strike in January 1916, emphasizing the steel companies' disregard for the workers' quality of life. The story cites the research conducted by J. M. Hanson for the Youngstown Charity Organization Society, and it blames the companies for paying insufficient wages. The conflict in East Youngstown, according to the *New Republic,* resulted from "resentment and bitterness born of years in which excessively long and arduous labor had alternated with the shame and humiliation of begging for work and bread." Noting the successful negotiation between Republic Steel and its striking workers, the article goes on to criticize Youngstown Sheet and Tube for refusing to negotiate with the strikers, leaving the workers without "living wages, . . . untrained in collective action, helpless, subservient, not only in the plant but in the community."[87]

The 1937 "Little Steel" strike is both the most well-known and also, perhaps, the most hostile of the major strikes of the period. The "Mohawk Valley formula" was put into full play in Youngstown, with local police helping to guard mills, a company-organized back-to-work movement, and a variety of actions by mill representatives and guards to provoke the strikers to violence. While oral histories with rank-and-file workers and union leaders who were involved in the strike include repeated claims that the strikers tried to maintain a peaceful protest, the "Little Steel" strike is probably best known for the violence that erupted between strikers and guards. One evening that June, guards shot tear gas and rifles into a crowd of strikers and their families. Two people were killed and many wounded. Not surprisingly, both local and national reports described the events of the strike in terms of a battle. In an article for the *New Republic,* Mary Heaton Vorse described the steel mills as "arsenals filled with machine guns and tear gas."[88] In the *Federated Press,* Vorse quoted Sheriff Elser as saying that the strikers have "asked for war" and warning that "They'll get it." She also described local police and vigilantes "shooting down defenseless workers before our eyes." The essay ends with a litany of casualties: "A little boy. A woman who lies with her eyes still closed. A man. Three more women. . . . Two dead here. Ten dead there. Twenty-seven wounded here, a hundred there." [89] An abbreviated version of the same text from Vorse appeared along with photos in the July 1937 issue of *Photo History*. The photos emphasize the feeling of struggle. One shows two women and a man, all with handkerchiefs tied over their mouths and noses to block tear gas, holding rocks or clubs, as if ready for battle. In one, three women stand in defiant poses, one holding a brick, another a gun, the third a large stick. Their faces are grim and angry. In another shot, several men holding sticks and clubs lead another man away. He appears to have been injured on his leg. A small photo in the middle of the page shows Vorse herself, with blood trickling down her forehead. The spread shows no images of the police or guards, only strikers and their sympathizers, but the written text describes women being harassed on the picket line, guards firing shots and grenades into the crowd, and strikers running from the bullets. At the hospital, Vorse writes, "the wounded are arriving by carloads." The images and text together present the "Little Steel" strike as a battleground. [90]

The *Nation* apparently agreed. "It's War in Youngstown" a headline there announced in early July 1937, warning that the strike would soon bring "bloodshed and murder." Writing, like Vorse, from a pro-labor perspective, Rose M. Stein vividly describes the fight between strikers' wives and the local police. Stein ends by describing the Youngstown situation as a "war of resistance" between the CIO, "fighting desperately to maintain and augment the phenomenal strength and power it has so far attained," and the "enraged employers and frightened, muddle-headed, subservient officials, whose absolute power is being curbed." [91] Stein's language clearly positions the strikers as the protagonists, valiant fighters who sought to maintain their hard-won solidarity and force the "Little Steel" companies to accept the unions.

Stein's article is followed by a two-page spread of drawings by William Gropper, an artist known for using images as a form of social and political commentary. His drawings show various scenes of the strike-torn community, including three workers throwing bricks at passing cars, a woman shielding a small child with her body and holding a fist defiantly in the air, three plant guards firing guns at an unseen target, a peaceful cluster of men, women, and children talking among themselves, and two police officers holding billy clubs, waiting for something to happen. Gropper's written description says that his "introduction to Youngstown" included witnessing the scene at Gate 5, where the women were teargassed, observing union-sponsored bread delivery in a "poor colored section" of town, and watching Youngstown strikers mingle with workers from Akron and Pittsburgh who had come to show their support. Most of Gropper's line drawings show people in action, both workers and officials, and conflict shows clearly in all of the scenes. The strikers here are both victims and activists, attacked by the guards but also organizing for mutual aid.[92]

One of those drawings may have inspired Gropper's 1937 painting, *Youngstown Strike*, which Howard E. Wooden claims is intended as a depiction of the 1916 strike.[93] In both the black-and-white line drawing and the color painting, Gropper shows a cluster of men and women who appear to be under attack from a mostly unseen threat just beyond the left frame of the image. In the painting, we see several men in dark clothing, wielding large sticks, bearing down on the unarmed crowd, but the crowd seems to be looking farther to the left, perhaps to a larger group of attackers. The strikers occupy the center

Youngstown Strike, William Gropper, 1937, *Butler Institute of American Art*

of the painting, and they are its focus. The light picks up the white shirt of a man who looks as if he's just thrown something and the upraised arms and distraught face of a woman just behind him, who appears to be yelling in protest. Two figures, one clearly female, the other less distinct, lie injured as others bend over them, apparently offering aid and comfort. The strikers are presented as both active and injured, the objects of attack but not passive victims. They are clearly under attack, fighting off dark and rather anonymous forces, but some are also throwing things. The mill is in the background, in between the strikers, who occupy most of the frame, and the shadowy but menacing guards to the left. Also in the background, apparently standing to the side and observing, stands a single police officer, so dark that he's almost not noticeable. The painting invites sympathy for the strikers, but it also shows them as active participants in the struggle.[94] Few people living in Youngstown would have seen this painting during the period, though in 1985, a few years after the mills closed, the Butler Institute of American Art bought the piece for its permanent collection.

By the 1950s, when a series of strikes hit the steel industry around the country, images of labor conflict had a less local focus, and the conflict was presented as more subdued. Conflict remains, but it is more legalistic, more a battle of words and ideas than a battle of clubs, tear gas, and guns. In a 1950 Labor Day editorial, the *Vindicator* accused organized labor of using its "monopoly power . . . against the government and the public more ruthlessly than did corporate monopolies in the old days of the trusts."[95] A 1959 editorial in the *Vindicator* notes the rise in unionism since the 1930s and organized labor's "rightful role in the American scene," yet it also calls upon "the responsible majority" of labor leaders to resist the "irresponsible power in the hands of unprincipled leaders," a reference to charges of racketeering and corruption in big unions.[96] Letters to the editor during this period commented on labor legislation, the treatment of labor demands by the press, the effects of labor negotiations on inflation, and the complacency of union members.[97] A *Time* magazine story on the 1959 steel strike emphasizes the effects of the strike on workers' daily lives, describing how strikers were managing household budgets and how they were handling "the burden of too much time." The only hint of struggle here is a brief comment that "Youngstown's steelworkers and their families are neither angry nor restive—not yet, anyway."[98] Labor conflict was clearly a subject for discussion, and at times the language of these battles was heated, but the conflict was also diffused, shifted from specific local sites to the national landscape, from plant gates to union offices.

CONCLUSION

During the years when Youngstown was a vibrant steel community, public images of the mills and steelworkers defined steelmaking as an important element of community life, a source of identity and solidarity, an activity that brought pride and fulfillment to individuals and the community. At the same time, these images reveal some central divisions and tensions. While the community's elite wanted to highlight the city's civic and cultural accomplishments, the smoke and grit of the mills could not be erased. While work gave people a sense of pride and brought them together, it could not bridge the gap between workers and managers, nor could it fully erase differences of race and ethnicity. Work brought benefits of physical health and spiritual strength, yet it also brought risk and bitter, even violent struggle. Everyone may have seen Youngstown as a steel town where work was absolutely central, but the meaning of work and even the identity of the place were sources of conflict.

While it is easy—probably too easy—to assume that workers and the elite would see the meaning of work and conflict differently, it is important to remember that individual images are themselves contradictory, and audience members may have used them in multiple ways. Steel mill owners and other community leaders may have wanted to emphasize the community prosperity made possible by the mills, yet they were also keenly aware of the social divisions between those who did the labor and those who built the fine homes and museums that illustrated promotional books such as *Youngstown in Pen and Pencil.* In attempting to manage the potential conflict of class inequality, the elite created images that both flatter and manipulate the working class. Workers resisted the erasure of differences, yet they also sought recognition as individuals who were just as good as anyone else. They may well have taken pride in images that valorize labor, even as those same images call for conciliation with management. They embraced solidarity and class conflict while at the same time writing poems and creating monuments that emphasized the virtue of individuals. They may have been skeptical of Labor Day ads that emphasized community harmony, yet they expressed patriotism and built their own communities. For both the elite and the working class, the public images and personal stories that describe their experiences embody the complexities of work and place and provide the basis for multiple communities of memory.

Those complexities would be further challenged in the last decades of the twentieth century. When mills began to close in the late 1970s, the core of community and individual identity shifted, and the meaning of Youngstown and the meaning of work in Youngstown would be first transformed and then deformed. Once a site of productive labor and class struggle, Youngstown would become a place known for loss but also for resistance. The struggle for meaning in Youngstown would not end with the closing of the mills.

3

Deindustrialization and

the Struggle over Memory

❖ ❖ ❖ ❖ ❖ ❖ ❖ ❖ ❖ ❖ ❖ ❖ ❖ ❖

We're still here, we're still here
Now the mills have gone away,
But we're still here.
With our neighbors and our kin,
Right here where we've always been,
Now the mills have gone away
But we're still here.
—*Si Kahn, written for* Shout Youngstown

On September 20, 1977, just days after the *Youngstown Vindicator* reported on a "slight upturn" in steel sales and expanded production at two local mills,[1] the Youngstown Sheet and Tube Company announced that it was closing its Campbell Works. Over the next few months five thousand workers would lose their jobs; within five years, more than fifty thousand people would be displaced because of the mill shutdowns in the Youngstown-Warren area. Unemployment would reach over 20 percent and remain in double digits for more than a decade. As steelworking jobs became scarce, the meaning of steelwork changed, as did Youngstown's identity. "Steel town" was about to become the heart of the Rust Belt, and local pride would be challenged as insiders and outsiders alike redefined the meaning of this place. Once known for productivity and hard work, Youngstown became, as a *CBS Morning News* reporter would put it twenty years later, a "symbol of the failure of American industry." During that same twenty years, however, Youngstown also gained fame for its refusal to give up without a fight. As steelworker John Barbero commented in a film about the fight against the mill closings, people around the country looked at Youngstown and shook their heads, saying "that Youngstown is sure dying hard."

Representations of deindustrialization from 1977 to 2000 reflect these changes. The meaning of work itself shifted. While the old image of steelmaking as meaningful and skilled work persisted, new images devalued steelworkers and highlighted the danger and disillusionment of steelwork. Many of the representations from this period focus on job loss. Both those immediately involved and others who were drawn to Youngstown to tell the story struggled to make sense of what the mill closings would mean for individuals, their families, the community, and the nation. At the same time, writers, artists, and journalists raised questions about what Youngstown would mean now that its work was disappearing. While some saw Youngstown as a place of loss and failure, others found hope in the community's determination and struggle. While earlier representations reflected conflicts over class and work, by the 1990s, the conflict focused on how to remember the community's past. Would Youngstown be remembered as a site of loss or as a place of struggle, a symbol of failure or an image of resilience? This chapter traces the struggle over memory in Youngstown by examining the dialogue among representations of work, loss, boosterism, and activism.

WORK

During the heyday of the steel industry in Youngstown, representations defined work as a source of identity for the community, as well as an activity that created individual identities and a sense of belonging. Work represented virtue, expertise, power, and conflict. Few of the images of work during the first seven decades of the twentieth century focused on individual workers. A few noted the dangers of steelwork and many emphasized conflicts over class, race, and ethnicity. Yet the importance of work and of the steel industry in Youngstown was never questioned. It may have been a source of conflict, but it was so central to the community's economy and day-to-day life that Youngstown could not be imagined as anything but a steel town. Even images of work that emphasized problems related to steelworking could not imagine Youngstowners doing anything else.

As steelworking jobs began to disappear, however, their meaning became at once more practical, more spiritual, and more problematic. For the first time, Youngstown and its workers had to ask themselves what their community and their lives might mean without the steel mills. The tensions that emerged during this period no longer focused so clearly on conflicts based in class and race, although much public criticism was aimed at the steel corporations and the unions. Rather, the conflict began to focus on questions of how to define Youngstown and what it meant to be a steelworker, both in the past and in the present, when the job no longer existed. While economic struggle was at the heart of deindustrialization, a parallel struggle emerged over representation itself. What did the work mean when the workplace shut down? In a community that had built its identity on work, what did it mean to be out of work?

While initial news reports emphasized the economic value of steel jobs, citing the effects on other businesses, local taxes, and church collection plates as well as the pockets of the laid-off workers, additional reports soon followed, noting, as a *Vindicator* headline put it, "Campbell Works More Than Jobs; Steel Way of Life Is Disappearing." Working in a steel mill was not just about earning a paycheck, and steelmaking skills did not translate easily to other kinds of jobs. As an unnamed steelworker explained to reporter Sergio Lalli, what could he tell a prospective employer: "Can I tell him that I've seen men's trousers catch on fire because they got too close to the furnace, that you have to wear longjohns in July to keep the heat off your legs, that I've seen men faint from the heat, that our crew received orange windbreakers because we set a production record?" As this comment suggests, some steelworkers who once felt proud of the special skills and knowledge they brought to the mill now came to feel shame that they did not have enough education or expertise to get another job. YSU philosophy professor Tom Shipka, whose father was president of United Steelworkers Local 2463 at the Campbell Works, told Lalli that steelmaking was "hard and dirty work, and [steelworkers] take pride in it. It's what they do best." Laying off a steelworker, he said, was "like an athlete being told he can't compete or an artist being told that he can't paint."[2] While the local paper's first response focused on economic costs to the community at large, job loss for these workers was clearly about more than money.

The national press also recognized that the steel mill closings were not simply an economic issue. In a 1984 op-ed piece in the *Washington Post,* for example, Mark Shields described Youngstown's experience as a "human tragedy." A large part of Shields's argument rested on the value of work, not simply because of lost income but also because jobs "confer status and self-esteem." He invited the presidential candidates to come to Youngstown to better "understand the pain" of deindustrialization. "Let the visitor walk by the Campbell Works," Shields suggested, to get a close-up view of the pain of unemployment: "The loss of a job, especially a coveted industrial job such as that of a steelworker, hurts. The steelworker was the contemporary counterpart of the American cowboy. He used and tested his muscles daily. He worked with danger and he worked hard—no three-hour lunches with clients and customers."[3] Writing for an audience that was, for the most part, far removed from steel mills, Shields valorized steelwork to emphasize the significance of its loss, and he subtly put down more privileged and (at that time) less endangered forms of work.

Shields's approach exemplifies a pattern that was played out in different ways over the next fifteen years. As writers and artists attempted to make sense of the meaning of work during deindustrialization, they often used work and the loss of work as mirror images, each reflecting the other. Representations of work during this period were almost always shadowed by the implied threat of job loss, while images that focus on the loss of work usually include powerful statements about the meaning of work. For example, the *Mill Hunk Herald*, a journal of creative writing, essays, photos, and artwork by steelworkers, published a poem by Youngstown steelworker John Martin in 1980, in which Martin writes of the mill closings: "I don't have a place. / my contribution / they tell me is not needed / who will give my hands / their natural right? / who will engage my mind / in the wrenching from nature / of goods?" The closing of Martin's poem suggests that its speaker does not easily accept the idea that he is no longer valuable. "Has it all gotten so sick," he asks, "that men and women must walk / these streets in despair / told the hideous lie / that we don't need them?"[4] In a 1985 issue, the *Mill Hunk Herald* ran an essay by Teresa Anderson, telling the story of Mike Bibich, who struggled to understand the shutdowns. She quotes Bibich's response to the term "rust bowl": "What in the hell is that supposed to mean? Look at me. You see any rot on me? I keep looking for something wrong with me, everyday in the mirror, but I don't feel any different." Bibich clearly resisted defining himself as something of lost value, yet Anderson describes how he spends his time sitting on his front stoop, drinking beer and watching over the now abandoned church across the street. In both pieces, we see laid-off steelworkers at once questioning and defending their own value, insisting that they should not be disposable but also wondering where they fit into a world without steelwork.[5]

Similarly, representations of work during this period always include the idea of potential loss, as we see in a profile of Brier Hill open hearth worker Carroll Megginson, in *Real Men*, a 1980 book on masculinity. The photo essay emphasized the dangers of steelwork, yet it also highlighted the threat of job loss, portraying Megginson as both rugged and vulnerable. One of Megginson's "responsibilities," author Frank Rose notes, was to "scramble out of the way of the molten steel" when a charge goes off, "taking care not to get splashed by the metal itself or blown away by its accompanying blast of hot air into the ladle that's waiting below."[6] Steel may be, as the article says, "a hellish substance to make," but Megginson "is lucky to have a job," and he makes "good money." That's not enough to "translate into the good life," but "it's still possible to have a good time on Friday night, assuming you're a steelman and you haven't been laid off yet."[7] The narrator explains that "steelmen . . . are a breed apart." They are "midwife gnomes who officiate at the birth of a metal that helps separate humanity from the animals. They pride themselves on their ability to take punishment, but still they are twisted by it into alien shapes, gnarled and toughened. It is their readiness to risk not only health but existence for its manufacture that marks them as different from other people. They possess a straight-on sense of authority."[8] Rose's words represent steelmaking as powerful, even emotional work, creating a tone reminiscent of some texts from earlier in the century. But Megginson distances himself from this, explaining that he has "no fetish for tapholes blowin' out—no fetish at all. Not even the least bit of pyromania." He's there, he says, for the money. He thought for a while about trying to become the first black supervisor at Sheet and Tube, but decided that it wasn't worth the effort. He was content to be a second helper on the open hearth. And he noted confidently, "As a blue-collar worker, you're guaranteed that as long as they're working, you're gonna have a job. The only way I'm gonna leave there is if they shut the place down." Confidence is revealed as bravado, however, when Megginson explains that he stays at Brier Hill, even though it's likely to close sometime soon, "because I'm honestly afraid to venture forth right now."[9] As this admission suggests, the emotional disinvestment Megginson assumes mirrors the economic disinvestments he sees elsewhere in the community. That point is emphasized by the ending of the story, a scene in a local steelworkers' bar, with the bar owners complaining about how the shutdowns were ruining their business and debating with customers whether the mills would ever come back. The implication is that Megginson, too, will soon be out of work, and by the time the book appeared in print, he was.[10]

The profile is accompanied by a dozen black-and-white photographs of Megginson on the job: walking into the cavernous open hearth section of the Brier Hill Works, inserting an oxygen lance into the hearth to begin the tapping process, being showered with sparks as molten metal breaks through and starts to flow, taking a sample of steel to be tested, and washing up around a large sink with other workers at the end of the shift. The images make steelwork look dramatic, dangerous but also exciting. The images are the work of George Bennett, a New York photographer with family ties to Youngstown. Fifty of Bennett's photos of the Brier Hill Works were displayed at the Butler Institute of American Art in 1986, under the title *Youngstown Steel: A Tribute to the American Open-Hearth,* though Bennett's own title for the series is *The Last Days of Youngstown Steel.* The photos highlight the activity of making steel, with many images of the huge steel mill machinery, molten steel being poured, and workers tending the open hearth.

Yet what is most striking about Bennett's photos is not how they present the work but rather how they present the workers. While many industrial images, especially those from the 1960s and 1970s, focus on machinery and the industrial built environment, nearly all of Bennett's photos include steelworkers, and in most the workers are the primary subject. Several show groups of workers talking, sometimes laughing and sometimes more serious. These clusters of men suggest the camaraderie that ex-steelworkers regularly say is one of the things they miss most about their work. Others focus on individuals. In one, a man stands with his back to the camera, in a rectangle of light cast from a window above. His arms are raised wide above his shoulders and his hands are positioned so that they appear to be points of light or fire, a pose that suggests both crucifixion and celebration. He appears to be motioning, perhaps directing the activity he watches—a twenty-foot-high ladle tipping to dump hot metal into a vessel. The image captures both the impressive mechanical process of steelmaking and the power of steelworkers. Another photo shows Megginson crouching over a small white-hot sample of steel, grasping a small chunk with a large set of tongs. The brightness of the molten metal and the light it casts on Megginson's hard hat and gloved hands are the focal points of this image, and his body almost fills the photo frame. This image, and several others that focus on one or two men doing specific tasks, work effectively with others that emphasize the large scale of steelmaking. Together, the images make clear that despite the oversize machinery, human beings are the heart of the steel mill. As reviewer Jay Paris remarked, Bennett's photos show the "remarkable dignity" of steelmaking.[11]

Dignity is presented most clearly in Bennett's portraits of individual workers, close-ups of them looking directly at the camera, with the mill setting blurring in the background. Some of these workers look tired or grim, though one younger man smiles impishly while another stands almost defiant beside a huge ladle, head high and tools slung casually over his shoulder. They are presented as individuals, identified as workers by their hard hats, safety glasses, sooty clothing, and sweaty faces. In one of the collection's most powerful images, Megginson stands just out of a slanting shaft of light, the kind of light that in a sentimental movie would symbolize hope or faith. The light catches Megginson's shoulder, neck, part of his face, and the top edge

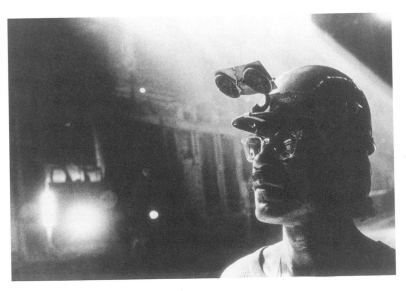

Untitled photograph of Carroll Megginson, George Bennett, c. 1980

of his hard hat, and light from another source creates a glare on his glasses so that we cannot see his eyes. Most of his face is in shadow as he watches something or someone else. The image brings to mind the juxtaposition of heaven and hell, cathedral and fire pit, that steel-workers often use to describe their work. The next two images suggest that what Megginson is watching so intently is the aftermath of an accident in the open hearth. In the first, the viewer looks down from a catwalk as an injured worker is carried away on a stretcher by six other men. Then we see a white-clad nurse, sitting on a bench that is draped with an American flag. Her face shows concern, and her hands seem to grip each other as if tensed, yet she sits, watching something that we cannot see, just as Megginson does in the earlier image. The images remind us, again, of the danger involved in steelmaking, and in doing so, they suggest the limits of the worker's power in the mill.

Taken as a whole, the series offers a complex image of steelmaking. Workers operate as a group but also separately. The mill is run by men, yet it can overpower them. The machinery itself is fascinating and beautiful, but Bennett's focus on the workers reminds us of the human labor and commitment that operates the equipment. Steelwork is celebrated but, as the exhibit's title reminds us, it is also doomed. The tension between these different ways of viewing the work is echoed in the two titles for the exhibit. *The Last Days of Youngstown Steel* suggests an elegy for something that is about to be lost; *A Tribute to the American Open-Hearth* suggests a celebration of something that is gone.[12]

A similar tension emerges in *The Steelmakers*, a large commemorative piece on steelwork commissioned by the Youngstown Area Arts Council and created by George Segal, an internationally known sculptor whose work positioned very lifelike human figures—often created from molds shaped on the bodies of the people who were being represented—in realistic environments. Segal came to Youngstown in the midst of the first wave of mill closings. Both the arts council and Segal himself were conscious that the work they were commemorating was changing dramatically, if not disappearing altogether. The sculpture and community responses to it demonstrate the complicated tensions that emerged surrounding the meaning of work as the mills were clos-

The Steelmakers, *George Segal, 1980, photo by Michael Williamson, 1985*

ing. The piece features an open hearth from the Brier Hill Works, with two life-size bronze figures, modeled on men who worked at Brier Hill, testing the molten steel for carbon levels. It was originally installed on Federal Plaza in downtown Youngstown, ironically next to the welfare office, in 1980. As Segal explained in an interview, the sculpture was meant to celebrate "the human spirit. Sure, if the steel mills have closed, yes, it's important, but I think the strength of the people who live in a town is equally important." He constructed the piece from unfinished steel, using elements taken directly from the actual mill, because he felt this would highlight "the natural, unconscious strength of the steel mill." He was intrigued by the power of the mill, describing its "impressive" and "massive" size, the "giant machines" that "delicately pick up steel beams that can crush you in three seconds." He was equally impressed, he said, with the workers, who "really loved the drama, the excitement, something spectacular about being in this gigantic space that's gloomy, dark . . . crashing cymbals, showering floods of sparks, and all these little guys controlling giant buckets and pouring molten steel, and loving it. Loving the drama, the excitement, the control over nature force." Segal explained how the elements of the sculpture were meant to evoke the power of both the mill and its workers:

> On the main street of Youngstown, you'll be able to see the massive door, the chain—one link of the chain is thicker than my fist—that sort of thing. It's incredible, oversize, overweight, but a small segment of a real open hearth furnace. Two guys in bronze, dark bronze, are going to be standing, doing the real thing in front of the furnace. . . . Something about the relationship between guys who are flesh, vulnerable, ordinary people like you and me—I don't want to glorify them. . . . These are regular guys, with all the vices and virtues of people.[13]

Like the sculpture itself, Segal's comments emphasize his respect for the power of both the mills and the workers. Yet both his words and his artwork carry multiple, even ironic meanings. The comment about the "unconscious strength" of the mill acknowledges the physical power represented by the massive mill structures, but it also indirectly reflects the massive power of the corporations over the lives of people in Youngstown. Segal's admiration for the workers emphasizes their strength, as demonstrated in their ability to control the forces of nature, but he also acknowledges their vulnerability. As Segal notes, the steelworkers were "big, tough guys who wouldn't let you push them around for a second, but they were poetic talking about how beautiful it was to make steel. And how they cried at the closings." They were vulnerable, of course, not just to the dangers of steelmaking but also to the pain of job loss.

Community response to the sculpture suggests that it represented both appreciation for the power and beauty of steelmaking and the loss and anger associated with the mill closings. Even as it was being installed, some Youngstowners loved it and others reacted bitterly. An untitled documentary on the making of *The Steelmakers* includes an interview with a former U.S. Steel worker who liked the piece because it brought back the feeling of being in the mill, though another said, "I sure liked it better when it was making steel." Another viewer noted that the sculpture made her think about her father's stories about working in the mill. Yet someone else commented bitterly, "It is a lot of money, and for what? The Valley's gone to hell, isn't it?"[14] Over the next few years, vandals stole pieces of the sculpture, bent the metal rod that the workers hold, spray painted it, and threw trash around it. Thus, despite the efforts of the local arts council to commemorate and valorize steelwork, Youngstown did not have the resources to protect the piece. Not only was there not enough money to provide police presence downtown that might deter vandalism, the community also did not have the will to protect the memory that the sculpture represented.

That lack of investment in remembering steelwork was made clear in the early 1990s, when the piece was dismantled and moved to the new Youngstown Historical Center for Industry and Labor, the "steel museum." The open hearth section was installed on the front lawn of the museum, and the sculptures of the two workers were moved to the museum's lobby. The move marginalized and fragmented the piece, removing it from a downtown pedestrian mall, where office workers and people going to the county courthouse would see it closely and daily, to a corner with almost no foot traffic. Drivers passing the museum see the steel mill section, without people, as abandoned and meaningless as the mills themselves. The two worker figures inside are protected and revered, part of the museum's commemoration of the history and labor of the community, but like the displaced steelworkers who posed for the sculpture in 1980, they have also lost their purpose. The comment of one of the models seems both resonant and ironic. "I don't feel that I'm representing me," he explained, "I'm representing all of the men that came in steel and worked in steel, past, present, and future."[15] But instead of representing them as actively engaged in meaningful work, what Segal termed "the real thing," the figures now stand in a mostly silent space, seen by the museum's relatively few visitors, and the tools they hold reach out to nothing. The sculpture's meaning has changed dramatically, transforming Segal's representation of power and vulnerability into an image that highlights the loss of work. The mill section has no workers, and the bronze figures inside the museum have no work.

The fear of losing a job haunts Frank Rose's profile of Carroll Megginson, and George Segal's sculpture was inadvertently reconstructed into an image of job loss. Loss of work is the central theme in *Journey to Nowhere: The Saga of the New Underclass*, a 1985 photojournalism study by writer Dale Maharidge and photographer Michael Williamson. In the early 1980s, Maharidge and Williamson traveled all over the United States talking with unemployed men and women, many stranded by deindustrialization. The book begins in Youngstown, using the steel mill closings to show how industrial change affected people's lives. To emphasize the impact of job loss, Maharidge and Williamson begin by telling their readers "How It Was." The first paragraphs of the book tell how steel dominates life in Youngstown. Maharidge describes the mills as the "deities of the industrial revolution," where looking into the "inferno called the soaking pit" is like looking into hell, and "hell is beautiful."[16] As in the profile of Megginson, Maharidge's text defines steelwork as both powerful and dangerous, killingly hard but also central to the life of the community. "Steel has been good to Youngstown," he writes. "The American Dream is wrought in steel for the city of Youngstown." Work is a source of pride and success, a point that takes on added significance at the start of a book on the loss of work. "We are the best damn steelmakers in the world," Youngstown workers proclaim, but readers know already that no matter how good they are at their jobs, these bragging men are about to be made obsolete.[17]

The story is made all the more poignant by Williamson's black-and-white photos, most of which link images of workers and their families with images of the destruction or abandonment of the mills. One shows Joe Marshall and his son, whose stories are told in the

Ken Platt Jr. and Sr. at the "Jenny," photo by Michael Williamson, Journey to Nowhere, *1985*

book's first chapter as examples of the effects of the mill closings, standing in the middle of a pile of rubble—pieces of wood, slate, a section of brick wall, their heads bowed in sorrow. The two men occupy the center of the photo, though they are also a relatively small part of the picture, overshadowed by the vast field of "ruins of the mill where they used to work," as the caption says.[18] In another, Ken Platt Sr., a burly man in a denim shirt, stands inside the mill, in front of the cold, abandoned Jenny, holding his young son in his arms. Father and son bear expressions of sadness, yet they also stand tall, looking directly at the camera. Like the written text, the photo captures the contradictory mix of pride in the work that was done here and sadness at its loss.[19]

Bruce Springsteen picked up on that irony when he read *Journey to Nowhere* almost ten years later as he was working on songs for *The Ghost of Tom Joad.* As he writes in the introduction to a reissue of the book in 1996, he read it through one night when he couldn't sleep and wrote three songs based on it. In "Youngstown," Springsteen writes in the voice of Joe Marshall Jr. He sings about the significance of steelwork, a "job that'd suit the devil," in a song that focuses on the loss of work in Youngstown. Using many lines straight out of Maharidge's text, Springsteen begins with the early history of the local steel industry, the furnace built by the Heaton brothers at the start of the nineteenth century, positioning his character as part of a long tradition of shared work. He emphasizes the patriotism of steelworkers by noting that "my daddy come on the Ohio works / When he come home from World War Two" and "I come home from Nam, worked my way to scarfer." He also reminds the listener that the products made by steelworkers contributed to national efforts: "These mills they built the tanks and guns that won this country's wars." But the work mattered for personal reasons, too: "Taconite, coke, and limestone fed my children, made my pay." The song's chorus addresses Jenny, the Jeannette Blast Furnace, as if it were a lover, "My sweet Jenny, I'm sinking down." Through images that combine natural forces—heat, smoke, and dirt—and religion, the song evokes a powerful but contradictory vision of the meaning of work as emotional, elemental, and spiritual but also ultimately disposable. The song describes "smokestacks reachin' like the arms of God / Into a beautiful sky of soot and clay," and it ends with the character commenting that he doesn't "want no part of heaven / I would not do heaven's work well / I pray the devil comes and takes me / To stand in fiery furnaces of hell." In the context of deindustrialization, work here represents both personal and national pride, and as in Segal's sculpture, the individual worker is both powerful and powerless, someone whose work defended the nation but whose employer is now "rich enough to forget my name."[20] As Nicholas Dawidoff commented in a *New York Times Magazine* article on Springsteen two years later, the song not only expresses the "bitterness" of job loss, it also juxtaposes "a mythical America where anything is possible with the crushing reality of a country that keeps letting hard-working people down."[21]

As Springsteen's song about the spiritual power of work and its loss suggests, the struggle to define the meaning of work after deindustrialization continued long after most of the mills shut down. A decade after the mill closings, artists and writers who were affected only indirectly by historical events that had shaped their community and, in some cases, their families' lives, began to create their own representations. While loss still haunts their work, this younger generation nonetheless holds on to the idea that steelwork held contradictory meanings. Working from a more distanced perspective, they emphasize the dangers of steelwork as well as its almost aggressive beauty, and their work suggests in almost elegiac ways that steelwork remained a powerful, imaginative force in Youngstown despite job loss, economic hardship, or even personal tragedy.

Local artist Bryn Zellers never worked in the mill, nor did his family members. But growing up in Youngstown, he was always drawn to the massive mill buildings and the image of steelmaking. Zellers's paintings, prints, and sculptures emphasize machinery rather than workers, yet he uses this imagery to examine the meaning of steelwork. While the local landscape now contains almost no mill buildings, his work frequently uses internal and external views of the mills and furnaces, often in bright yellows and oranges that visually suggest the heat and violence of steelmaking. His sculptures feature scrap, cast, and molded metal elements that evoke the machinery inside the mill. In two pieces, appropriately titled *Anxiety* and *Panic*, Zellers links individual emotions with the noise and danger of millwork; both pieces are set into motion when an observer approaches, giving off heat, sparks, and noise, and moving in ways that tell viewers to "stand clear," as one of them is subtitled. Ironically, when these pieces were exhibited in a gallery in New York, they were shut down by the local fire department because they were seen as hazardous. Zellers also notes that fellow exhibitors have sometimes complained that the noise and fireworks of his art distract from theirs.[22] His representations of steelwork emphasize both its danger and its fascination, creating a sense of natural forces that are just barely contained, just barely controlled.

A similar mix of fascination and awareness of danger appears in several poems published in a 1993 anthology of local writing, pieces written by individuals who did not work in the mills but who recog-

Anxiety (Unbalanced), *Bryn Zellers, 1995, from the collection of Eryn Schaefer*

nized the strong link between the worker and the work. While these poems include images that remind us of how deeply steelworkers valued their work, they also, like Zellers's sculptures, emphasize danger and hint at loss. In "Open Hearth," local poet M. Lisa Shattuck describes "Uncle Dominic," who "fed that furnace / his health and comfort. / The broad sweep of flames / over such raw potential: / his liver and lungs." Like Carl Sandburg in "Smoke and Steel," Shattuck acknowledges the dangers of steelwork, describing "three men at J & L who fell / when a catwalk buckled / to the crucible / and how their screams melted." But she also imagines steel and steelworkers as "fused like his memory, / just as tightly as those steel wires / that wrap his rod metal soul."[23] Kelly Bancroft describes how working in the mills captured her grandfather, ruining his hearing but shaping his life: "My mother's mother's husband's ears kept the sound of his work like a conch keeps the Pacific. Break it into one hundred pieces as I am told work broke my grandfather and each fragment still holds the sea. The sea and my grandfather are never free."[24] Both poems commemorate the worker's commitment to the job but also note the risks and losses involved.

Joe Gorman similarly suggests the contradictory nature of steelwork in "Days Since Last Accident." The poem begins with a description of what the steel mill used to be like:

> There used to be an orange
> glow in the sky, accompanied
> by a din of pounding
> hammers, tooting whistles,   ·
> and rumbling trains. Rats emerged
> from the depths of the mills
> as big as small dogs, forming
> packs, scrounging for
> food. The sign on the
> bridge over Wilson Avenue
> read
> "DAYS SINCE LAST ACCIDENT."

Gorman goes on to describe how "Grandpa made the light by / feeding pieces of soul / and flesh into the furnace." The poem describes the mill as a place of both beauty (the orange glow) and ugliness (the rats and pounding hammers), while work required not just physical effort and risk but a part of one's humanity. The poem closes, however, by expressing a sense of loss. Grandpa quit working at the mill, so "now, the light in the sky / is gone. Nothing / can ever replace it. / Even the / rats have abandoned / us for fresh / meat."[25] Steelwork here is valuable but also dangerous, costly to the individual but essential to the community.

In her ceramic sculpture *Certain Death,* local artist Betty Lambert, the daughter of an ex-steelworker and herself an industrial worker, represents a combination of loss, anger, and pride about steelwork. The sculpture depicts a human skull wearing a hard hat; the neck on which the skull rests is surrounded by a blue work shirt and a ring of barbed wire. As Lambert explains, the skull represents "the frailty and vulnerability of the human body" as well as the many steelworkers who were killed on the job "due to the poor, hazardous working conditions." The hard hat is worn backward, as many workers wore theirs in a gesture of defiance against management. Together with the barbed wire, Lambert says, these elements reflect the ongoing conflict between workers and management. The hard hat is cracked, an accident that Lambert decided not to repair, in reference to the steel companies' choice not to invest in or repair the aging mills of Youngstown. Inscriptions on the hard hat are based on workers' graffiti in steel mill locker rooms, a reminder that they claimed a kind of ownership of the workplace despite the conflict and risk involved in the work. The hat also bears a quote from Samuel Gompers that comments on the dignity of labor: "The labor of a human being is not a commodity or article of commerce. You can't weigh the soul of a man with a bar of pig iron."[26] In a small piece, no more than eighteen inches tall, Lambert captures a complex mix of attitudes about work and the loss of work.

That complicated and often ironic mix of ideas appears in many of the images of work and the loss of work created in the twenty years after the mills shut. As work became less certain, and as Youngstown ceased to be dominated by one kind of work, the meaning of work became increasingly intertwined with the idea of nonwork. The result was a bittersweet image of work that emphasized its difficulties as well as the pain of losing a job and the identity associated with it. While images of work and the loss of work often focused on individual struggle, the idea of loss became a dominant element in representations of Youngstown itself.

POSTER CHILD FOR DEINDUSTRIALIZATION

Deindustrialization challenged and reshaped long-held visions of the meaning of work in the Youngstown area, but it also disrupted the way Youngstown saw itself and was seen by others. As Tom Shipka put it, a few days after the announcement of the first major mill closing in 1977, "The community's identity is up for grabs."[27] Over the next two and one-half decades, Youngstown became known as a key site of deindustrialization, but what that meant was indeed up for grabs, as writers and artists, filmmakers, and journalists told various versions of the story of what happened when the mills shut down.

In the days following the initial announcement from Youngstown Sheet and Tube, workers were, as the *Vindicator* put it, "befuddled." Even though some had had an "'inkling' that the end was coming," they expressed surprise, worry, and confusion. Some worried about making house payments and finding new jobs. One commented that he had "no place else to go." While workers were concerned about their own survival, many also worried about how the shutdowns would affect the community. An African-American woman who had only recently gotten her job in the mill commented, that "It's all wrong, but I don't know who's wrong. Youngstown won't do anything when the people don't have any money. It will be hard on everybody."[28]

Local leaders recognized how devastating the mill closings would be. The mayors of Youngstown and Campbell, school board leaders in Campbell and Struthers, and even ministers and priests all spoke out in the days immediately following the Youngstown Sheet and Tube announcement, predicting major problems because of lost wages and taxes. A banner headline in the *Vindicator* on the day after the first closing was announced summarized the problem succinctly: "Loss of S&T Taxes to Hurt Area." The story goes on to quote Campbell city finance director John Kadilak, who pointed out that 80 percent of that city's taxes came from Sheet and Tube workers. Youngstown's mayor Jack C. Hunter commented that the closing was the "worst possible news that your elected public officials, straining to meet the challenge of major problems, could have received."[29] On the Saturday religion page a few days later, Leon Stennis reported that local religious leaders were worried about how the shutdowns would affect church collection plates.[30] As an editorial in the paper reflected, the closings were "The Worst Blow," presenting a challenge to the community as a whole as well as to individual workers and their families.[31]

Over the next five years, many national news reporters would come to Youngstown to tell the story, in part because Youngstown was one of the first major sites of deindustrialization. Early reports in national newspapers position the Youngstown story as a warning for other communities and for the national economy. Stories in the *Washington Post* during the week after the Youngstown Sheet and Tube announcement in 1977, for example, cite Youngstown as the first big plant closing in what business leaders and workers alike rightly feared would be a long series of job losses. A September 20 story focused on the problems of foreign competition in the steel industry, as well as concerns about environmental policies.[32] The timing of Youngstown Sheet and Tube's shutdown made Youngstown the national symbol, this story suggests, but that was, on some level, a matter of bad luck. Another community might just as easily have been the first to receive the blow. As if to reinforce this idea, a longer piece run on the following Sunday focused on the fear of job loss in nearby Steubenville, Ohio, as workers responded to the Youngstown shutdown announcement. As Steubenville mayor William Crabbe explained, what happened in Youngstown "broke the dam on the rumor mill" that had been predicting layoffs for several years.[33] During the 1980 campaign season, Ronald Reagan capitalized on Youngstown's struggle by coming to town and charging Jimmy Carter with responsibility for Youngstown's "tales of misery" and "lack of work."[34] Here, too, Youngstown served as an example, the worst-case scenario for national-level discussions of economic policy and deindustrialization.

By 1983, *New York Times* reporter Peter Kilborn could easily include Youngstown along with Detroit and Akron in a brief list of cities that represented "the clichés of unemployment and shut-down factories in the nation's depressed industrial core."[35] Earlier that year, *Wall Street Journal* reporter James M. Perry described the Youngstown-Warren area as "a necropolis," citing the miles of "silent, empty steel mills" up and down the Mahoning Valley. Perry caught the community's fear and loss through interviews with laid-off workers, one of whom explained that "We're just mill hunks. . . . We can't do anything else." Perhaps most important, though, Perry recognized the community's failing sense of hope, noting the "widespread concern that the economic recovery, when it comes, will pass the valley by."[36]

According to one version of the Youngstown story, those fears were justified. As Michael Williamson, the photographer for *Journey to Nowhere,* commented years later, Youngstown became a "poster child for deindustrialization," a symbol of the devastation of economic change.[37] This image of Youngstown as a place of loss is probably the most powerful and enduring representation to emerge from deindustrialization. While many voices have offered alternative stories, as we will demonstrate, this one carries an especially powerful force.

One reason may be that images of devastation tend to be framed in absolute terms, creating images that are easy to understand because they are fairly simple. A good example is a poem published in the 1993 anthology of local writing by Jeff Ortenzio, "Degrees of Gray in Youngstown." The poem addresses a Youngstown native, who "might come here some weekday because you / have to," someone in search of work and uncertain about how to imagine his hometown now that its past is disappearing. "Nobody likes to be here," Ortenzio writes, because

> The city speaks of unemployment.
> The mills stand alone. The beautiful
> stone courthouse. Homeless standing in its shadow.
> Shadows of great mills, once spewing smoke
> and flame. Nothing but shadows. Gray. Nobody
> likes to be here.

The image is desolate, hopeless. We are reminded by contrast of the power of the huge mills, which now stand as "skeletons" and "dinosaurs," relics of a past that leaves only "shadows."[38]

A much darker image of despair in Youngstown is offered in "Ten Years Later," a song by the local band Sister Ray on an album they produced in 1990. Songwriter Sam D'Angelo tells the very simple, straightforward story of Joseph, who was laid off on Black Monday. When his unemployment ran out and he could no longer support his family, Joseph "took his gun and one round" and "went on foot for a mile or two / To the place that killed this town. / Put the gun in his mouth / Pulled the trigger, hit the ground." This stark tale is only half of the song, however. The song's narrator "was too young" to understand Black Monday, ten years before, but he sees the mills, "ruins dark and gray, / Their metal panels rust and decay." Taking a camera and some beer, he and some friends go into one of the old mills one day, "hunting for souvenirs," and find "Joseph lying in his rusty tomb."[39] The song suggests both the despair of those who lost their jobs and the next generation's lost sense of history and identity.

Abandoned mills are a common motif in artwork from the late 1970s through the early 1990s. A number of painters and photographers have documented these structures and their destruction. In contrast to D'Angelo's use of the empty mill as a setting for a dramatic story, however, some visual artists emphasize form over function, viewing the buildings as "visually interesting" without focusing on the story surrounding them. Yet when those images are seen by people from Youngstown, stories cannot be entirely erased. Viewers bring stories with them. Regardless of the artists' intentions, both the documentary work and the more abstract images produce a sense of Youngstown as a place of stillness, silence, emptiness, and death.

The paintings of George Dombeck offer a good example. He first came to Youngstown in 1979, during the period when mills were closing, and he was taken with the shape and scale of the mill structures. While he noted in a 1988 interview that his images did not "have a lot to do with anything outside of the work," his stark paintings, many featuring images of stacks, cranes, and huge mill structures, create an image of the mills as uninhabited and forbidding.[40] The light gray or rosy backgrounds cast the mills in silhouette, as if the sun were setting behind them. In nearly every case, the mill structure is presented without context—no surrounding landscape, no entrances, no people. For Dombeck, framing the images in this way may have emphasized the "visual experience" of looking at the mills, but for those who attended his 1988 exhibit at the Butler Institute of American Art, the separation of the mills from their setting may well have suggested a

Steel Mill South, *George Dombeck, 1986, Butler Institute of American Art*

narrative of abandonment and desolation. Dombeck acknowledged that the images of the mills had a special appeal for him because he had watched coal mine closings in his hometown in Paris, Arkansas. He insisted that he did not intend for his images to be read as stories or commentaries, but he also noted his concern for the erasure of the mills from the Youngstown landscape: "Unless some small part of the steel mills is saved as a reminder of the history of this town, Youngstown is about to become just like a hundred other cities in America, and the grandchildren and their children will have lost part of their roots."[41] His paintings help preserve a "small part" of Youngstown's history, and in their stillness and emptiness, they offer an unintended comment on the loss of work as well.

We see a similar tension between viewing the mills as simply "visually interesting" and seeing them as meaningful representations of work and place in a collection of photographs of northeastern Ohio, presented in a book-length photo essay, *Images of the Rust Belt,* published in 1999, by local photographer James Jeffrey Higgins. The book contains forty-eight color plates, a little more than half of them images of industrial sites in Ohio, Pennsylvania, and West Virginia. The other images in the book are nature scenes, such as a pink-hued view of the Shenango Reservoir or shots of wooded areas near Higgins's hometown of Hubbard (about five miles northeast of Youngstown) in different seasons. Higgins explains the combination in his introduction, writing that he wanted to dispel the ideas he had grown up with, that the Youngstown area "was just a steel town and that nothing good could come from here. Nothing special or beautiful." He writes that he wanted to create images that would help viewers see that "rusted old steel mills and abandoned city streets" could be beautiful.[42] The book contains one image of the Jeannette Blast Furnace, with the brown, rust, and gray of the mill softened by the green of the trees and weeds that have grown up around the site since the mill shut down. But most of the book's steel mill images come from Weirton, West Virginia, where mills still stand. Additional industrial scenes from East Liverpool, Ohio, feature water tanks and other structures. Thus, while the book commemorates the past, it also highlights how the past is being erased, either by buildings being torn down or by nature reclaiming the landscape.

The relationship between these images and deindustrialization is made even more complex by the juxtaposition between Higgins's explanations of his work and the comments of his mentor, Robert Glenn Ketchum. Ketchum writes in his foreword to the book that the photos offer "no visual commentary about the successes or failures these transitional relics symbolize" and they "hold no message beyond the photographic beauty of the artist's vision." Higgins's own introduction, however, reminds readers of the history that created those "transitional relics." He comments on the dramatic change in the meaning of work since the late 1970s, from his father's and grandfather's expectation that they would work for the local steel mills for forty years to his own experience as a worker: "I have not worked for a single employer for longer than five years, and during the early eighties I had as many as six or seven jobs in one year." He goes on to express a skeptical response to newspaper articles about "the soaringly rich stockmarket" that are juxtaposed with stories about "someone who is struggling to keep a roof over his head." The government claims that "everyone who wants a job is working. But what sort of jobs are these?"[43] For Higgins, the beauty of the images he creates seems to be closely connected with his sense of history and his frustration with the postindustrial economy.

Yet the biggest irony here lies in the images themselves. Many seem almost romantic. Steel mills are seen at sunrise, suffused with a warm, nostalgic glow. Photographs of river scenes are explicitly identified as tributes to the Hudson River painters, and the soft edges and warm colors seem to belong to places far from the smoke and noise of industry. The smoke hovering over an East Liverpool concrete plant provides a sort of filter, creating an image that gains some of its beauty from smudging the edges of factory buildings and rows of small houses in the background. Photos of neighborhoods are perhaps the most contradictory. Swing sets, window fans, and parked cars suggest the presence of people, and the condition of the buildings suggests their poverty, yet we do not see people in any of these photos.

We do not see people in the mills, either, but we do see the smoke pouring from cooling tanks or the bright colors of fairly new equipment, and many of these industrial sites seem more active, more inhabited, than the neighborhood scenes. Taken as a whole, Higgins's photos and the introductory statements to the book offer a contradictory vision of the Rust Belt as derelict and depopulated but aesthetically beautiful, a place of memory rather than activity, a place to be looked at but not lived in.

The sterility of both Dombeck's and Higgins's images of Youngstown is all the more striking when viewed in comparison with the dark, impressionistic, and almost violent images created by journalist and painter Agis Salpukas. A business reporter for the *New York Times,* Salpukas was assigned in the 1970s to cover the steel industry and deindustrialization. As he noted in the artist's statement for a 1993 exhibit of his work, he was taken by the "clamor and clang of steelmaking" but also by the steelworkers, who "trudged up the hill at the end of their shifts at Campbell" and stopped at bars such as the Towne Tavern in Struthers for a beer before going home. He wrote hundreds of newspaper articles about the steel industry, but the "images that were left after many visits demanded expression." In 1978, he began learning to paint, and he started to make sketches and paintings of the mills. Salpukas viewed Youngstown as "an exotic place," which for a reporter from New York looked as foreign and interesting as Tahiti must have looked to Paul Gaugin.[44] Salpukas's statements make clear that unlike Dombeck, his response to the mills was as much about the way of life they represented as it was about their visual elements. At first glance, his paintings of the steel mills look so muddy that they are almost unintelligible, yet on closer examination, the shapes of mill buildings and stacks emerge. Salpukas's slightly rough brush strokes in brown, rust, gray, and black, with carefully placed patches of lighter grays and yellows, suggest movement and, in some places, fire. The effect is to give a sense of turmoil and struggle, which is matched by the smouldering, smoky skies that sit low over the mills that fill most of the canvasses. While his images do not depict the literal struggles to save the steel mills, which were taking place during the years when

Blast Furnace, *Agis Salpukas, c. 1980*

he was painting many of these images, they suggest a much more conflicted and active vision than what we see in Dombeck's work. As an amateur painter, Salpukas may have been less influenced by trends in the art world than Dombeck was, while his own struggle to come to terms with deindustrialization may have had a stronger role in shaping his vision. Salpukas's position as a journalist, who would have been expected to report objectively on what was happening but who was clearly moved by the story personally, may have led him to create such dark, almost tortured images of Youngstown.

Representations of Youngstown often highlight that sense of abandonment, and as the city struggled during the 1980s and into the 1990s without making serious recovery, Youngstown was increasingly seen as a site of failure. In some cases, Youngstown's failure was used as a persuasive tool for projects focused on social change and liberal politics. For example, images of the locked gates of steel mills and the deteriorating Brier Hill neighborhood helped to dramatize the effects of job loss in a 1990 documentary produced by the Catholic Conference of Ohio. *Patchwork of Poverty* calls for individuals and parishes to provide better support to their unemployed neighbors. Scenes from Youngstown are used frequently in the film, in part because they offer powerful images of economic loss. The documentary positions Youngstown as representative of changes in the national economy, although it also discusses the loss of mining and farming as other major economic shifts that have created an increased need for charity and social services in many communities. The piece ends with a call to service, inviting viewers to get involved in efforts to help others survive and recover from the hardship of job loss.[45]

Similarly, a 1999 documentary, *Michael Harrington and Today's Other America: Corporate Power and Inequality,* uses the Youngstown story as a representative example of how corporate power harms ordinary people. In a section entitled "Downsized," filmmaker Bill Donovan uses Springsteen's song about Youngstown together with images of abandoned mills, closed businesses, relief offices, and empty lots to portray Youngstown as a site of loss. Scholar and activist James Chapin explains that Youngstown's story illustrates the power of private, business-oriented decision making, noting that it was "possible for four to five people in a room to make a decision to shut down Youngstown, Ohio." This emphasizes Youngstown's role as a victim, a point that Donovan further emphasizes by showing how conservative critics want to downplay the significance of deindustrialization. The film includes an interview with neoconservative critic Irving Kristol, in which he dismisses Youngstown's struggle: "What's happened to Youngstown since? Everyone remembers the sixteen thousand people who lost their jobs. So far as I know, things are not so bad in Youngstown." Although Kristol acknowledges the powerful memory of loss associated with Youngstown, he denies the long-term effects of the shutdowns. When the unseen interviewer points out that crime rates in Youngstown have skyrocketed, Kristol brushes the problem aside: "Crime is up everywhere."[46] Kristol's effort to erase the problems of corporate greed is clear, but we should also take note of Donovan's use of Youngstown's struggle to promote the issues championed by Harrington and to critique capitalism. The video defines Youngstown as a representation of how ordinary people and communities are victimized by corporations. Like so many versions of the story, Donovan's shows Youngstown only as a site of loss, completely ignoring the community-wide struggle to save the mills. Such images make Youngstown an object of sympathy, yet they also exploit the community's difficulties.

In part because Youngstown was so widely known as a representative example of a deindustrialized city, people around the country know about what happened here. When they travel around the United States, people from Youngstown are often asked whether the city has yet made a comeback. Several news reports asked the same question when Springsteen's song came out in the mid-1990s, and especially when he visited Youngstown in January 1996. These stories reviewed the history of the mill closings, and their reports on Youngstown in the 1990s comment sadly on the city's failure to "pull itself up by its bootstraps." The community's continued economic struggle contributed to its identity as a "symbol of the failure of American industry," to use the phrase from a CBS reporter.

The *CBS This Morning* report on Springsteen's January 1996 performance in Youngstown told the story of how the songwriter picked up *Journey to Nowhere* one sleepless night, wrote his songs, and started Maharidge and Williamson on a return trip to update the state of the unemployed and homeless in the United States. The report describes how Youngstown is now in much worse shape than it was in the early 1980s, as the downtown is "just fading away." Interviews with Springsteen, Maharidge, Williamson, and the Marshall family all emphasize that Youngstown's experience is not unique but, rather, representative of difficulties facing the nation at large, including the large numbers of middle-class and white-collar workers being "downsized" during the mid-1990s. As Williamson put it, "Now the rest of the country knows what only Youngstown knew then." While their comments focus on the national economy and the "failure of American industry," the story's focus on Youngstown and on the Marshall family serves at once to humanize the issue and to deflect attention from the role of industry. The segment includes almost no discussion of why the mills shut down, nor any critique of the business decisions that led to widespread downsizing in the 1990s. American industry failed, yet the emphasis here is on Youngstown as a "symbol of failure." *CBS This Morning* looks at Youngstown twenty years after the shutdowns, and it sees only economic and cultural disaster, highlighting the way prisons are replacing steel mills as well as the boarded-up stores downtown. At the end of the report, another shift occurs when host Mark McEwen comments, "For some people, having your heart in the right place is just a cliché, but for Bruce Springsteen, no cliché, it's a way of life."[47] Youngstown is left behind, then, erased by the virtue of Springsteen's good intentions.

While CBS emphasized the empty landscape of Youngstown, highlighting the "mile-long meadows" that had replaced the twenty-five-mile stretch of steel mills along the Mahoning River and the vacant lots around the city where homes had been burned or torn down, other reports on Springsteen's song focused on the desolation of what remained in Youngstown. An *Akron Beacon Journal* story from December 1995 draws attention to the "strange, silent hulks of steel" that represent "the remains of a lost civilization," inviting readers to imagine Youngstown as a kind of museum of the industrial past. Journalist Bob Dyer notes in the article that Springsteen's version of the story honors the dedication of steelworkers but also emphasizes the devastation and betrayal of losing a job. Near the end of the article, Dyer comments, "Although portions of Northeast Ohio have experienced a significant rebirth in mass steel production . . . the trend has not touched Youngstown."[48] So while, on the one hand, Youngstown's story represents a common tale of deindustrialization, and while Dyer creates a poignant portrait of the community, the final message emphasizes Youngstown's identity as a site of failure.

Youngstown's long-term economic struggle also made the community a useful symbol of the devastating effects of widespread job loss. In 1998, that image was used as an implied threat to workers and communities facing further economic restructuring in a *Nightly Business Report* segment during the GM-Flint strike. Reporter Stephen Aug examined the way workers at the Lordstown plant outside of Youngstown were being affected by the strike. The report suggested that workers and business owners who still remembered the economic devastation of the early 1980s felt especially sensitive to the economic effects of layoffs. At the same time, the report emphasized Youngstown's worries that Lordstown might close or significantly reduce its workforce as the company moved to modular production and increased outsourcing. According to the report, GM workers were right to worry; the Youngstown area had already lost more than seven thousand jobs from Delphi Packard, a GM parts supplier with several plants in the Youngstown area. In this clip, images of deindustrialization in Youngstown both validate workers' fears and hint at the dangers of workers asking too much. The opening images and words of the report shift the emphasis from "local issues" in the Flint strike to larger long-term interests involving outsourcing. It asks where the work will be done, pointing out that the cars made at Lordstown are also made in Mexico. Viewers are reminded that Delphi Packard Electric in Warren had already moved seven thousand jobs to Mexico. Perhaps most important, Aug reminds us that Youngstown "has seen all this before"; Springsteen's "Youngstown" plays while we are shown images of the broken-out windows of the abandoned Youngstown Sheet and Tube Company office building. As Aug points out ominously, Youngstown never recovered from the mill closings. In linking the past with the present situation, the report juxtaposes the Flint strike with deindustrialization and job loss in Youngstown and emphasizes fears about permanent plant closings. Autoworkers in the 1990s, the story implies, are just as helpless as the steelworkers were at the end of the 1970s. "They may have jobs now," Aug says. "But what about next year, or the year after?"[49]

While Youngstown was clearly devastated economically by the mill closings, images that focus on Youngstown as a site of loss or even as the victim of distant corporate decisions and globalization miss an important piece of the area's history: its community-wide fight to save the mills. That struggle laid the foundation for plant closing legislation and new uses of eminent domain, but this part of Youngstown's history is forgotten here. What we see is only the aftermath—a community still struggling to recover from the loss of the steel mills and afraid of further job loss.

BOOSTERISM AND ERASURE

A different kind of struggle emerged in public discussions of Youngstown's economic future as the community tried to attract new businesses and maintain a sense of hope. Even early on, some local leaders, journalists, and residents resisted the idea that Youngstown was failing economically, though the sense of struggle was never entirely erased. While the *Vindicator* described the steel mill shutdowns as "the worst blow,"[50] and while many local leaders publicly worried about how massive job loss would affect the local economy and the lives of Youngstown residents, others insisted that Youngstown would not be destroyed by deindustrialization. In its October 1977 issue, just weeks after the Youngstown Sheet and Tube announcement, the Youngstown Area Chamber of Commerce newsletter headline proclaimed "Not Our Valley! No Place for Doom and Gloom." The article argued that the closing of Youngstown Sheet and Tube was "NOT the end of the Mahoning Valley. Without downplaying the seriousness of the situation we do not want to allow ourselves to be talked into the worst depression our area has ever seen." Chamber president Ken McMahon explains, "Now is certainly not the time for anyone to take a defeatist attitude. If we all work together constructively the Mahoning Valley can and will emerge a stronger region."[51] Local business leaders offered a positive response to the shutdowns, refusing to admit to local economic struggle. Over the next year, alongside articles that acknowledged the significance of the decline in the steel industry, the Chamber of Commerce newsletter ran articles that highlighted every possible piece of good news, as if focusing on the positive would erase the economic devastation around them.

Local boosters were not alone in looking for recovery rather than suffering. National newspapers and magazines began to report that

Youngstown was recovering well as early as November 1978. A *Washington Post* article that month began with a scene in Mayor J. Philip Richley's office, with Richley handing out "green and white buttons proclaiming that Youngstown is 'Alive and Well.' The words are underlined twice and punctuated with an exclamation point." Richley explains to his visitor that despite the "tragic blow" of the shutdowns, "the area has absorbed the blow." He cites low unemployment figures and increased retail sales, and he paraphrases Mark Twain's famous line, saying that "the story of our demise has been greatly exaggerated." Despite this upbeat opening and the headline "Youngstown's Vital Signs Encouraging after Plant Shutdown; Youngstown Didn't Die, after All, when Steel Plant Shut Its Doors," the story documents the continuing real problems in the city, and it ultimately questions Richley's claims. Urban studies specialist Steve Redburn points out later in the article that the effects of the layoffs were delayed because most workers were still receiving financial support. He predicts "significant hardships—financial and emotional—this winter." The article also profiles a half-dozen laid-off workers, giving brief glimpses into their lives a year after the shutdown. Several have found new jobs, most at less pay, while others remain unemployed. The article closes with a poignant quote from William Sullivan Jr., president of one of the economic development groups formed in response to the shutdowns: "How do you measure what might have been? The economy of the area is less sound today than before the closing. Buildings where steel was once made are now idle. A lot of people who used to make steel now do nothing. Should we just accept that?"[52] Despite the optimistic headline and the mayor's enthusiasm, the article reflects the difficulty of Youngstown's economic struggle. The piece takes on added significance when we note that it appeared just as Lykes-LTV was about to announce the closing of the Brier Hill Works and a year before the Ohio Works would close.

Even before the mill closings, Youngstown business leaders had begun to try to attract new business to the area. While a number of those efforts in the 1980s failed, business leaders tried to remain upbeat. At times, community development projects took on an air of

desperation as promoters asked the community to support development projects that seemed ridiculous or to behave in humiliating ways
to persuade companies to move to the area. For example, community
pressure was put on local banks and the state and local government
to build a $10 million facility to manufacture airplanes whose design
was unproven and unsafe. Ultimately, no planes were ever built at
the plant. Another project focused on developing financial support for
the manufacture of blimps for use in commercial transportation. Even
when the projects were more serious, economic development activities were sometimes extreme and embarrassing. For example, in an
attempt to attract the GM Saturn project in the mid-1980s, development leaders had schoolchildren, parents, and community members
write two hundred thousand letters to Roger Smith, president of GM;
organized a one-hundred-car caravan to Detroit to deliver the letters;
and bought billboard space and television time, all beseeching the
company to build its Saturn plant in Youngstown. A ten-year-old
wrote:

> Dear Mr. Smith,
> I hope that you will consider building the Saturn plant in
> the Mahoning Valley. I would like it to be here because it
> would make thousands of jobs and it will ease the 32.9% un-
> employment rate. Please do not rule us out because Lordstown
> is here. The Mahoning Valley is well suited for the Saturn
> plant. Some reasons are is it is near transportation and re-
> sources and our people are willing to work and work real hard.
> I hope your car beats the imports and brings many Americans
> a job.[53]

No doubt, such efforts were designed to show that Youngstown
had a sympathetic business and investment climate. Unfortunately,
when deindustrialized communities go to desperate lengths to attract
new business, critical understanding of the relationship between plant
closing, unemployment, and corporate disinvestments is undermined.
In Youngstown, one result of failed efforts such as the Saturn campaign has been that the community has increasingly looked inward,

blaming itself for economic problems, and opened itself to a type of economic blackmail in the form of tax abatements and other accommodations to attract business. As this example suggests, economic development efforts sometimes undermined the community's sense of itself and its history.

Even efforts to commemorate Youngstown's steelmaking history sometimes erased the community's past, choosing to promote a hopeful but largely inaccurate vision of success instead of dwelling on what was lost. On the twentieth anniversary of Black Monday, for example, the *Youngstown Vindicator* ran a series of commemorative articles. One focused on the reminiscences of steelworkers, another on the efforts of community leaders to redevelop the area by building industrial parks on the sites of the dismantled mills, and a third on the revitalization of the American steel industry. The series included a front-page graph under the headline "Steel Valley/Still recovering?" which contrasted the increase in the total number of jobs in the valley with the significant decline in the number of manufacturing, metal industry, and blast furnace jobs. Inside, a small photograph from the 1940s shows "smoke roiling" from the Campbell Works, described in the caption as "a sign of life for Youngstown and the surrounding communities." Beside it, a larger photograph shows two men probably in their late sixties, looking at a scale model of the works inside a glass case at the steel museum. The two workers, both former mill supervisors, and several of their colleagues comment nostalgically about the work of making steel: "It was hot, nasty, and dirty, but we loved every minute of it," says one, while another speaks even more emotionally: "My heart aches for the old mills." As the reporter notes, the former steelworkers speak with "reverence, respect, and romance in their voices." The article suggests that Youngstown's attitude toward the old mills is tender and bittersweet. The accompanying articles emphasize recovery, the hopeful attitudes of local politicians, and the increased wages of the town's workers.[54]

Yet we should also note what is missing from this set of articles. The article on former steelworkers focuses on men who were supervisors and office workers, men who have gone on to find new jobs, in consulting, railroading, recruiting, and public relations. Their memories of the hot, dirty work of steelmaking come from the early part of their careers. The article does not include the voices of ordinary production workers, laborers, bricklayers, and scarfers, nor does it include those who left Youngstown or who didn't find better work. Instead, the *Vindicator* tells a story of success: workers who found other, possibly even better jobs; a community that added more jobs even as its population has declined by almost one-half; local leaders who were actively and successfully pursuing redevelopment options; an industry that was, as the headline notes, "stronger than ever." The article ignores the local unemployment rate, still among the highest in the state; the city's exceptionally high murder rate—among the highest per capita in the nation; and the continued decay of the city core amid the growth of the suburbs. This forward-looking emphasis suggests that thinking about the past is a pastime for old men, a matter of memory but not, apparently, an incident of real loss. Boosterism is, of course, one of the missions of a local newspaper, and the *Vindicator* is not without respect for the past. Yet its reporting on the anniversary of Black Monday also seems to advocate forgetting that past. Indeed, the Jeannette Blast Furnace is literally erased from the series. The illustration for the article on the redevelopment of the land where the mills once stood features a map indicating the current use of the land. The map of the Brier Hill Works cuts off the south end of the old mill grounds, leaving the empty lot where the Jenny stood off the map entirely.

REMEMBERING THE STRUGGLE

The *Vindicator*'s look back at the mill closings also downplays the community's resistance to the shutdowns, presenting an image of acquiescence and sadness rather than struggle or anger. Yet Youngstown steelworkers and the community at large did not simply accept the shutdowns. Less than twenty-four hours after Youngstown Sheet and Tube's announcement on September 19, 1977, that the Campbell Works would close, local protests began. Steelworkers organized a petition drive, asking the federal government to provide better trade protection for the steel industry. Four days after the closing was announced, five busloads of Youngstown-area workers and their families, 250 people, headed to Washington to stage a protest. The *Vindicator* featured photos of the group on its front page, with placards bearing slogans such as "Save the Steel Valley," "Steel Town to Ghost Town," and "Don't Export Steelworkers' Jobs." As an accompanying story explained, the protesters would join 750 area workers who were already in Washington to "make known their anger and frustration over the plight of the steel industry and job situation." They brought with them petitions bearing the signatures of 110,000 Mahoning Valley residents, the results of the petition drive begun just two days earlier.[55] The large number of protesters and the thousands of signatures on petitions demonstrate the rapid community response to the shutdown announcement.

While many turned their anger outward, joining with neighbors and coworkers to organize community protests, others had a more tempered response, turning to religion for spiritual solace rather than to activism. The *Vindicator* ran a large photo feature with images of a monument to the valley's steel history, erected just a year before. The accompanying story ended with this statement: "So devastating has been this past week, so catastrophic, that a special Mass will be celebrated at St. Nicholas Church in Struthers." The Mass was aimed at helping laid-off workers and their families find the strength to survive: "We have to turn to God for help and guidance. As a parish community we are turning to Youngstown Sheet and Tube. Some may be tempted to make rash and sudden decisions. Others will become depressed and worried. In community we find our strength. In our Lord's hands we must place ourselves as never before."[56] While on the one hand, this response suggests that people turned inward, seeking individual strength and comfort, in a largely Catholic community, a special community mass suggests that people found hope in gathering together.

While many Youngstown residents admitted that they were not completely surprised by the announcement, their responses suggest a range of attitudes. A September 25 article in the *Vindicator* featured short vignettes describing how various people in the community heard about and responded to the shutdown announcement. While many expressed grief, confusion, or anger, ex-steelworker and mayoral candidate Ron Daniels, who would later become a leader of Jesse Jackson's Rainbow Coalition, insisted that he "rejected the notion that Youngstown will become a ghost town."[57] In the same vein, letters to the editor that day expressed local residents' sadness but also their anger and their determination that Youngstown not become a "ghost town." Several of the letters criticized the government, either for not providing effective trade protections or for enforcing environmental rules and leaving local families with "clean air to breathe, pure water to drink, but nothing to eat." Another writer noted that it was "morally wrong for industry to pull out and leave thousands of families with nothing. Shame on You!" A third criticized the *Vindicator* for not digging deeper into the cause of the shutdown: "This giant of our Steel Valley, who has so drained its human resources down through the years—and left nothing but tears—is there no one to question WHY?"[58] These comments suggest that while some people tried to remain upbeat, others were angry, although they were not sure whom to blame—the government, the steel companies, or local leaders.

By September 26, the city of Campbell had formed a task force to "seek ways for this community to pull itself up by its own bootstraps, including the possible purchase of some Youngstown Sheet & Tube Co. property here." A *Vindicator* editorial praised the community's quick organizing: "Mahoning Valley's crisis has impregnated the community with a sense of mutual responsibility. All the meetings, protests, petitions and heartbreaking trauma haven't produced genuine results as yet. But the stage is set. Responding to 'last chance' appeals for action, administration officials acknowledge the 'beginning of an ongoing dialogue,' and have set in motion several studies aimed at providing both short- and long-term assistance."[59] Meanwhile, Campbell mayor Michael J. Katula Jr. called for people to join a shared struggle to find appropriate responses to the shutdowns: "Remain calm. Have faith. Be strong. We must stand together and see this time of tragedy through. We must help one another, as help will be needed. We must unite as this community has never united before."[60] As the *Vindicator's* reports on protests, masses, and the actions and thoughts of local leaders show, the immediate responses to the shutdowns were not passive or accepting but, in many cases, angry and active.

Indeed, while many images of deindustrialization in Youngstown emphasize job loss and community failure, others highlight the incredible struggle staged by local unions and churches. Filmmakers, journalists, labor historians, and others have told the story of Youngstown's response to the mill closings. Most of their work focuses on union activism and the almost-successful efforts of the Ecumenical Coalition to buy one of the local plants and run it as a community-owned venture. These stories define Youngstown as the site of an important and, in some ways, successful battle against deindustrialization.

Youngstown's battle against the shutdowns drew attention largely because it was so unusual and so well organized. In 1978, ABC News sent a crew to Youngstown to report on the activities of the Ecumenical Coalition. Reporter Dan Cordtz commented:

> There is nothing new about plant shut downs or corporate decisions to abandon workers and communities in search of greener and more profitable pastures. But there is something new, something very new and therefore of national importance, in the response of Youngstown to the crisis it faces. Youngstown is a town which is refusing to die. In that refusal to die, and in the effort to overcome the social and human consequences that flow from massive unemployment, the people of Youngstown are posing sharp and difficult questions that go to the heart of the American way of doing business.

Later in the report, economist William Sullivan comments, "Right now, the strength of this valley is in the steelworker, an extraordinarily resilient guy with a lot of common sense. He's not prone to panic.

There's no panic in the streets in Campbell or anywhere else that I see." Housing and Urban Development (HUD) undersecretary Jay Janis describes the federal government's support for Youngstown's efforts, noting that "we'd like Youngstown to be a showcase, a showcase of self-help and a showcase of community involvement, that somehow can be an example for the rest of the nation." He describes Youngstown as "a community that wants to chart and plan its own future. It wants to take matters into its own hands and find a way to deal with what is a devastating blow to its economy." Janis's comments indicate that the federal government was happy to see the community taking action in response to the shutdowns, in part because this relieved both the government and industry from taking responsibility.[61]

The story of Youngstown's fight also inspired artists, who saw the organizers of the fight against the shutdowns as heroes. Songwriter Mike Stout, who had been the grievance chair of the USWA local at Homestead before the shutdowns there, offers a romantic vision of the union leaders who were central in the Youngstown struggle. "Flowers of the Working Class" offers a musical tribute to John Barbero and Ed Mann, two of the central activists in the Youngstown struggle, whom Stout describes as "steel warriors," "prophesizers," and "human resisters" who "were never afraid, when confronted with an enemy." The song's chorus exhorts listeners to join the battle:

> Then let your heads and your conscience arise;
> The rain and wind are swirling outside.
> Seize the time, grab hold of the day;
> Pick up their swords, we have dragons to slay.
> Hear what they said, remember their names;
> They may be dead, but their message remains.[62]

"Flowers of the Working Class" preserves a memory of resistance and invites listeners to join a continuing struggle, yet it does not acknowledge that the effort to save the Youngstown mills was not successful.

Bryn Zellers was also inspired by the struggle, and in the mid-1980s he created a metal assemblage in tribute to Mann. *Homage to Ed Mann (Man of Sorrows)* features a cast-lead human heart, suspended within

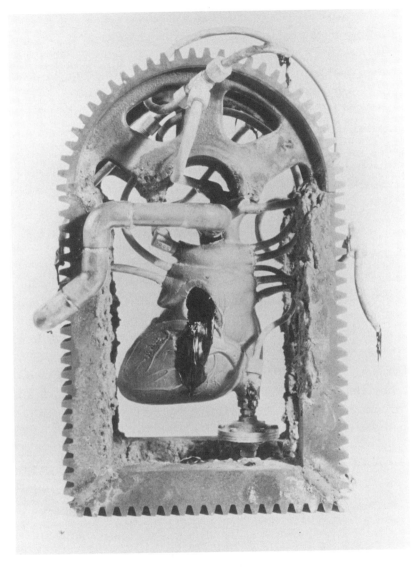

Homage to Ed Mann (Man of Sorrows), *Bryn Zellers, 1996*

an open frame of gear racking and gears. The piece links Mann's work as a union organizer and activist with his work in the mill, positioning the heart of a man at the center of an industrial frame. Copper tubing and black tar emerge from holes in the heart, visual markers of Ed Mann's struggle to keep the Brier Hill Works open in the late 1970s. As Zellers comments, the piece represents Mann's struggle and dedication but also the sadness of knowing that his efforts did not succeed. In contrast to Stout's heroic vision, Zellers offers a more mediated image, representing Mann as a tragic hero. As Zellers explains, "Here's a guy that's spending so much time and energy, and with such a passion and conviction about work, and he dies after having realized that it's just not going to happen. It's almost like a sort of martyrdom."[63]

One of the most moving versions of the story of Youngstown's struggle is told in *Shout Youngstown,* a documentary by Carol Greenwald and Dorie Krauss, a Youngstown native who returned to her hometown to make the film. The film uses interviews with steelworkers, especially local union leaders, who describe the efforts of the Ecumenical Coalition. From its opening sequence, the film defines Youngstown as the home of dedicated fighters, workers, and organizers who did not back off from the struggle and who did not simply accept defeat. The film's opening sequence shows a row of four mill stacks being demolished. We hear the person directing the demolition beginning a countdown. Then, an unidentified steel company official (a later scene shows that the voice belongs to David Roderick, U.S. Steel chairman) comments that "the closings were needed because, in today's environment . . . these facilities were no longer competitive and therefore needed to be phased out." The count continues, stops again, and we hear one of the local protesters commenting on the steel companies' disregard of their workers and the community: "And then, when they decide to leave, it's 'tough luck, follow us,' and it doesn't matter what they leave behind." The demolition crew finishes the countdown, we hear a blast, and we see the stacks begin to fall. The image is frozen with the stacks halfway down, and another voice interrupts. This time we hear local union leader Ed Mann speaking at a rally: "We're gonna let the politicians know, we're gonna let U.S. Steel know, we're gonna let the whole country know, that steelworkers in Youngstown got guts, and we're gonna fight for our jobs!" This juxtaposition of the image and the multiple, contradictory voices highlights the contestation over the production and, in this case, destruction of space and place. From the opening moments, *Shout Youngstown* puts the community's struggle, especially the activism of steelworkers who did not quietly or passively accept the loss of their jobs, at the center of the story. At the end of the sequence, Si Kahn begins to sing "We're Still Here," one of several songs he wrote for the film. His words remind viewers that even though the mills may be gone—as shown in the long opening image—the workers cannot simply be erased by the shutdowns. They may no longer be "competitive" and "need to be phased out," but they are "still here."

From there, the film chronicles the organizers' efforts to stop the shutdowns and later buy one of the plants, beginning just weeks after the initial Campbell Works announcement and continuing for several years until a final judgment from the government that ended the battle to buy the Ohio Works. Clips from local news and video footage of church services, organizing meetings, and rallies help to tell the story. Interviews with local union and community activists, and union leaders, including Mann, John Barbero, Ron Daniels, June Lucas, and attorney Staughton Lynd, fill in the details of the effort to organize community ownership efforts and protests against steel corporation actions. Their reflections, recorded a few years after the struggle, suggest their continuing anger but also their fierce commitment to the cause. Through these interviews, the film emphasizes the humanity of the fight, focusing on individuals but also positioning their efforts in the context of the steelworkers' unions. Many scenes show meetings and rallies in union halls or workers' protests outside plants and steel company offices. Another Si Kahn song emphasizes that these efforts reflected the collective energy of the workers and the community: "We are the future, we are the nation, we are the people, we are the union."

At the end of the film, we view scenes of empty mills and piles of rubble, while Kahn begins to sing: "All the mills stand in silence, all the jobs gone away, the storefronts are empty as I walk up and down, but everywhere I go, I will shout Youngstown." Several of the participants comment on how the mill closings have devastated the community's economy. As one older man points out, pointing to the clear sky above downtown Youngstown, "We have no more mills, and no more smoke, and no more prosperity." Two African-American teenagers comment on how difficult it is to find a job in town, and then two older women who identify themselves as office cleaners comment on how the downtown area is becoming increasingly empty.

But the film does not end with images of desolation. Rather, the final words and images are those of the men and women who were most active in the struggle, and their comments emphasize not the failure of their efforts but rather the excitement and strength of people working together. Joe Gavini reflects that Youngstown's experience might help prepare other people for the possibility of job loss, urging people to "try to keep it from happening." Jim Davis says that he counsels workers "that all is not lost. As long as you work and demand your rights, fight for what is correct, and don't lie down and play dead. We still have a union. I believe that, because the union is the people." Bob Vasquez says proudly that his local "retained the dignity of the guys who were members of this local. That may sound like a corny phrase, but I hear it time and time again—we went down fighting." Ed Mann points out that each round of the struggle was better organized, and ends by saying "maybe next time." Ron Daniels emphasizes the anger of realizing that "these kinds of things can happen in America." John Barbero explains that he feels compelled to "shout Youngstown" wherever he goes, to tell the Youngstown story everywhere: "We shouldn't let the country forget what industry did to Youngstown." As a closing song plays, we see a series of smiling faces, brief glimpses of some of those who have helped tell the story. They do not look defeated; their smiles suggest that they will keep on fighting. Together, the visual images, comments, and song represent the story of Youngstown's struggle not just as memory but also as a force for action and unity. Moreover, the closing sequence offers a distinct contrast with the opening, which presented competing voices with conflicting perspectives. At the end, multiple voices express similar ideas, emphasizing a sense of unity and hope, suggesting a foundation for future struggle. While the film acknowledges the ultimate failure of the buyout efforts, it closes with the message that the struggle itself was valuable because it left Youngstown with a sense of pride and because it offered a model for other communities.[64]

In his book, *The Fight against Shutdowns: Youngstown's Steel Mill Closings*, Lynd provides a detailed report on the organizing efforts and the battles between the steel companies, the federal government, the international offices of the United Steelworkers of America, and the local groups who tried to stop the shutdowns and establish a community ownership plan. For Lynd, as for Greenwald and Krauss, the heroes of the story are steelworkers. As he notes early on, rank-and-file steelworkers (most of them officers in area locals) were the ones who initiated the key ideas and activities of the struggle.[65] While Lynd acknowledges that the group made some tactical errors in timing and approach, he ends his book with a call for direct action led by rank-and-file workers. Collective bargaining and lawsuits were not effective, but those involved in the Youngstown struggle agree that "what little they accomplished was by direct action."[66] Lynd's version of the story offers a less hopeful conclusion than we see in *Shout Youngstown*, but like the film, *Fight against Shutdowns* emphasizes the significance of struggle.

These versions of the story make clear that in the first years of deindustrialization, Youngstown workers and religious leaders actively resisted the shutdowns. Not only was Youngstown not a site of failure, its experience served as a crucible for future activism. In fact, it launched what Lynd called "the most sustained struggle against disinvestment and downsizing anywhere in the United States."[67] Those who had been active in Youngstown's struggle went on to work with other communities that were facing plant closings. The legal theories developed by Lynd and others have been used throughout the country in court cases involving plant closings and community takeover efforts, and Lynd himself has been involved in many of those cases. Barbero and Mann became involved in efforts to resist shutdowns around the country and were instrumental in organizing the TriState Conference on Steel in 1979. Built on the model of the Ecumenical Coalition, TriState held informational meetings for public officials, church groups, and academics throughout the Rust Belt and nationally. As deindustrialization spread to the Pittsburgh area, TriState members organized unemployment committees, participated in community actions, and developed a legal theory for the use of eminent domain for the community takeover of mill sites. According to Charles McCollester, one of the leaders of the TriState Conference, these activities had Youngstown roots: "The Mon Valley Unemployed Committees were based on support groups that had first developed in Youngstown. TriState members marched with Youngstown steelworkers and community members that took over the U.S. Steel building in Pittsburgh. We worked closely with Staughton Lynd and his young legal assistant, Jay Hornack, who developed the legal theory that ultimately led to the development of the Steel Valley Authority."[68] A legal entity involving twelve communities in the Pittsburgh area, the Steel Valley Authority used the threat of eminent domain to keep plants open or to influence corporate decision making.[69]

Other key players in the Youngstown struggle also went on to further activism to protect the interests of workers. In 1977, June Lucas was an organizer for the Ohio Public Interest Campaign, and she worked with the Ecumenical Coalition helping to develop grassroots support.[70] In the late 1970s, Lucas lobbied in the community and with politicians to build support for plant closing legislation. As a state senator in 1986, she joined with state representative Robert Hagan to introduce a plant closings bill in the state legislature. That effort helped lay the foundation for Ohio senator Howard Metzenbaum's successful passage of the nation's first plant closing legislation in the U.S. Senate in 1988.[71]

Bishop James Malone was one of the leaders of the Ecumenical Coalition. The son of a Youngstown steelworker and former steelworker himself, Malone had a long-standing concern for workers' rights. Outraged that "capital could unilaterally decide the fate of so many work-ers and their families," he believed that the church had few options: they could deplore what was happening, offer comfort to those involved, or take action. When the closing of the Campbell Works was announced, Malone helped write an open letter to the steel companies from the community's religious leaders. The Ecumenical Coalition grew out of that initial effort, and Malone played an active role all along. Later, as head of the National Conference of Catholic Bishops, Malone was the driving force in the development and passage of the U.S. Bishops Pas-toral Letter on the Economy, published in 1985. In that letter, the church "bears witness for the need for change," critiques capital for its treat-ment of workers and communities, and reaffirms the value of workers and their unions in a democratic society.[72]

REMEMBERING STEEL TOWN AND "THE OLD NEIGHBORHOOD"

Within ten years after the mills shut down, local groups began to orga-nize museums, preservation efforts, and community activities to com-memorate Youngstown's working-class steelmaking history. As with the immediate responses to the closings, projects focused on construct-ing public memory reflected continuing tensions about how to think about the past, and how the community's relationship with its past would define its future. Official sites such as the Youngstown Histori-cal Center for Industry and Labor as well as more informal, grassroots projects such as the annual Brier Hill Italian Fest demonstrate the community's struggle with its own memory. Whose stories should be preserved? What form should representations of the past take?

The most official version of the Youngstown story is told at the Ohio Historical Center for Industry and Labor. Created by the Ohio Historical Society (OHS) in the 1980s, the "steel museum" was de-signed by one of the most prominent contemporary architects, Michael Graves, who worked with a local architectural firm, Raymond J. Jaminet and Partners. Graves incorporated industrial shapes into the design,

Youngstown Historical Center of Industry and Labor, designed by Michael Graves, 1982–1989, photograph by William Taylor, courtesy of Michael Graves & Associates

such as turrets that echoed the shapes of mill stacks and a section shaped like a coal tipple, which was not actually built in the end. In addition, Graves linked the industrial shapes to the peopling of Youngstown, borrowing the octagonal shape of towers often seen in southern and eastern European architecture for a two-story staircase in the museum. The roofline in the front of the museum echoed the arched roof of St. Columba's Catholic Cathedral across the street.

The building was completed in June 1989. The 32,000-square-foot museum provided space for exhibitions, classrooms, archives, and a research library. Built at a cost of $3.9 million, the historical center immediately won an award from *Progressive Architecture,* whose critic Philip Arcidi noted that the building itself, even before exhibits were installed, "documents the development of Ohio's steel industry and commemorates a vanishing way of life."[73] Arcidi predicted that residents would flock to the museum because "the people it serves and represents—those who worked in the mills and the school children who will come to learn about Youngstown's past—are proud to identify the museum as their own institution, on a par with the art museum, civic buildings, and, specifically, the Cathedral of St. Columba across the street."[74] Like much of the artwork that emerged during the period of deindustrialization, however, the museum created a somewhat distanced, even shadowy version of the steel mill. While it appealed to architecture fans, many local critics complained that it simply didn't capture the scale or experience of the real thing.

But in an ironic twist on Youngstown's economic struggles, art followed life. The historical center could not open because no funds had been allocated for a permanent exhibition. As a 1989 article in *Newsweek* suggested, the building sat empty, mirroring the empty steel mills that its postmodern design reflected.[75] To make matters worse, during the design phase, a struggle within the OHS began over control of the museum itself. Much of that struggle focused on what would be in the museum's permanent exhibit. Ultimately, museum director Donna DeBlasio set up a small, temporary exhibit in the lobby and began to develop a permanent exhibit by collecting equipment, furnishings, photographs, and mementos from former steelworkers, steel companies, and the OHS. LTV (formerly Republic Steel) donated a blooming mill pulpit and mill models; an iron industry display and the Youngstown Sheet and Tube photographic collection were provided by the OHS; and a steelworkers' locker room complete with washbasin was donated by McDonald Steel, formerly part of U.S. Steel. These materials were woven together into a permanent display titled *By the Sweat of Their Brow: Forging the Steel Valley*, which combines a history of the steel industry and technology with displays of labor both at work and home. Using artifacts, oral histories, photomurals, and historical film footage, the exhibit blends labor and industrial histories with elements of working-class life and culture. No doubt, the permanent exhibit reflects DeBlasio's sensibilities. DeBlasio grew up in Smokey Hollow, a working-class neighborhood that abutted Republic Steel, just blocks from the museum. In developing the permanent exhibit, DeBlasio tried to "achieve the proper balance between the development of the iron and steel technology, the representations of industrial and labor organizations, and working-class life and culture."[76]

While the museum waited for the resources to develop a permanent exhibit, DeBlasio began to collect oral histories from individuals associated with the steel industry and the city's history. She understood the importance of gathering stories from a diverse cross section of the community—whites, blacks, and Puerto Ricans; men and women; workers, supervisors, and city officials. According to DeBlasio, the oral histories provide information that is hard to get from other historical documents. While steel company documents may emphasize technological developments or the company's successes, the oral histories provide a highly personal view of what it was like to be a steelworker and a union member, with all the grit, danger, and struggle involved.

When the museum's permanent exhibit and archives were finally opened in 1992, however, relatively few people visited. Those who did come were largely architectural groupies interested in Graves's work and visitors from outside the area. Local people seemed to avoid the historical center. DeBlasio believes the extended development period and the still-fresh memories of the impact of the steel mill closings kept locals away. The memories represented in the museum may simply have been too painful for some. For others, though, it was not a question of memory but of image. Many business and economic leaders had not supported the museum, DeBlasio notes, because they thought Youngstown should shed its Rust Belt image. They feared that the museum would only contribute to the community's antiquarian attitudes. Despite this "get over it" attitude, attendance increased somewhat in the 1990s as marketing efforts improved.

The museum's permanent exhibit received largely positive reviews and only minor criticism. Despite DeBlasio's efforts to foreground working-class culture, critic Curtis Minor noted in a *Journal of American History* review that "in dignifying the value of labor under inhuman conditions and in reconstructing aspects of everyday life, [the exhibit] fails in places to convey the full breadth of the industrial experience, particularly the role of working-class culture."[77] Mike Wallace, on the other hand, praises the historical center for avoiding one of the key problems that face industrial museums: the tendency to focus on "nostalgia" and to rely on "banal and vacuous categories" of development (such as preindustrial and postindustrial) that imply that deindustrialization is part of a natural economic process. According to Wallace, industrial exhibits typically lack critical understanding of "human agency" and conflict. These museums would look different, he argues, if deindustrialization were reconceptualized as capital flight and/or a global redivision of labor.[78] As Wallace points out, the Youngstown Historical Center is better than most in dealing with these issues: "It was good to see a museum finally grappling with the issue of deindustrialization, even if this exhibit does not cut terribly deeply."[79] As these critics suggest, while the exhibit does represent aspects of working-class life, it also downplays the role of conflict in shaping both the community and working-class culture.

For many in the community, the museum itself became a source of conflict. They agreed with Minor's criticism that the museum failed "to conjure up a true physical presence, a sense of the gritty sights and smells of industrial life; even the physical reconstructions rarely transcend the sterile, modern exhibition space."[80] For those familiar with steel mills, the scale of the historical center itself symbolized the diminution of the industry. In an effort to preserve a local structure that did reflect the massive scale of the steel mill, the Jeannette Blast Furnace Preservation Association (JBFPA) was organized in 1993. The organization was led by J. Richard Rollins, a young railroader who was attracted to industrial history and technology. The JBFPA was dedicated to preserving the industrial heritage of the Youngstown steelmaking district by ensuring that the Jenny was not torn down.

As other Youngstown mills were being razed, the Brier Hill site, and the Jenny, remained standing into the late 1990s, twenty years after it was shut down, so the site came to be seen as an emblem of Youngstown's steelmaking past. Following the model of the Sloss Furnaces National Historic Landmark in Birmingham, Alabama, where a preservation group had raised funds through a bond issue to preserve the furnaces and build a museum and community arts center, the JBFPA launched a preservation project to turn the Jenny into a historic site and museum. The JBFPA effort brought to the surface the underlying debate over Youngstown's past. In writing about the controversy to save the Jenny, *Philadelphia Inquirer* reporter Jeff Gammage wrote, "For some, it is a monument turned grave site, no less hallowed than the green fields of Gettysburg or the hushed waters of Pearl Harbor. To others, it is a rusting reminder of a past best forgotten, an eyesore that binds this downtrodden town to memories of bygone industrial glory."[81] Clearly, the Jenny had become the last important symbol of the past and, in the eyes of some, its destruction represented hope for the future. The Jenny and the past that it represented was, at once, something to be remembered and overcome. As with the historical center exhibit, some local business and government leaders questioned the value of holding on to the past. Rufus Hudson, an analyst for YSU's Cushwa Center for Entrepreneurship and later a city councilman, spoke for many who believed that "we've been on a 20-year pity party. As long as we keep looking backward, we'll never keep going forward."[82] Mayor Pat Ungaro concurred, arguing that the destruction of the Jeannette Blast Furnace was necessary for future economic development. After all, some economic development had occurred around former mill sites. But for JBFPA supporters, the Jenny was the key to understanding the city—a reminder of past prosperity, nationalism, and what happened on Black Monday, a role that was heightened when Springsteen's song came out in the midst of the community debate, with its chorus addressed to "my sweet Jenny."

The JBFPA was unable to build community support for the project, however. Many believed that the Jenny was simply beyond repair and unsafe from almost twenty years of neglect. Others felt the economically strapped city could not afford to purchase the property. Still others worried that the project would compete with the existing historical center. James Allgren, a member of the JBFPA and former employee of the historical center, wondered why anyone would want to go to the historical center and look at a model of a blast furnace when they could look at the real thing. Less obvious, Allgren claimed, was the concern that the proposed museum would also compete with the "official history as handed down by [the OHS in] Columbus."[83] Unable to save the Jenny, the JBFPA turned its efforts to saving other industrial artifacts. They succeeded in preserving the Tod Engine, one of the oldest stationary steam engines in the nation that was used for rolling steel. In 1998, the U.S. government declared the Tod Engine a historic mechanical and materials and engineering landmark.[84] Ultimately, when the demolition of the Jenny was completed in 1997, the most visible reminder of Youngstown's steelmaking past was erased from the landscape.

In the adjacent Brier Hill neighborhood, community members would develop another grassroots version of public memory, the Brier Hill Italian Fest. Some of those who lived in the area had organized informal Brier Hill reunions starting in the 1980s. In 1991, Dominic "Dee Dee" Modarelli, who owned a tavern in the old neighborhood, decided that before he died, he wanted to "revive the spirit of the old Italian neighborhood and offer his friends and neighbors an opportunity to enjoy a weekend of festivities, fellowship, and memories."[85] Modarelli and his friends decided to try to hold the Brier Hill Fest each year around the feast day of St. Rocco. St. Rocco is a patron saint of many Italian immigrants, especially those from Calabria, and is thought to protect individuals from misfortune, disease, and hardship—all common to immigrants and steelworkers. This interpretation of St. Rocco was perhaps most widely seen nationally in the film *Rocky*.

Along with organizing the annual street fair, the creators of the Brier Hill Italian Fest publish a program booklet commemorating "the old neighborhood." The booklet consists primarily of ads from local businesses and neighborhood families, many of which are dedicated to the memory of various family members and are illustrated with family photos, including wedding and baby pictures. The programs also include biographies of the "Brier Hill Fest Man of the Year," greetings from the organizers, and, in the early years, maps, photographs, and newspaper clippings from the 1920s to the 1950s, representing community life in "the old neighborhood." The 1992, 1993, and 1995 programs also include histories of Brier Hill, focusing on the experience of immigration, St. Anthony's Roman Catholic Church and St. Rocco Episcopal Church, and the neighborhood's contributions to community and national history. For example, the program says of the parish sons who enlisted in the military during World War II: "Proud to serve their Country, the brave and sacrificing men of St. Anthony's answered the call to arms. Many of these young men

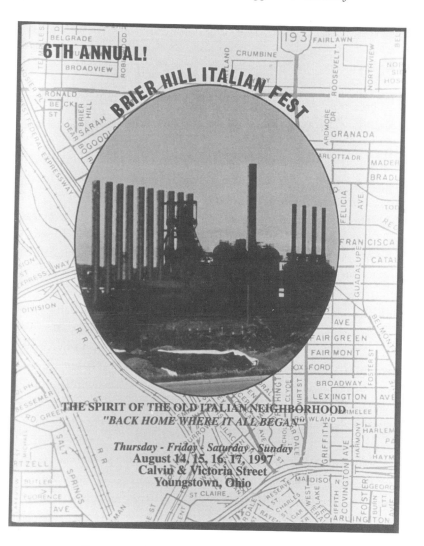

Program, 6th Annual Brier Hill Italian Fest, 1997

were immigrants, eager to pay a debt of gratitude to their adopted Country." The program also describes the churches' role as a "source of solace" during the Depression and World War II, and how the pastors "guided their flock . . . as, once again, devoted sons and husbands gave their services and their lives to their Country. As before in hard and fearful times, St. Anthony's was an unfailing source of spiritual help to those who remained behind."[86] None of the programs comment directly about the steel mills, whose smoke shadowed the area throughout its heyday. Rather, emphasis is placed on relationships among neighbors and the central role of the neighborhood churches. This neglect of work might be read as evidence of the power of working-class community life, which endures even when the work disappears, or it might be seen as an effort to erase the memory of the mill closings, what must have been an especially "hard and fearful" time.

Since its inception in 1992, the Brier Hill Italian Fest has grown. By 2000, it ran for four days, with dances, live Italian music, displays, games, and food in the one-hundred-square-yard area at the corner of Calvin and Victoria Streets in the heart of Brier Hill. Over five thousand people regularly attend the Fest from across the United States, returning to the neighborhood as the Fest's motto suggests "back home where it all began," and indulging in "the spirit of the old Italian neighborhood." While ethnic festivals are a staple of the summer calendar in Youngstown, none compares with the Brier Hill Fest. In covering the Fest, Youngstown reporters frequently marvel at this persistence of place. As Bob Black, anchor for a local newscast, has said, "On every corner, there are neighborhoods full of memories of who once lived there. Many of these communities are ghosts of what they once were. But one neighborhood just refuses to fade away."[87]

Clearly, the neighborhood is not what it once was, and, in fact, many neighborhood landmarks have been torn down or become dilapidated. Yet the Brier Hill Fest helps to ensure that memory endures. Many of those who attend the Fest are like Dan Pecchio and Mary Frances Carol. While both moved out of Brier Hill over fifty years ago, they can still name almost everyone who lived in each home on a one-mile stretch of Dearborn Street and what happened to each of them.[88]

Another former resident, Fred Ross, recalls the pain of how his father was forced to change his name, from the Italian Rossi to the more American-sounding Ross, in order to purchase a home. His wife, Josephine, remembers family members jumping on coal cars passing through Brier Hill to steal enough coal to heat their homes. But despite the poverty of the neighborhood, Brier Hill residents stress how everyone helped one another. Thus, as Josephine Ross comments, they "never thought they were poor."[89] Still, given the neighborhood's working-class history, the inclusion in the Fest of a "Man of the Year" award to celebrate local boys who made good seems especially important. The Brier Hill Fest provides an opportunity to remember and celebrate the struggles, sacrifices, and indignities that family members endured. Through its dances, food, and storytelling, the Fest helps those attending to build and rebuild networks, allegiances, and a community of memory. In Youngstown, the Brier Hill Fest represents how closely identity, community, and place are intertwined.

Nor is Brier Hill the only site where the working-class community of memory is preserved. But while the Brier Hill Fest downplays the role of work, across the river at the Sam Camens Steelworkers' Center, work still plays a central role in working-class memory. The center is the former USWA Local 1330 (U.S. Steel, Ohio Works) union hall, home of the strongest steelworkers' local in the area, and a center of community outreach and labor support activities ranging from the integration of the city's swimming pools in the 1950s to assisting in the organization of teachers' unions. Unlike other local union halls that were either placed in trusteeship by the international union or sold when the mills were closed, the members of Local 1330 fought to keep the hall, and it has since been turned into a social center for steelworkers and the neighboring community. The center is named after a former president of the Local, who for thirty years served as special assistant to the USWA president.

The Sam Camens Center has long served as a meeting place for steelworker retiree organizations, such as the Steelworker Organization of Active Retirees, as well as for individuals. Retired steelworkers congregate at the center as early as 6:30 A.M., the traditional starting time for the day shift in the steel industry, "to meet their buddies" and reminisce about their days in the mill. By serving as a gathering place for retirees, the center has become a repository of steelworker memories. At the same time, the center serves other functions. It offers bingo games several nights a week, and at the end of the 1990s, it was the most profitable bingo parlor in the state of Ohio. Neighbors gather there, and it serves as a union hall for active steelworker locals. It has also sponsored men's and women's golf and bowling leagues and summer league baseball, softball, and soccer teams for high school students. Local residents rent the hall for weddings and banquets. Thus the center helps to maintain its working-class community by serving the neighborhood.

Twenty years after the mill closings, though, the memory of steelwork is fading because, as Joe Gavini, the center director and former steelworker, suggests, "Many of us have retired or died." Talking about the mill is simply too painful. Yet the center still serves as a place where people can come together and talk about family and relationships. As Sam Camens himself suggests, "This turned out to be a social center, really, where retirees basically can come down and communicate, relate to, and be with their buddies. They worked together for forty years." For others, the center serves as a physical reminder of their own histories. Almost every day, Gavini and Camens come to the center because, they say, they built it through their labor at the mills and rebuilt it after the mills closed. Gavini says, "It has a lot to do with feeling like we've accomplished something." For Camens, spending time at the center that bears his name is "something I want to do . . . I have a continuing desire to be involved with people I worked with for so many years."[90]

❖ ❖ ❖

CONCLUSION

In the years after the mills shut down, Youngstown found its identity, as Tom Shipka had warned in 1977, "up for grabs." Both locally and nationally, the meaning of work in Youngstown, the significance of deindustrialization, the community's hopes for the future, the importance of resistance, and the meaning of place were all sources of struggle. Representations of Youngstown in the 1980s and 1990s reflected local efforts to come to terms with the closings and national conflicts about changes in the economy. While locals sought to understand the changing meaning of work and how their community was being reshaped by deindustrialization, representations produced for a national audience found the Youngstown story useful for everything from critiquing the excessive power of corporations to warning union members against fighting too hard for better treatment. Meanwhile, the community struggled over how to remember the past. A continuing dialogue between versions of Youngstown developed, reflecting conflicting views of how to define and remember this place. Was it a site of work or nonwork? Loss or struggle? Hope or despair?

As deindustrialization came to define Youngstown's image, many resisted the idea of remembering the past, arguing instead that the community should move on. Such conflict over memory leaves a community vulnerable, not only to having its image exploited by outsiders but also to internal strife and uncertainty, the loss of leadership, and a lost sense of shared purpose. It became much too easy to blame Youngstown for its own losses, forgetting the significance of corporate responsibility and even the long-term effects of deindustrialization. Yet the road to the future passes through the past. If the past is disrupted or erased, moving ahead becomes much more difficult. Youngstown was indeed vulnerable: the changes that developed during the 1980s and 1990s further undermined the community's stability and invited a new and even less positive image to emerge, as Youngstown came to be seen as a site of crime, corruption, and failure, a place that is almost beyond hope.

4

From "Steel Town"

to a "Nice Place to Do Time"

❖　❖　❖　❖　❖　❖　❖　❖　❖　❖　❖　❖　❖　❖

Beneath a brick skyline still smudged with soot
from long-gone mills, a drama is unfolding that
makes The Sopranos *look like choirboys.*
—*Kathy Kiely,* USA Today

Twenty years after the mill closings, Youngstown's national reputation as a steel town and poster child for deindustrialization receded, replaced by images of crime, political corruption, and corrections. In the 1990s, national news stories about Youngstown emphasized the rising murder rate, white-collar crime, the corruption of public officials, and the emerging prison economy of the Mahoning Valley. At the same time, this image of Youngstown largely ignored the significance of deindustrialization and institutional failure, suggesting instead that the community somehow brought its troubles on itself by too easily accepting crime and corruption. As Youngstown came to see itself as a site of loss and corruptibility, its sense of hopelessness increased. At the same time, the community refused to take responsibility for its own contributions to its struggles. As this chapter argues, because Youngstown refused to deal critically with its own history, it was unable to develop effective solutions to its continuing problems.

Although the *Saturday Evening Post* first defined Youngstown as "Crime Town, USA" in a 1963 article on local mob violence, that image resurfaced in the 1990s. Filmmaker Adam Bernstein drew on it when he set his 1999 independent film *Six Ways to Sunday* in Youngstown. The film tells the story of an unemployed nineteen-year-old who becomes an enforcer for the local mob. The film shows old industrial areas, decaying neighborhoods, and a largely abandoned downtown. As reviewer Joe Williams noted in his *St. Louis Post-Dispatch* review, "Harold's initiation into this middle-market mob is the most enjoyably offbeat aspect of the movie. The bars, bordellos and back offices of this Rust Belt Babylon became an effectively seedy backdrop for the unspooling of Harold's fragile personality."[1] The film was not actually shot in Youngstown, but Bernstein apparently relied heavily on viewers knowing something of the city's reputation.

That reputation was not unwarranted. In the 1990s, a series of stories appeared about crime and corruption in Youngstown, starting with a dramatic increase in the local murder rate, followed by tales of white-collar crime and reports on a large-scale investigation of corruption among public officials. Like the film, most stories on crime in Youngstown made use of familiar elements of Youngstown's image. The cover of a July 2000 issue of the *New Republic* is a good example: a battered "Welcome to Youngstown" sign full of bullet holes stands before a silhouette of smokestacks, a gray building, and telephone poles, providing a background for "A Story of the Mafia, the FBI, a Congressman, and the Most Crooked City in America."[2] Like most representations of Youngstown, this visual image refers to deindustrialized landscapes but gives only a very superficial and stereotypical image of what happened in Youngstown. Most of the stories read like the *Rocky Mountain News* report titled "High Crime, Low Hopes in Youngstown": "Youngstown had everything it needed to succeed— coal, railroads and an eager workforce—as the industrial revolution roared into town 100 years ago. Now poverty, drugs, gangs and hopelessness are what this crumbling northeast Ohio city is left with as the

Steeltown U.S.A.

New Republic, *Kevin Dresser, 10 & 17 July 2000*

century ends."[3] In this quote, as in so many of the stories about Youngstown, the relationship between Youngstown's economic and social struggles and its industrial history are erased.

This chapter examines how Youngstown's image as "Crime Town, USA" resurfaced in the 1990s and how that image erases important aspects of the community's history and culture. We examine stories of Youngstown as a "murder capital," the downfall of two local business leaders, and ongoing investigations and convictions of organized crime figures, public officials, attorneys, and the area's most prominent politician, Congressman James A. Traficant Jr. We also look at local redevelopment and promotional efforts and the growth of Youngstown's prison economy. As our discussion of these narratives shows, media representations of Youngstown's troubles rarely acknowledge the powerful long-term effects of deindustrialization. The picture that emerges thus seems to blame Youngstown for its difficulties and erases the economic violence caused by unfettered corporate behavior.

CRIME IN YOUNGSTOWN: BLAMING THE VICTIM

In the 1990s, Youngstown became known as a "murder capital." The *Vindicator* chronicled the carnage periodically, reporting that Youngstown's per capita murder rate was in the top ten in the nation for cities larger than fifty thousand for much of the 1990s. Youngstown's murder rate was eight times the national average, six times higher than New York, four and one-half times higher than Los Angeles, and twice as high as Chicago. The paper noted that criminal justice experts define anything over three times the national average as a homicide epidemic. It also cited a study by local researcher C. Allen Pierce, who found that convicted killers from Youngstown were becoming younger and after their first murder they also became less · inhibited. Pierce also noted that despite the fact that young men like themselves were the most common victims, the young killers in Youngstown "were almost proud of the fact that they were [from] a high homicide city."[4]

Such reports created an atmosphere of fear in the local community, presenting the city of Youngstown as a dangerous place and the rising murder rate as a mysterious trend, explainable only by the declining morality of those involved. Although the relationship between persistent high unemployment and per capita murder rates is well established, it was rarely discussed in the local media. The *Vindicator* compared Youngstown with Gary, Indiana, and Compton, California, whose murder rates were often higher, without mentioning that both of those cities had also experienced high levels of unemployment and deindustrialization. This version of the story fed into divisions between the city and surrounding suburbs, giving middle-class residents outside the city another reason to avoid the crumbling downtown and to blame the city for the area's problems.

Furthermore, the *Vindicator* failed to recognize that most of the murders occurred in the African-American community, a point that was highlighted by a story in the *Cleveland Plain Dealer* in 1999. An analysis of death records from the Centers for Disease Control and Prevention from 1988 to 1997 found that black women in Youngstown were murdered before their sixty-fifth birthday at higher rate than anywhere else in the nation. In addition, black women in Youngstown were murdered at a rate nearly eleven times higher than white women—the largest racial disparity in the country. The high murder rate was attributed to the women being "long abused by husbands and boyfriends or caught in the middle of drug deals gone bad." Further, for all causes of death, Mahoning County had one of the widest overall racial health gaps in the thirteen hundred counties with large numbers of black residents. The study also found that "homicides, heart disease, and lung cancer—all considered preventable and treatable by public health officials—killed blacks at a much higher rate than whites."[5] Unfortunately, by highlighting racial disparities, the *Plain Dealer*'s portrayal of murder as a "black problem" also fed into existing racism. This may explain why the *Plain Dealer*'s revelations came as such a surprise to many in Youngstown. Most had ignored what was happening in the city's African-American neighborhoods. They simply didn't care.

Not all accounts ignored the connection between economic struggle and rising crime rates. *The Human Factor,* a 1992 Instructional Television Services (ITV) documentary production for the BBC, focused on the effects of deindustrialization on crime in Youngstown fifteen years after the first mill closings.[6] The film opens with the dramatic statement, "There's a war going on in the streets of Youngstown, Ohio." The film starts with images of a deserted downtown Youngstown street. "This is Saturday afternoon on the main street of a city that illustrates with dreadful clarity the urban decline that's blighting America as old industries die," the voice-over tells us. Moving backward through time, the scene then shifts to a widely used image of mill stacks falling, and then to clips from the 1945 film *Steel Town,* showing the once busy and prosperous downtown. Youngstown today is full of problems, we're told: "Street corner dealing in drugs is rife. Violent crime, particularly among youngsters, is horrific. There's an irony about the name of this city: Young's town, a place where killing has literally become child's play." The film highlights the increased racial tensions of a depressed economy by contrasting the comments of white police officers and African-American residents. Several white police officers and detectives are quoted, including one who remarks that there are some parts of the city that "you just don't visit." Speaking from inside one of those areas, African-American mother Rita Agee describes her home as a sort of fortress, where "everybody else is the enemy" because "nobody else gives a damn."

The documentary draws a clear and direct connection between the widespread job losses related to the mill closings and increased crime and despair a decade later. Yet it also suggests, indirectly, that the poor people who remain in the city, especially African Americans, do not have an adequate sense of right and wrong. So while on the one hand, the piece blames Youngstown's problems on deindustrialization, on the other hand, it also points a finger at those who remain in the city. This shift from blaming large-scale economic factors to blaming individuals for not being strong enough or good enough to persevere through hard times is repeated in many images of Youngstown, and over time, it has been applied increasingly to the community itself.

While media reports on Youngstown's high murder rate offer varying versions of the story, researchers and local residents suggest that the local African-American community not only has suffered because of unemployment and crime but also has been undermined by racism. In *When Work Disappears: The World of the New Urban Poor*, William Julius Wilson showed that the disappearance of work aggravated poverty, racial tensions, and class and social isolation among the urban poor in Chicago. Crucial to his research was the staggering impact of structural impediments to economic and social renewal, such as lack of jobs, health care, and support networks, and the cumulative impact of the environment in shaping the lives of inner city residents.[7] The same understanding is necessary to grasp the chaos caused by the mill shutdowns in the Youngstown area and its relationship to criminal activity.

Deindustrialization and disinvestment exerted an enormous cost in terms of employment, earnings and fringe benefits, and destruction of the social fabric of the local community. Prior to the mill closings, despite Youngstown's reputation for mob activity, the local crime rate did not stand out. In fact, according to criminologist C. Allen Pierce, crime rates were fairly low because organized crime figures threatened petty criminals and burglars, especially in those areas where crime figures continued to live in the city.[8] When the mills closed, the crime rate did not initially increase dramatically in Youngstown. Rather, according to local economists and criminologists, after an initial lag, two later periods of increased crime could be tied directly to reduced income and long-term unemployment. Six to ten years after the mill closings, nonviolent crimes and traditional domestic violence increased.[9] The increase in the murder rate came fifteen years later.

Youngstown led the state of Ohio in unemployment and per capita welfare costs for almost two decades after the mills closed. The city's population declined as younger residents left and the mortality rate increased among its aging population. As economic conditions and population declined, services and education also deteriorated as public employees were laid off and public schools fell into bankruptcy. In turn, the structural changes in the community contributed to out-migrations of stable working-class and middle-class families who traditionally reinforced conventional patterns of work, family, and education. As economic conditions worsened over time, traditional families and neighborhoods disintegrated through divorce and migration, and the city saw a rise in the number of single parent families led by females. As Wilson found in Chicago, stable and employed families, social networks, and ethnic and racial communities in the Youngstown area were disrupted but have not been totally eliminated.[10]

The most significant increase in crime came some fifteen years after the first mill closings as the children from these broken families and neighborhoods became both perpetrators and victims of the wave of homicides in Youngstown. Lacking economic opportunities and access to real wealth, these young adults turned to selling drugs, especially crack cocaine, to largely suburban residents who do "drive-bys" into poor neighborhoods. Most young adults in Youngstown do not have the money to purchase drugs; rather, they have opportunities to sell drugs, purchase guns, and join gangs to protect territory and profits. Some of those who are not directly involved in drugs purchase guns and join gangs just to protect themselves. But researchers found relatively few drug-related homicides. In interviews with youthful offenders who were convicted of homicide in the mid-1990s in Youngstown, most said the homicides were over disagreements, minor disputes, disrespect, and the prevalence of deadly weapons.[11] Interestingly, there is little evidence that organized crime was directly involved in drug-related violence. However, while organized crime does not control the supply and distribution of drugs in the Mahoning Valley, it is involved in both the sale of guns and judicial protection. By influencing a network of prosecuting and criminal defense attorneys and judges in the Mahoning Valley, organized crime could control bonds, prosecutions, trial dates, and sentencing.[12]

As stories such as *The Human Factor* suggest, most of this activity was centered in African-American neighborhoods, and most of the killers and their victims were black. Yet most media reports also ignore important parts of the story, even those that acknowledge the role of economic struggle in rising crime rates. The experience of the African-American community on Youngstown's lower north side is instructive. As the twentieth century began, Youngstown had a relatively small African-American population, but this changed as increasing numbers of black workers migrated from the rural South seeking work during the first half of the century. Many gained economic footholds and formed small enclaves. These African-American communities grew larger and economically stronger by midcentury as white workers began to seek work outside the steel industry and more African Americans were hired to work in the aging steel mills. While African Americans often held the worst jobs and endured racism from both companies and unions, rising industrial wages in the postwar era provided increasing numbers of African Americans with a middle-class lifestyle.[13]

In the late 1940s, one of the first public housing projects in the United States, Westlake Terrace, was built on Youngstown's lower north side adjacent to Brier Hill and near the Ohio Works to house returning veterans and the increasing black population. Born in Westlake Terrace, Dr. Homer Warren, a professor of marketing at YSU, remembers that the apartments were neatly kept. Residents were expected to cut the grass, make minor repairs, clean laundry rooms, and pick up paper. In essence, Westlake Terrace reflected and reinforced the values and work ethic of the community that lived there. Soon, however, Westlake residents began to move into housing that was being vacated by middle-class families who where moving to the upper north side and to Youngstown's suburbs. Like Brier Hill, Westlake Terrace functioned as a portal community before becoming "the projects," a permanent home to low-income families who saw little hope of moving up or out.

Warren recalls how the growing African-American community attracted new black businesses in the 1950s. Small black-owned business, such as the Colored Store grocery, the Allison Hotel, Dills and McCullough-Williams funeral homes, Goldie's Flowers, Sonnyboy's barbecue, and a myriad of barbershops and small businesses located in the area known as Westlake Crossings represented the growing economic strength of the neighborhood. Likewise, black professionals located along Belmont Avenue adjacent to St. Elizabeth's Hospital and Westlake Terrace and the lower north side. Black nightclubs, such as the Casablanca, Soso's, the Elms, the Ritz, and the Elks, brought leading national performers and nightclub acts to entertain residents of Youngstown. Black women, who were largely excluded from industrial jobs and most clerical, sales, secretarial, and other jobs associated with white women, helped support their families by doing cleaning, laundering, and other service work for families on the upper north side. Others engaged in entrepreneurial activities, such as the network of hairdressing salons and "beauty schools" in the neighborhood. Finally, many well-attended churches, largely Baptist, dotted the north side of Youngstown, building a network of support and community as ethnic churches and clubs had done for white immigrants earlier.[14]

In the 1950s and 1960s, however, the African-American community was disrupted by changes in transportation and "urban renewal." When State Route 422 and the Interstate Route 680 beltway were built, housing was demolished and the African-American community on Youngstown's north side was literally torn apart. Sarah Brown-Clark, local politician and former director of the black studies program at Youngstown State University who grew up on the north side, remembers Westlake Terrace and the lower north side as actually being split into two sections by the highway. Many of the displaced residents were moved to older white areas where the housing stock was aging and in disrepair. As Brown-Clark explains, before the highway and urban renewal projects, "the lower north side was an economically strong and occupationally diverse African-American neighborhood with high levels of home ownership." But when the highway bisected the area and urban renewal projects tore down older housing, displaced African-Americans moved into the areas being abandoned by white flight. Poorer African Americans, especially those from the "monkey's nest" area adjacent to the Ohio Works (which was completely destroyed by the highway projects), moved into the stable middle-class African-American neighborhoods on the north side. But because they had less money to invest in their homes, housing stock deteriorated further, and as white flight expanded, property values on the lower north side declined. This combined with the city's economic decline at the end of the 1970s made it much more difficult for families to move up out of Westlake Terrace. According to Brown-Clark, the housing project ceased to be "generational." Earlier, she said, "people had moved there and left once they got an economic foothold. With the building of the highway, it became poorer and intergenerational. It became what we think of as 'the projects.'" At the same time, black businesses in the old neighborhood lost many of their customers, in part because the shops were simply less accessible now that State Route 422 ran through the area, and the entire process hastened white flight to the suburbs, increased residential segregation, and disrupted shopping patterns. The geographic and demographic disruption largely destroyed Westlake Crossings as a growing economic center for black businesses and destabilized largely African-American neighborhoods. As Brown-Clark suggests, the demographic and geographical changes were not so much about urban renewal as "Negro removal."[15] This also benefited local mall developers, who wanted to control all retail activity by moving it to the margins of the city.

But like Youngstown's other working-class areas, it was the mill closings that had the most dramatic impact on the African-American community. The mill closings and the downsizing of support industries and other manufacturing occurred at a time when African-American steelworkers were just beginning to benefit from increases in job opportunities resulting from the civil rights movement and, more specifically, the steel industry's Consent Decree that attempted to overcome past discrimination in the mills by expanding job ladders for minorities and women.[16]

As unemployment in Youngstown increased in the late 1970s and 1980s, so did the poverty rate, which remained over 20 percent for twenty years. And as the poverty rate increased, a continuous cycle developed of economic dislocation, unemployment, outmigrations of middle- and working-class families, and the decline of the work ethic, values, neighborhoods, and community. The economic and community destabilization was reflected in the rise of broken families, antisocial behavior, and loss of control over the social behavior of children and adults. This contributed to the kind of culturally destructive behavior and attitudes that Wilson found in Chicago and might be found in other economically distressed areas. As was happening in other low-income neighborhoods throughout the city, the vital, stable, and well-kept working-class neighborhood on the lower north side and Westlake Terrace became a place of instability, decay, despair, and danger. While similar changes were felt throughout the Mahoning Valley, they had a disproportional effect on the African-American community. The lower north side thus became one of the primary areas associated with crime locally, one of the neighborhoods that, as the police officer in *The Human Factor* commented, "you just don't visit."

To briefly summarize, the representation of Youngstown as a crime town persists, and it has been exacerbated by the high homicide rate. But while some media reports offer no explanations and others place blame on those who are most directly involved, at heart Youngstown's crime problem was directly related to unemployment, poverty, failed urban policies, and racism. Violent crime in the 1990s was rooted in a combination of the urban renewal and transportation projects of the 1960s and the corporate economic violence of the late 1970s and early 1980s. Yet most representations of Youngstown as a murder capital pay only lip service to the lingering effects of displacement and deindustrialization.

❖ ❖ ❖

WHITE-COLLAR CRIME

Along with dramatic stories about the murder rate, white-collar crime and mob activity also played key roles in defining Youngstown's reputation as "Crime Town, USA." When two local business leaders were charged with fraud and bribery in the 1990s, media reports focused not only on their individual activities but also on the significance of their position as local heroes in a community that was desperate for economic hope. The rise and fall of Michael Monus and Edward DeBartolo Jr. were significant not just as examples of individual failure but also as stories about a community that was betrayed by the local businessmen in whom it had placed its hopes and trust. On the one hand, media reports emphasized the personal success but also the psychological and moral failures of these local entrepreneurs. On the other, they suggested that the local community bore some of the blame. The Monus and DeBartolo stories added to Youngstown's image as a site of corruption, and they contributed to the idea of Youngstown as a community that accepted bribery, conspiracy, and carefully targeted generosity as the price of doing business. As *Newsweek* suggested in one report, "the public is almost a co-conspirator."[17]

In what the PBS documentary series *Frontline* called the largest corporate "fraud of the century," the executives of the Youngstown-based Phar Mor company swindled $500 million from its stockholders.[18] The film traces Phar Mor's history as a deep discount retail and drugstore that rivaled Wal-Mart in the 1980s. Formed in 1982 by local entrepreneur Michael Monus, the company attracted many local investors and grew rapidly by forcing suppliers and manufacturers to accept lower profit margins for bulk purchases and by offering consumers lower prices. So successful was the deep discount retail format that between 1982 and 1992, Phar Mor grew to over three hundred stores nationwide and became a retailing phenomenon. Soon major investors, such as Westinghouse Credit Corporation and the investment house Lazard Freres, were eager to provide the necessary capital for future Phar Mor expansion.

The documentary also showed that Monus did not limit his entrepreneurial activities to retailing. Like local entrepreneur and mall magnate Edward J. DeBartolo Sr., Monus entered the sports business. He founded the summer professional World Basketball League (WBL) that was made up of athletes under six feet, five inches tall. He also owned the hometown team that he named the Youngstown Pride. The team's moniker suggested courage, strength, self-esteem, and the solidarity of family and community, ideas that had powerful resonance in a town struggling to overcome the ravages of deindustrialization. Monus also established a Ladies Professional Golf Association (LPGA) tournament in Youngstown, which would become one of the first LPGA tournaments to be covered by ESPN. The proceeds of the tournament were used to fund a summer camp, Camp Tuff Enuff, for children who were at risk for drug abuse. Building on his involvement in the LPGA and WBL activities, Monus won the right to become a general partner in a new major league baseball expansion franchise, the Colorado Rockies. Monus's emphasis on the business of sports had much to offer the local community. Not only did his ventures promise to bring new business to the area, they also provided a rallying point for community solidarity and hope. Youngstown residents who formed the fan base for the Pride, the LPGA tournament, and even the Colorado Rockies could imagine themselves as partners in Monus's efforts. While relatively few in the community had actual financial investments in these projects, many were invested emotionally, and that investment added to Monus's reputation as a local hero. It helped that Monus gained a national reputation in the late 1980s as a successful entrepreneur. In 1988, *Venture* magazine honored Monus as a top entrepreneur, and *Newsweek* reflected that Monus had become an "icon in the American cult of the entrepreneur."[19] Such accolades played well in Youngstown—a town that had become increasingly distrustful of outsiders and frantic for economic development.

Phar Mor's success offered evidence of vitality and hope for a community in need. As the *Frontline* documentary suggested, Monus became a "favorite son" whose creation of thousands of jobs, renovation of an abandoned retail store, and relocation of his national corporate offices to downtown Youngstown were seen as acts of loyalty to his hometown. He became a leader in community and philanthropic activities. He was appointed to the board of trustees at Youngstown State University, where he established the University's first academic chair, the Monus Chair of Entrepreneurship. As *Newsweek* noted, "For downtrodden Youngstown, Mickey, as everyone knew him, was a savior."[20] Especially for those in the business community who stressed entrepreneurship as the source of redevelopment, Monus's success became a source of community pride and direction. And in a community that tolerated "greasing the palm," a little corruption did not raise any eyebrows.

As with many businesses in the so-called go-go 1980s, Phar Mor and Monus's other ventures were highly leveraged, and growth was imperative because of low profit margins. When Phar Mor started hemorrhaging money, Monus turned to questionable and sometimes illegal activities to keep the company afloat. As the *Frontline* documentary reported, Monus pressured Coca-Cola to enter into a $10 million exclusivity agreement to assure that Pepsi would not be sold in Phar Mor stores. Phar Mor negotiated agreements that called for suppliers to accept deferred payments. Such arrangements amounted to short-term loans to Phar Mor by suppliers, which soon became long-term loans. But as Phar Mor's debt grew to over $18 million by the late 1980s, Monus turned to fraud and embezzlement. Phar Mor hugely inflated the value of its inventories to make the company appear more profitable than it was. With the company valued at twice its real worth, Phar Mor easily gained additional investors and working capital. But as the swindle reached over $350 million by 1992, the fraud was uncovered. Investors found that money invested in Phar Mor was being used to prop up the WBL. Within months, 50 percent of Phar Mor stores were closed, thousands of employees were laid off, hundreds of suppliers went unpaid, investors suffered enormous losses, and 129 indictments were filed against Phar Mor officials.

In June 1994, despite overwhelming evidence against him, the trial of Mickey Monus ended in a hung jury. The prosecution suspected jury tampering and upon investigation found that Ray Isaac, the star quarterback on the first YSU national championship football team who had been befriended by Monus, had influenced a jury member. At a retrial in May 1995, Monus was found guilty of 109 counts of fraud, tax evasion, and embezzlement and was sentenced to twenty years in prison.[21]

The Monus story was told in newspapers and broadcast media around the country, where it was picked up as "a modern morality tale."[22] *Frontline* referred to the story as "the fraud of the century," yet it also questioned whether Monus was a "crook or a classic entrepreneur."[23] Other reports implicated both Monus and the community. *Newsweek's* version of the story included a long analysis from Steve Berglas, a psychologist from Harvard Medical School who specializes in working with high-level businessmen. According to Berglas, Monus's corrupt behavior was typical of top executives, who were "often desperately insecure beneath the pinstripes" and who often become self-destructive. But in the next paragraph, the article suggests the community's responsibility, noting that people who are deeply invested in the "Horatio Alger myth" sometimes display "a profound will to believe." Youngstowners, the story hints, should have been more suspicious. But as local newspaper columnist Nancy Beeghly explains, the community had high hopes for Monus: "We were the fifth largest steelmakers in the *world.* . . . I don't think we ever got over that. People wanted something magical again."[24] As Beeghly's comment suggests, the community was betrayed by Monus, but because it was so desperate to believe in him, it also helped to make his rise and fall possible.

Indeed, local news reports early on praised Monus for bringing hope to the Mahoning Valley. In 1989, for example, an editorial in the *Youngstown/Warren Business Journal* offered a glowing summary of Monus's good works for the community, including both economic development and service on numerous boards. For all this, the editorial argued, Monus deserved "not just the praise of [*the*] community— and the thanks that accompanies it."[25] Even after he was convicted, some continued to view him as a local hero. After all, he was not an outsider, like those who had closed the mills, nor had he abandoned the community. In July 2000, Monus's attorney, Don Hanni Jr., wrote a letter to the editor of the *Vindicator,* praising Monus and suggesting that he had served enough time. Noting that the LPGA Ladies Golf Classic had raised over $2 million for eighty charitable organizations, Hanni wrote:

There is no question that Mickey Monus did wrong, but believe it or not, most of the money that he misappropriated was spent trying to put Youngstown, Ohio, on the map in a positive way in the area of sports. This stolen money was poured down a bottomless pit called the Youngstown Pride. As a result of his love of sports and a lot of poor judgment, Mickey has already served more time than many people convicted of murder. Not one word has ever been mentioned about a group of New York investors who invested $200 million despite the fact that the auditors to whom they paid $350,000 advised them not to buy Phar-Mor stock. "Greed is a terrible thing to waste."[26]

Monus's embezzlement might be portrayed as an extension of normal business practice, or it might be seen as an example of how free enterprise requires a type of gambling. For another local family, however, the corruption and gambling that brought down one of its members was much clearer. Just as in the Monus story, representations of the downfall of Edward DeBartolo Jr. comment as much about Youngstown as they do about DeBartolo himself.

After the mill closings, the Edward J. DeBartolo Corporation became the most powerful influence on local business and the political community. [27] The DeBartolo Corporation was founded by Edward J. DeBartolo Sr. in 1948 and, until its purchase by the Simon Corporation in 1998, it was the nation's leading mall developer. As the company grew, the DeBartolo Corporation expanded into several highly successful diversified real estate investments and professional sport franchises, including the San Francisco Forty-Niners and the Pittsburgh Penguins, and the Thistledown and Louisiana Downs racetracks. In a time of local economic crisis, the growth and success of the DeBartolo Corporation was a source of economic stability and community pride in Youngstown.

While the DeBartolo Corporation had grown economically powerful throughout the nation, it remained faithful to economically depressed Youngstown. In fact, DeBartolo's pride in his hometown was often highlighted in news stories about his business, a point emphasized in a 1993 special Sunday section of the *Pittsburgh Press* devoted entirely to the DeBartolo family: "The world's largest developer of shopping malls, DeBartolo's success is in glaring contrast to the industrial boneyard of Youngstown's steel industry. His hometown devotion has rooted his house and headquarters just outside the city in Boardman township."[28] Furthermore, DeBartolo Sr. was proud that he was from Youngstown. Thomas M. Macioce, president and CEO of Allied Stores, called DeBartolo Sr. "a man who never forgot his roots. In the corridors of business all over this country, he makes it clear that his hometown is Youngstown."[29] DeBartolo Sr. frequently explained that his self-discipline and hard work were strengths he had developed from growing up and living in the area. News stories also noted that DeBartolo combined toughness with a "gift for personal gestures," ruthless business savvy with integrity, a deep sense of loyalty and "impeccable honesty" with a touch of corruption.[30] That devotion to Youngstown had its downside, as the *Pittsburgh Press* noted: "But DeBartolo's identification with Youngstown also may be the source of the shadow over seven decades of success—persistently linking him to organized crime."[31] Regardless of the accusations, DeBartolo unashamedly said of his hometown in the midst of its economic crisis:

> If I can create one job for one person with a family, I am going to do it. If I can create 200 jobs, by God, I want to do it. I have nothing to gain. Sometimes I wonder why I do it because sometimes it becomes so discouraging. But I get a lot of letters a day that would make you cry. People that are starving. Somebody's got to do something about it and if I can do something, by God, I'm going to do it no matter how much criticism I get about nationality and all this bullshit you hear about the rackets and all that crap.[32]

A number of profiles of DeBartolo Sr. have appeared over the years, and most tell a similar story of his life. He was born in 1909 in Smokey Hollow, a working-class section of Youngstown. Educated at Notre Dame in civil engineering, he was one of the first builders to understand the potential of post–World War II prosperity, highway construction, and suburbanization on retailing. The DeBartolo Corporation's shopping centers and malls dramatically changed the nature of general merchandising and the retail apparel business in the United States, and later his sports entertainment business would revolutionize professional sports. But almost from the beginning, the company was plagued with allegations of corruption ranging from the shorting of subcontractors to ties with organized crime. Brief histories of the DeBartolo Corporation mention that during the mob wars in Youngstown in the 1950s, the corporate offices and DeBartolo shopping centers were bombed six times. In the 1960s, the concessions and other elements of his racing interests were found to be controlled by companies that were fronts for organized crime figures. In the 1970s, DeBartolo's banking interests in Florida came under investigation when they were suspected of laundering money from gaming, narcotics, and other organized crime activities. A 1978 classified report by the Florida Department of Law Enforcement described DeBartolo Sr. as "a very wealthy, powerful, influential person with organized crime connections in Ohio."[33] Despite the numerous investigations and allegations, DeBartolo Sr. was never charged with any crimes. But his son was not so lucky. The national attention given to the corrupt activities of Edward J. DeBartolo Jr. would embarrass and divide the DeBartolo family and add to the community's association with criminality.

In 1977, DeBartolo Sr. bought the struggling National Football League (NFL) franchise, the San Francisco Forty-Niners, for $17 million and immediately sold it to his twenty-nine-year-old son. The team was a separate company from the DeBartolo Corporation until 1985, when, against NFL rules, the DeBartolo Corporation took over controlling interest. From 1977 until he was forced to turn operations over to his sister in 1998, DeBartolo Jr. was acknowledged as one of the best owners of a professional sports franchise. While he lacked his father's intelligence, judgment, grace, and shyness for the public spotlight, DeBartolo Jr. shared his father's deep sense of loyalty, responsibility to family, and gift for personal gestures with his Forty-Niners family. To help oversee the Forty-Niners' operation, DeBartolo Jr. asked a

Youngstown attorney, Carmen Policy, to be executive vice president for front office and league relations in 1983. Much is made of the close relationship between Policy and DeBartolo Jr., which developed during their early years in Youngstown. The *New York Times* described how the two men had met at a charity event in Youngstown in 1968, shared a common background in the Smokey Hollow section of Youngstown, and had grandparents who lived in villages in Italy only eleven miles apart. Policy remembers those days fondly, as he explained in the *Times* article: "We didn't have a lot when I was growing up but we weren't poor because we were rich in so many ways. My grandmother worked seven days a week at a tavern we owned and she went to church five days a week. Life was so simple then. It was so full of wisdom."[34]

To be sure, DeBartolo Jr. and Policy were considered the two best NFL executives in the last twenty years. DeBartolo had a reputation for hiring the best people regardless of the cost. The Forty-Niners was the first team to make coaching professional football a financially rewarding occupation and regularly had the highest player payroll in the league. Indeed, the NFL fined the Forty-Niners for doubling player bonuses during the 1985 players' strike to lessen their financial hardship. Policy was generally conceded as among the most intelligent, charming, and sophisticated men in professional sports. In 1994, the *Sporting News* named Policy NFL Executive of the Year. By hiring the best football people into administrative positions, revolutionizing the structure of football contracts, and using techniques that circumvented salary caps, Policy worked behind the scenes to help DeBartolo Jr. rebuild the Forty-Niners into an organization that won five Super Bowls in twenty-two years. In 2000, Policy was fined by the National Football League for violations of league rules regarding salary caps when he was with the Forty-Niners.

Youngstown took great pride in what DeBartolo Jr. and Policy accomplished with the Forty-Niners. Most newspaper accounts of the Forty-Niners' success included references to Youngstown and the DeBartolo family. A 1990 Associated Press story marveled that despite the "allure" of San Francisco, "DeBartolo's city remains Youngstown, where he lives with wife Candy and three daughters. It is from here that he runs the family business—mostly shopping center construction—and it is to Youngstown that he invited the 49ers, their wives and girl friends after last year's Super Bowl victory for what by all accounts was a lavish party."[35] Forty-Niners executives and players regularly visited the city and touted both the city's fighting spirit and the DeBartolo family. Even though San Francisco was two thousand miles away, the team's success was Youngstown's. A large sign in front of the DeBartolo Corporation proudly boasted that Youngstown was the "Home of the World Champion Forty-Niners." Given Youngstown's battered image, locals must have taken great pride in the words of President Clinton, when he told DeBartolo Jr. after the Forty-Niners won the 1995 Super Bowl, "I think the best thing I can say about the Forty-Niners is that I haven't met a single fan anywhere in America that resents all the success that you've had and that's a rare thing."[36]

In the 1990s, DeBartolo Jr. turned over daily operations of the Forty-Niners to Policy in order to devote more time to the DeBartolo Corporation, which had begun to experience some financial difficulties. The Forty-Niners had been a financial drag on the DeBartolo Corporation, which had subsidized the team in the 1980s. Despite its championship seasons, the Forty-Niners lost money in every year in the decade except 1983.[37] Worse yet, according to the *Wall Street Journal,* the nation's largest mall developer and manager had accumulated $4 billion in recession-related debt in the early 1990s.[38] At the same time, the DeBartolo Corporation's entertainment division was being threatened by the expansion of legalized gambling. Specifically, the DeBartolo Corporation anticipated that riverboat gambling would impact revenues at their Louisiana Downs racetrack. The company entered into a joint venture with Hollywood Casino Corporation to open a riverboat casino in Bossier City, Louisiana.[39] Given the difficulties, the DeBartolo Corporation sold most of its shopping mall construction and management business to the Simon Property Group, forming the Simon-DeBartolo Property Group. As a result, the Youngstown headquarters was downsized, and the real estate and construction business was moved to Simon's headquarters in Indianapolis. In 1999, the Simon-DeBartolo Property Group changed its name back to the Simon Property Group and began to remove all references to the DeBartolo Corporation at its Youngstown properties. At Youngstown's Southern Park Mall, just a few blocks from the Boardman Shopping Center, where many of DeBartolo Sr.'s original ideas about retail construction were established, the only reference is a small sculpture and tribute to Edward DeBartolo Sr. Thus has begun the slow erasure of one of Youngstown's most famous family names and the memory of a man who, as the authors of the *Pittsburgh Press* story put it, changed "the texture of American lives and perhaps the course of American politics."[40]

The downsized DeBartolo Corporation continued to operate its entertainment division. But in 1998, Edward DeBartolo Jr. was forced to plead guilty to concealing an extortion plot by former Louisiana governor Edwin Edwards. DeBartolo Jr. had paid Edwards a $400,000 cash bribe in return for his assistance in receiving a Louisiana riverboat casino license. Under the plea bargain, DeBartolo Jr. testified against Edwards and was given two years probation, fined $250,000, forfeited $400,000, and provided up to $350,000 in restitution. His testimony helped convict Edwards on seventeen counts of racketeering, extortion, and fraud. More important for DeBartolo Jr., he was forced to turn over operations of the Forty-Niners to his sister, Denise DeBartolo-York, who had become the chairperson and chief executive officer of the DeBartolo Corporation. In turn, this led to countersuits between DeBartolo and his sister over the family's and DeBartolo Sr.'s assets.

The Edwards affair received much media attention, with DeBartolo Jr. alternately portrayed as a fallen hero, victim, coconspirator, broken man, or snitch. According to Edwards, DeBartolo was a "new Linda Tripp."[41] During the first interview following Edwards's conviction, *USA Today* reported that DeBartolo Jr. felt obliged to pay the bribe for the casino license and admitted that he made a mistake that "very well could have ruined my life." Yet, he felt sorry for Edwards: "Isn't life strange. There was a little part of me that actually felt bad for everything (Edwards) did and for all the problems he caused me with the NFL, my family, with a lot of things. . . . But justice was served. Sometimes, it's served cold, sometimes warmed. But it was served." In his defense, the paper minimized DeBartolo Jr.'s complicity by suggesting that he "should have known better" and was "not on his game," inviting readers to feel sorry for a man who had paid a high price for his acts.[42] He lost the Forty-Niners and precipitated legal actions between family members that resulted in his removal from the DeBartolo Corporation board of directors. He later reduced his involvement in the construction business to relatively small-scale real estate interests in the Tampa–St. Petersburg area. At the same time, perhaps because of family tensions and public embarrassment, DeBartolo Jr. sold his Youngstown home and moved permanently to Tampa.

The media played up the tensions between DeBartolo Jr. and his sister, who had been appointed head of their father's company after he died in 1994. While *Forbes* magazine characterized the family dispute as a "spat" between the super-rich prompted by DeBartolo Jr. "soiling the family name,"[43] the *Wall Street Journal* suggested that the affair had exposed a "long-simmering rivalry" between the siblings.[44] The *San Jose Mercury News* described DeBartolo Jr. as someone who "loved fame and glory and attention," while his sister "wanted nothing other than to stay at home in Youngstown, Ohio with her four children and quietly run her late father's company."[45] Throughout the ordeal, the press emphasized DeBartolo-York's refusal to air the family's dispute in public: "It's been very hurtful. I've never told my side. I wanted to take the high road. I never said anything derogatory about him. I want to set an example for my children. After all, he is my brother."[46]

The fall of Edward DeBartolo Jr., like that of Michael Monus, was presented as a tale of individual avarice and greed, but at the same time, it suggested larger scale corruption that was supported, or at least accepted, by the local community. Some reports positioned such white-collar crime in the context of local corruption, pointing out that Monus and DeBartolo Jr. were raised in this atmosphere, and both were seen as local heroes despite their illegal activities. At the same time, however, both were portrayed as examples of personal failure—Monus led astray by an inflated ego and DeBartolo Jr. part of a dysfunctional family. As later reports demonstrated, the two explanations were never entirely separate, and both would later serve to characterize Youngstown.

ORGANIZED CRIME, ARSON, AND POLITICAL CORRUPTION

Organized crime has a long history in Youngstown, in part because the city has sat on the boundary line between major Mafia families in Cleveland and Pittsburgh for over fifty years. Local mob involvement in the rackets was made possible, to a large extent, because the community tolerated close ties between organized crime and public officials. As former mayor Patrick Ungaro explained in 1999, bribery was normalized and mob influence "was so overwhelming, so ingrained. Either you are intimidated by it or you join it."[47] While there is nothing new about such ties in communities touched by organized crime, in Youngstown the corruption took on multiple meanings in the 1990s and resulted in the community being portrayed as "a European City-State in a time warp" and compared with the dysfunctional mob family of HBO's series *The Sopranos*.[48]

A spate of investigations and convictions of local political leaders and lawyers in the late 1990s only added to the lingering representation of Youngstown as "Crime Town, USA." In 1998, *George* magazine named Youngstown one of "The Ten Most Corrupt Cities in America."[49] In 2000, the *New Republic* ran a cover story on Youngstown, referring to Youngstown as "the city that fell in love with the mob."[50] *USA Today* suggested, "Beneath a brick skyline still smudged with soot from long-gone mills, a drama is unfolding that makes *The Sopranos* look like choirboys."[51] A *U.S. News & World Report* story on the investigation of local representative James A. Traficant Jr. made the connection even clearer: "The cast of characters sounds like a real-life version of HBO's popular show about a low-rent mob family, *The Sopranos,* starting with the disheveled Traficant, who is best known for shouting intemperate speeches in the well of the House." *U.S. News* also quotes the head of the FBI office in Cleveland, who described Youngstown culture as an example of "the 'broken window syndrome.' If you neglect quality of life and accept less than what's right, it chips away and erodes the windows of the judicial system."[52] A town long associated with organized crime was now being likened to a dysfunctional mob family—"a low-rent" one at that.

Many of the national news stories on corruption in Youngstown focused on the FBI's extended investigation of Traficant, who served as both the most visible example of Youngstown culture and a lightning rod for the media. *USA Today* suggested that while his oddball appearance and one-minute rants on the House floor against government institutions, corporations, and hypocrisy have not enamored him with his House colleagues, his defiant populist sentiments and "junkyard dog" approach to politics have resonated with the media. In the 1990s, Traficant appeared regularly on the talk show circuit, including the nightly news, the *Larry King Show,* and the Rush Limbaugh radio broadcast, and *USA Today* labeled him the "star of C-SPAN."[53] The *Cleveland Plain Dealer* wrote, "There's a fictional quality to the life of U.S. Rep. James A. Traficant Jr., a Dickensian character whose rise from the gritty streets of Youngstown to football stardom and the halls of Congress is the stuff of legend."[54] The media's fascination with Traficant and his populist politics have brought additional national attention to Youngstown and increased the community's image as a place where corruption and crime are accepted parts of everyday life.

Traficant's legend is based, in part, in Youngstown's struggles after the mill closings. A *Sixty Minutes* profile traced his rise from local football hero to Mahoning County sheriff, a position that had historically come under mob influence. Traficant's reputation for disdain of government and institutions began during his stint as sheriff, when he refused to enforce eviction orders for unemployed families. When charged with contempt of court, Traficant chose to go to jail. Similarly, the *Plain Dealer* tells the story of how Traficant defended himself when the Justice Department charged him with accepting bribes from the Cleveland and Pittsburgh mobs. Despite enormous evidence against him, including his own written confession, Traficant was acquitted because he claimed that the bribes were part of an elaborate "sting" operation that he had planned to trap local mobsters. The Justice Department was incensed at the acquittal, but the community cheered Traficant's "up yours" attitude toward the federal government. The Justice Department continued to hound Traficant and got a measure of revenge when the federal tax court found him guilty in 1984 of income tax evasion for the $163,000 in bribes and held him liable for $180,000 in back taxes and penalties. But Traficant's "legend as a hero of the little people" was launched, and he was elected to the U.S. Congress in 1984, where he became the most visible representation of Youngstown's anti-institutional sentiment.[55]

Traficant represented the Youngstown-Warren area for more than fifteen years. He was seen as an iconoclastic populist who for many years had a near-perfect labor voting record while supporting a highly conservative social agenda on illegal immigration, capital punishment, and the involvement of the military in drug intervention. Throughout his term of office, he remained deeply suspicious of the government, especially the Justice Department and Internal Revenue Service (IRS), and angry at government support of large corporations. He was one of the most outspoken critics of free trade, especially the North American Free Trade Agreement (NAFTA), and he frequently told corporations that if they were moving jobs overseas, they should be responsible for their own defense. At the same time, his amendments in 1998 to the tax reform bill curtailed the ability of the IRS to seize the property of tax evaders.

The late 1990s investigation of Traficant was part of a highly publicized ten-year federal investigation of public and private corruption in Youngstown that resulted in more than eighty indictments and convictions. According to Andrew Arena, head of the local FBI office, Youngstown in the late 1990s had more FBI agents per capita than anywhere else in the nation. The investigations involved organized crime, drug-related violence, public corruption, and white-collar crime, including health care fraud. In explaining the large FBI presence in the community, Arena said that the local corruption was deeply rooted and that "the rest of the world does not accept the behavior that's accepted here." Cynically, he suggested that the crime-ridden locale provided "the best job security for an FBI agent" nationally.[56] Francis X. Clines of the *New York Times* picks up on this theme: "The fact that the only obvious growth industry is in the special federal task force indictments underlines Youngstown's failure to share in the suburban economic boom, which leaves it encircled like some ossified European city-state in a time warp."[57] As these stories suggest, the success of this investigation, in which Traficant was repeatedly implicated, added to Youngstown's reputation as a haven for corruption.

Among those convicted were the local sheriff, several county prosecutors, a county engineer, a city law director, the coroner, several municipal and county court judges, and numerous local attorneys. Most of the public corruption involved case fixing and bid rigging. But the investigation also led to several major organized crime convictions, including local mob boss Lenny Strollo. Several of his associates also pled guilty to the attempted murder of prosecuting attorney Paul Gains, who had a reputation for not cooperating with the mob. Other Strollo associates included former fire chief Charles O'Nesti and George Alexander, both Traficant aides, who pled guilty to racketeering and conspiracy charges. Traficant told the national media that he also expected to be indicted and that, once again, he would defend himself in court.

In May 2001, Traficant was indicted. The ten-count indictment charged that he had engaged in bribery, accepted illegal gratuities (kickbacks), obstructed justice, defrauded the government, filed false tax returns, and with his office staff engaged in a pattern of conduct that violated the Racketeer Influenced and Corrupt Organization Act. Following the indictment, he railed in public against "government bureaucrats," vowed to defend himself, once again, in court, and warned prosecutors that "If I defeat you, you'll be working in Mingo Junction," a reference to a poor rural area in southeast Ohio near the West Virginia border.[58]

But his defiance did not gain the usual support. In its "Winners and Losers" column, *Time* magazine pictured Traficant as a loser in a broken glass frame and sneered that there are "no plaid suits in the pen."[59] The *Cleveland Plain Dealer* noted that powerful political allies were distancing themselves from Traficant, and some were even willing to testify against him. For example, John J. Cafaro, a member of one of the most powerful and influential political families both locally and nationally, pled guilty to one count of conspiracy to bribe in return for testifying against Traficant: "The family's proud political history is what makes J. J. Cafaro's predicament so incongruous: That a millionaire who helped the careers of so many politicians would help the government try to bring down U.S. Rep. James A. Traficant, a nine term congressman who holds folk-hero status in the valley."[60] Jason Vest, writing in *The American Prospect,* argued that public opinion was also changing and that Traficant's "working-class shtick" and "working-class demagoguery" were no longer "resonant." As proof, Vest argued that traditional supporters, such as organized labor, were "distancing themselves from Traficant and what he stands for." In explaining the lack of union support for Traficant, United Auto Workers Local 1112 president Jim Graham said "a lot of our members are tired" of the factors that have made Youngstown one of the most disreputable cities in America.[61]

But Traficant has proved to be an agile politician. Some would call him a political terrorist or a renegade, willing to change his political stripes as necessary. For example, in spring 2000, during the most hotly contested primary campaign of his career so far, he secured $25 million in federal funds for a new convocation center for Youngstown, a success that was hailed even by his local detractors. He did this by moving to the right politically, voting 70 percent Republican, and openly supporting Republican Dennis Hastert for Speaker of the House. His actions were particularly vexing for the national Democratic Party in the 2000 presidential election, because no Democratic candidate had ever won in Ohio without a 60 percent Democrat vote in the Youngstown area. National party leaders feared that local voters would follow Traficant's move to the right. But Traficant had grown tired of leaders who promised federal largesse but delivered nothing. Jimmy Carter, Walter Mondale, Ronald Reagan, and Bill Clinton had all visited Youngstown during their presidential campaigns and promised to help ameliorate conditions. Despite the promises, very little was done. Youngstown may have been a long-standing Democratic stronghold, but as Traficant pointed out in his 2000 campaign, the area's support for "new Democrats" had not yielded much in terms of federal support for a community that was still struggling economically.

Traficant's limited success in bringing federal dollars to Youngstown doesn't fully explain why someone widely identified as a fool in the national media and associated with corruption would be seen as a local hero. To understand why local voters continued to support Traficant even though he contributed to the community's image as a site of corruption, we need to take a closer look at local attitudes and local history.

Traficant's populist politics reflect local attitudes toward the federal government and large institutions. The simmering resentment of government intrusion has a long history in Youngstown, based largely on class conflict, dating back to the role of the state in protecting the interests of steel mill owners and the upper class during strikes throughout the century. It developed further during deindustrialization, when the government was blamed for imposing environmental regulations and failing to protect the interests of the steel industry. Other institutions also failed to provide real help during deindustrialization. Big business, especially businesses outside the Mahoning Valley, were clearly suspect after the steel companies pulled out. The Ecumenical Coalition's move to buy one of the local mills failed, leaving some doubting the effectiveness of both churches and unions as sources of support. The result was distrust of institutions and a belief that individuals and groups that challenged and even violated traditional rules were the community's best hope. Overall, this politics of resentment is best summarized by Don Hanni Jr., an ex-steelworker, criminal defense attorney, and longtime Mahoning County Democratic chairman, who told the *Washington Post* that "a lot of people around here are hurting economically, and they're tired of a lot of phony promises from people like Bill Clinton." In Hanni's eyes, this explained Traficant's popularity: "Jim is competitive and combative, and people around here like that."[62]

As the *Washington Post* story illustrates, news stories often present Traficant's popularity as a mystery. One explanation they offer is that Traficant effectively represents the community's populist resentment. In many cases, however, such stories also explain Youngstown's support for Traficant as part of its acceptance of crime and corruption, describing both as part of Youngstown's working-class culture: "In this gritty, shot-and-beer town where the mob has proved more durable than the steel industry, the prospect of being indicted by a federal grand jury does not intimidate Rep. James A. Traficant Jr. (D), the flamboyant House member who favors polyester suits and dominates politics here."[63] A *Plain Dealer* story on mob activity in Youngstown cited YSU anthropology professor Mark Shutes, who explained that Youngstown's immigrant working class saw mob leaders as heroes because—like Traficant—they "had found a way to beat the larger, more corrupt outside world." The idea that corruption close to home was acceptable because it provided protection against outside threats was, according to Shutes, part of the working-class experience of Youngstown's immigrants: "The roots of Youngstown's mob problem can be found in those old steel mills, which were largely manned by European immigrants who had grown up in small, close-knit rural villages where governments and the outside world were viewed with suspicion." In such villages, Shutes noted, "closed cultural groups encouraged the idea that it is OK to pay someone, be it business or a politician, to get a job or some benefits."[64]

The idea that corruption could be explained, in part, as a symptom of working-class culture also emerged in a 1998 book by Rick Porello, which offered a history of organized crime in northeastern Ohio. In the book, Porello cites Steven Olah, the head of Cleveland's Federal Organized Crime Strike Force, who explained that organized crime resisted reform efforts and continued to prosper in the area because gambling and political corruption were accepted by the sizable "millworking population."[65] In fact, as Carmen Policy, former president of the San Francisco Forty-Niners and later the Cleveland Browns, said of his hometown, "This is a working-class area and gambling is not considered a vice. In fact, gambling permeates everything. For its size, I must admit, there is no city in America like Youngstown."[66] This popular mythology of the corruption of working-class culture is accurate in many ways, yet it also ignores the more complicated story of what happened in Youngstown. While some illegal activities, like gambling, were accepted as harmless, others were seen as survival strategies or ways of fighting back. Further, this version of the story ignores the active participation of Youngstown's professional-managerial and middle classes.

Youngstown has tried periodically to diminish mob influence on the local community. In 1947, Charles Henderson was elected mayor on a "smash the rackets" platform and hired Edward Allen as police chief. Allen moved aggressively to undermine gaming interests. For example, he closed the statewide racing wire, the Youngstown Empire News Service, and played a role in shutting down the notorious gambling mecca, the Jungle Inn. While the *Vindicator* supported Allen's efforts, openly criticizing the Jungle Inn's patrons as "suckers" and calling its operators "hoodlums,"[67] Allen gained little support from other public officials. In his 1962 book on organized crime in Youngstown, Allen acknowledges that Youngstown's district attorney and police department actively opposed the mayor and police chief, and the city council refused to increase jail time for racketeering offenses, settling on small monetary fines instead. Even the local U.S. Congressman Michael Kirwan, who at the time was a ranking member of the powerful House Appropriations Committee and headed the national Democratic congressional campaign caucus, worked to protect the interests of organized crime. Kirwan introduced legislation to cancel the deportation orders of major Mafia members, such as Detroit's Licavoli family leader Francesca Camarata.[68] When Allen publicly objected, Kirwan tried to get rid of Allen. He said cynically to Allen, "The faster the citizens of Youngstown deport you back to Erie, the sooner it will be a better city. I shall not take it up with the city council to stay your deportation."[69]

Local efforts to close down organized crime activities in Youngstown were episodic and largely ineffectual, in part because many in the community did not see mob activity as a problem. Gambling especially was simply not seen as a crime. In 2000, the *Vindicator* ran a feature story on the Jungle Inn, one of the most popular gaming establishments in the area, some fifty years after it was shut down. The Jungle Inn had been located just outside of Youngstown in Halls Corner, a village incorporated in 1936 with nine residents for the sole purpose of protecting the growing gaming operation. In the story, local residents nostalgically describe the Jungle Inn's fashionable lighting, comfort, spaciousness, elegant décor, and the two-story dining and bar areas where Dean Martin worked "before he hit the big time." Former employees mention the generosity of the Jungle Inn owners who "were good to everybody. If you needed a handout, they'd give it to you."[70] The article is wistful in tone, and it makes clear that for many locals, the Jungle Inn and similar gambling places were highly valued elements of the local social scene, much like the legal casinos that would begin to open in Las Vegas fifteen years later.

Simply put, it is generally accepted that gambling was just too popular to be shut down in Youngstown. But the influence of organized crime was hardly limited to the working class, nor was it limited to gambling. In fact, Youngstown's middle class and professional communities also participated in the rackets, accepted organized crime's influence, and, in some cases, contributed to local corruption. So long as the area prospered economically and no one felt threatened by violence, everyone seemed to accept mob influence and political corruption. But when the mills closed, unemployment severely reduced the profitability of gambling in the area. Organized crime and corruption became more visible as criminal activity shifted to public works projects, drugs, arson, and the fixing of legal cases. While the city's working-class history may well explain some of its reputation for mob influence and public corruption, by the end of the century, corruption in Youngstown would become more associated with suburban mobsters and professionals, including a number of local lawyers, judges, and politicians.

Given the high levels of unemployment and downsizing in various industrial sectors in the Mahoning Valley during the 1980s and 1990s, jobs had been at a premium, especially in the public sector. Corrupt politicians fought over those jobs, especially in the public schools, fire and police departments, and public works. Nepotism was a well-established tradition. For generations, young men got their first jobs in the steel mills or the building trades through the connections of a father or uncle, who would introduce the newcomer to his supervisor. As subsequent generations moved up economically and gained power in the community, many local politicians simply transferred that hiring practice into public life, using jobs as rewards for their supporters. Over time, as the local economy struggled, control over jobs became increasingly important to any economic development program. Anthropologist Shutes told local papers that residents had become accustomed to fighting for limited resources and wanted politicians who could deliver jobs: "You've got to have somebody who can broker for you. You've got to have somebody who is dirty, who can fight dirty, or you'll get nothing."[71] For many local politicians and voters, political favoritism was seen not as a form of corruption but as a form of public service.

But "public service" was not limited to job placement. It also involved "taking care" of the needs of citizens. During the years after deindustrialization, as both public and private institutions failed to protect individuals and the community from economic hardship, arson emerged as a key element of "public service" as officials overlooked and even assisted in burning down homes to protect home owners' financial investments. While no official rankings exist, local firefighters claim that Youngstown had one of the highest per capita arson rates nationally for almost four decades. Geographer David Stephens found that between 1960 and 1980, during a period when some areas of Youngstown were experiencing "urban renewal," arson increased sixfold in the city. In the 1980s, as the city's population dropped, its economic base crumbled, unemployment and business failures increased, and the real estate market crashed, Youngstown averaged 2.3 fires daily with an estimated dollar loss between $1.75

million and $9 million annually.[72] In the 1990s, Youngstown averaged 310 arson fires with an estimated loss of $2 million annually.[73] There is little doubt that residential, commercial property, and automobile arson fires became commonplace in Youngstown in the last two decades of the twentieth century.

With such dramatic numbers, the fire department might have been expected to keep careful records and aggressively investigate possible arsons. But quite the opposite happened. Youngstown Fire Department records from this period were sketchy and incomplete. Existing reports record only the total number of fires without making any distinction between possible arsons and clear accidents. Years later, fire department investigations found that the most common explanation in the few reports on individual incidents from that period that do exist is generally that the fire was "of suspicious origin" or "undetermined or arson." Between 1980 and 1989, however, only one person was convicted of arson. Despite widespread suspicion that many of the arson fires were professionally set, the only person actually convicted was a black woman, and hers was the only arson case in which anyone was killed. Rosalee Grant was convicted of killing her three children and burning down her own house to get the insurance money in 1983. Destruction of property and arson committed by professionals were tolerated, but death was not, nor were the unassisted actions of a poor black woman.

The dramatic increase in arson placed enormous pressure on Youngstown firefighters. According to firefighters, just after the mill closings many of the arson fires were amateurish, started simply "by papers in the corner."[74] But soon firefighters regularly faced professionally set fires where walls had been opened up, treads taken off the stairs, and accelerants used.[75] Professionally set fires were particularly dangerous. If they made it to the fire quickly, firefighters could enter buildings just as gasoline-filled garbage bags were ready to explode. As the number of fires increased, so did injuries such as facial burns, bruises, and sprains resulting from falling through floors. Furthermore, with arson occurring around the clock, firefighters got little sleep. Rather than attempting intermittent sleep, they would often engage in "perching," sitting on benches in the middle of the night awaiting the glow or smell of fires being set. To make matters worse, the city's economic collapse had forced some fire stations to close and some firefighters to be laid off, increasing the workload and slowing response time. Despite the increased danger and overwork, firefighters say that they still wanted to fight fires. They set aside their own suspicions about arson, both because they saw themselves as firefighters and not arson investigators and because they understood that the high arson rates provided a type of job security. Firefighters thus adopted a "don't ask, don't tell" attitude toward arson fires. Clearly, as public employees, they saw no reason to see their acceptance of arson as a form of public corruption.

The large number of arson fires raised suspicions of insurance fraud. Commercial and residential fires in the 1980s cost insurers millions of dollars, including claims from many failing local businesses. At first, since proving arson without seeing someone physically light the fire was very difficult, insurance companies made good on their policies. But by the mid-1980s, they began to develop their own special investigation units and refused to pay claims unless there was firm evidence that a fire did not involve arson. At the same time, insurance companies raised the cost of home insurance in the city dramatically, redlined poor neighborhoods, or insured properties only at their "actual cash value." The insurance companies' suspicions may have been well founded; members of the fire department could not name any houses or commercial establishments that were rebuilt as a result of insurance money.

Private demolition companies also benefited from arson. So many buildings required demolition that the city hired private contractors. Demolishing an existing building and removing debris could be expensive because of extra costs associated with environmental, removal, and dumping requirements. These costs are not incurred, however, if buildings have been torched and the debris can simply be hauled to the local dump. Consequently, a demolition contractor would charge the full fee, hire "scarfers" to strip the home of anything that could be sold, arrange for a fire of "undetermined origin," and simply haul away the debris. The contractor could then pocket the difference between the demolition and mere removal costs.

While individuals may have set many of the fires or committed insurance and demolition fraud, public officials ignored the problem, and in some cases they may have participated actively. Slumlords would buy a vacant home for one dollar, spend several thousand to fix it up, insure the home for one hundred thousand dollars, and then pay an arsonist to burn the building. According to firefighters, some of the slumlords had ties to the fire department, and one was the city official responsible for demolition. Despite the high number of fires and the number of fires reported as "suspicious" on incident reports, it is clear that fire chiefs and arson investigators in the 1980s chose not to investigate most cases. In addition, firefighters recall the sign on the firehouse wall, directing calls about investigations to go either to the arson investigator's office or to a local bar, Cyrak's, widely known as a mob hangout. The mob connection was made clearer in 1999, when Charles O'Nesti, who had been fire chief during the period when the arson rate was highest and record keeping at its worst, pled guilty of being a bagman for the mob. In 1999, O'Nesti was chief legislative aide to Traficant. While no clear evidence exists to link Youngstown's arson epidemic to the mob, many firefighters and community members believed that arson, and the demolition and insurance fraud that often came after a house was burned down, involved collusion between members of the fire department, organized crime, and public officials. Firefighters point to the fact that, lacking a public outcry, the only conviction involving demolitions was the individual who coordinated demolitions for the city. He was convicted of arson in 1990.

Why would a town that had long prided itself on high rates of home ownership watch its housing stock be destroyed by arson? The answer lies in deindustrialization. Economic decline led to unemployment and foreclosures. Lacking disposable income to maintain older homes, some individuals allowed their homes to fall into disrepair. Their home was their only major asset, yet the real estate market had stagnated. Without the hope of selling their houses, some turned to arson for the insurance money, the only way they could see to get something out of the house before it was devalued even further. In some cases, as people left town to seek work or lost their homes or businesses to foreclosure, buildings became unsold empty shells. Firefighters recalled incidents where two or three buildings in a neighborhood burned at once, in so-called clearinghouse fires, which often occurred in the spring when neighbors saw dilapidated housing at its worst. Citizens knew that the foreclosure process was lengthy and that it was impossible for the Youngstown Street Department to keep up with demolitions, especially in the winter when they could not spray to keep the lead down or when demolition teams joined the street crew doing shift work removing snow. Consequently, the city had a backlog of demolitions. But when a house burned down, it became a hazard—open basement, debris, rats, and so on—and thus became a priority to be cleaned up. In essence, arson served as a mechanism to speed up the demolition process. Certainly, residents did not want arson fires, but they did not want vacant houses that would become eyesores either. In some areas, then, arson may have seemed like a new version of urban renewal.

Arson, demolition, and insurance fraud contributed to the image of Youngstown as a place of public and political corruption, but few citizens seemed to care. While some community members may have seen the arson and demolition fraud as a public service, the fires resulted in more vacant lots, reduced housing stock, and declining property tax revenues in the city. In turn, the city had to rely more on income tax, which some claimed inhibited economic development. The loss of housing also had social costs. As houses burned and were torn down, neighborhoods and social networks fell apart, and the community lost part of its history and therefore part of its identity. No longer was Youngstown just a site of deindustrialization; it had become a landscape of decay.

Not all local residents were so willing to accept public and private corruption, and some recognized the connection between Youngstown's image and its future economic prospects. In a *Vindicator* article on mob influence, for example, former mayor Patrick Ungaro claimed that his administration's ability to develop former mill sites was inhibited by the region's reputation.[76] Independent businessman and Traficant rival Randy Walters told the *Washington Post* during the 2000 legislative campaign, "We have to change our image from being a mob-infested area with a corrupt, inefficient congressman, or no new business will never come here."[77] Tom Mock, vice president of the Youngstown-Warren Chamber of Commerce, told the *Akron Beacon Journal* that all the attention to criminal activity and political corruption in Youngstown created an image problem that might impact economic development: "As we all know, perception is reality. The reality across the rest of the country is [that] we are in a compromised position."[78] Outsiders agreed. In writing about the 2000 census and differences between Akron, Canton, and Youngstown, *Akron Beacon Journal* editorial writer Diane Evans suggested that despite population losses there was hope for economic growth in other Northeast Ohio communities: "On the other hand, the city that is really in bad shape is Youngstown, which lost 14.3 percent of its population in the last decade. With its reputation for mob influence and union militancy, who wants to do business in Youngstown?"[79] The answer was prisons.

A NICE PLACE TO DO BUSINESS, A NICE PLACE TO DO TIME

In late spring 2000, *Mother Jones* ran a major story on the growth of the prison economy in the Youngstown area. The article began with a two-page spread featuring a pair of contrasting photos representing the two halves of the article title, "Steel Town, Lockdown." On the left, a full-page black-and-white photo shows a pair of railroad tracks crossing in the empty field where the Youngstown Sheet and Tube Company once stood. Downtown Youngstown stands in the distance, and it is hard to tell whether the train on a side track is going into the city or leaving. The sky looks gray, and a bit of snow lies on the ground, which is scattered with a few pieces of debris from the long-gone mills. The image suggests a landscape that was once occu-

SteelTown Lockdown

CORRECTIONS CORPORATION OF AMERICA
IS TRYING TO TURN YOUNGSTOWN, OHIO, INTO THE
PRIVATE-PRISON CAPITAL OF THE WORLD

BY BARRY YEOMAN

Photographs by MICHAEL WILSON

"Steeltown Lockdown," Michael Wilson, Mother Jones, May/June 2000

pied but is now abandoned. On the facing page, a much smaller, more constricted image shows a scene from inside a prison. In about two square inches, we see another set of converging lines, here the walls of a prison hallway, reflected in the shiny, empty floor. Running through the entire image are the vertical bars of an interior prison gate. Neither scene shows a single person, nor does either suggest a hospitable location. Each image comments on the other. The larger photo suggests that the desolation outside parallels the austerity inside; the smaller photo hints that the outside space might be just as constricted as a prison. Together, they also emphasize the connection between deindustrialization and the growing prison economy in Youngstown. As the *Mother Jones* photos suggest, past, present, and future intersect in complicated ways in representations of economic development in Youngstown.

As in many deindustrialized communities, economic development efforts in Youngstown have a complicated relationship with the past. On the one hand, even though the area's last remaining basic steel furnace at WCI Steel in Warren is one of the most productive in the industry, promotional publications make few references to the steel industry. Rather, they emphasize the strong manufacturing base and the area's "skilled, capable" workers who are "willing to produce quality products to effectively and efficiently serve customer needs."[80] A *Vindicator* report looking back at the 1990s highlights that in 1998, *Industry Week* magazine ranked the Mahoning Valley as the twelfth best manufacturing area in the nation because of its tax abatements, target marketing, labor supply, and geographic location.[81] In *Ohio's Mahoning Valley: An Economic Resource Profile,* a pamphlet produced by the Mahoning Valley Economic Development Corporation in 1997, an opening statement briefly describes the area as "historically a producer of high-quality steel," but it goes on to emphasize today's "diverse economy which lends itself to consistent economic growth and prosperity." Later in the booklet, in a section headlined "Overview: Hardworking, Resourceful, Successful," the text refers only obliquely to the closing of the steel mills: "As the postwar steel industry declined, the resourceful workforce of the Valley sought other avenues for economic growth."[82]

In contrast with the images in *Mother Jones,* this statement is illustrated with small, colorful photos, including one of a woman putting together a wiring harness, most likely at the Delphi Packard plant in Warren, plus others of the Mahoning County Courthouse, an idyllic lakefront scene, and two men at work on an ice sculpture. The bright photos and illustrations fit well in a booklet that aims to promote the region by touting its cultural and recreational facilities, education and "skilled labor training," banks and development support resources, industrial parks, infrastructure, and location. A page of "facts at a glance" emphasizes that Youngstown sits at the center of a populous and economically active region with more than 6.8 million people, 11,700 manufacturing plants, 12,500 wholesale and distribution centers, the world headquarters of forty-six Fortune 500 companies, and the cities of Pittsburgh, Cleveland, Akron, Canton, and Erie all no more than seventy-five miles away. Forty-four percent of the U.S. population, 65 percentof all manufacturing, and 60 percent of all retail sales exist within a five-hundred-mile distance or a one-day drive from Youngstown. Moreover, the city sits at a major hub of the U.S. highway system.[83] As the statistics on location suggest, much of the emphasis both in promotional materials and actual development efforts focused not on the city of Youngstown but on outlying areas. In addition, the book does not acknowledge that, as in other parts of the country, most of the job growth in the last twenty years has been in the service and retail sectors. These sectors have traditionally provided short job ladders, contingent and part-time employment, and, of course, low pay and miserable benefits.[84]

A 1999 *Regional Guide,* developed by a newspaper chain as an advertising vehicle and "endorsed" by the Youngstown-Warren Regional Chamber of Commerce, makes not a single mention of Youngstown's industrial history. Rather, its pages are full of listings of local resources—parks, historical landmarks, restaurants, housing developments, schools, and businesses. A badge shown on the cover of the book touts the area's ranking as twelfth in *Industry Week*'s 1998 listing of "world class manufacturing communities." Inside, numerous charts highlight the area's low cost of living, its medical facilities, and economic statistics, including retail sales, labor force participation, and levels of education. As the guide's creator Holly Burnett acknowledged, the book shows the area "putting on its Sunday best."[85] This is, of course, the purpose of such publications, yet the erasure of the past leaves many aspects of both the social and the economic situations hidden from view.

These Hundred Years, a commemorative chronicle of Youngstown in the twentieth century created by the *Youngstown Vindicator,* offers a more critical view. The book describes the "economic meltdown" and betrayed hopes of economic development in Youngstown in the 1980s and 1990s. With unemployment over 20 percent and both company closings and personal and corporate bankruptcies at record highs throughout the 1980s, "residents grasped at every sliver of hope, as small, diversified industries expressed interest in the area, only to taste bitter disappointment as yet another plan melted away."[86] Yet, despite its central location, available workforce, history as a manufacturing center, the availability of industrial sites, and even the city's generous program of tax abatements, the Mahoning Valley has not attracted a substantial amount of new business investment since the steel mill closings.

Others blame the lack of development on competition among deindustrialized cities generated by a government policy called "new localism," developed during the Reagan administration. In an article examining Youngstown's struggle for economic redevelopment, urban studies researcher Frank Akpadock argues that "new localism" resulted in cutbacks in federal government appropriations to cities and shifted the burden for economic development to state and local governments. As a result, like other deindustrialized cities, Youngstown was put into a bidding war against other cities and regions. Using economic incentives, such as tax abatements, industrial revenue bonds, and land guarantees, economically weakened cities were forced to compete to retain old and attract new economic development at brownfield sites.[87]

But brownfield redevelopment proved problematic. Over time, many of the mill structures were demolished and the landscape transformed into long meadows that belied what had existed and what remained in the ground. The Mahoning River and mill areas adjacent to it were found to be environmentally unsafe as a result of over one hundred years of largely unregulated iron and steelmaking and the dumping of industrial pollutants. According to the American Youth Hostel canoeing guide for the area, the Mahoning River "is one of the most polluted streams in the U.S. and no one is trying to clean it up."[88] The cost of cleaning the brownfield sites was prohibitive because disturbing the polluted soil would stir up the toxins and there is no place to dump the polluted soil and sediment. Yet the community was so desperate for economic development that former mayor Ungaro argued that it was necessary for the local government to "hold harmless" would-be developers and financial institutions from responsibility for environmental contamination. He advocated selling brownfield sites for one dollar in exchange for promises to clean the site and hire unemployed residents, purchase adjacent polluted properties, and offer generous abatements.[89] Yet these incentives were largely unsuccessful in attracting new development, and attempts to turn brownfield sites into industrial parks or to introduce riverfront development failed. So twenty years after the mill closings began, a *Vindicator* article on brownfield redevelopment notes only limited success, especially at former Youngstown Sheet and Tube sites, where after $7 million in tax abatements and limited infrastructure improvements, only about fifteen hundred jobs had been created. As the *Vindicator* explained, "it's hard to share the optimism of development enthusiasts" when many brownfield sites are littered with scrap metal lying "twisted in heaping mounds not far from the banks of the Mahoning River."[90]

Promotional images from both business leaders and local politicians describe the brownfield sites quite differently, however. The Mahoning Valley Economic Development Corporation's 1997 promotional booklet featured several pages of profiles of growing companies and developments, with ads offering financial assistance in the form of bank and public loans, developers and realtors, and the area's nineteen industrial parks.[91] A 1997 editorial in the *Cleveland Plain Dealer* praised Youngstown for devising a "formula for turning a deserted urban wasteland into an oasis of job-rich manufacturing sites. Land that once contained abandoned, heavily polluted steel mills now holds light manufacturing plants and expansive warehouses for Federal Express, Toys 'R' Us and other major American companies."[92] Such representations emphasize the success of brownfield redevelopment, but they ignore several key aspects of the story. The Salt Springs Road Industrial Park that the editorial described was not located on a former mill site, but rather on property a mile or so away, where U.S. Steel had dumped its slag. Slag is a by-product of the steel-making process and was long considered an industrial hazard, but in the mid-1980s, it was reclassified by the Environmental Protection Agency. This meant that the slag heaps at the Salt Springs site could simply be cleared, leveled, and topped with concrete—a much less complicated, less expensive process of reclamation than would have been required for the old mill sites. In addition, as geographer Thomas Maraffa and members of the local buildings trades have pointed out, the long aluminum warehouses built on the site were not designed to last. Maraffa predicted that they would probably last about as long as the tax abatements.[93]

The promotional representations do reflect another problem with local redevelopment efforts, though in the context of economic development publications, it is presented as an asset. Most of the economic growth in the Mahoning Valley during the 1990s took place outside of the cities of Youngstown and Warren. Along with the warehouses, retail and service businesses opened in the suburbs, especially in Niles, Boardman, Austintown, and Canfield. This suburban development resulted in small increases in the wholesale and retail trade sectors and a doubling of service sector employment. Even further out, "greenfield" sites also saw growth, as former farm fields became host to new industrial parks. The Youngstown Commerce Park, for example, was developed on land owned by the DeBartolo Company a short distance from the GM Lordstown plant, more than ten miles from the city limits. In exchange for promises of future jobs for city residents, the city of Youngstown provided support for the development, paying for the extension of water lines to the Youngstown Commerce Park.[94] The area did create new jobs, but few of them went to city residents. Yet again, efforts to bring new economic opportunities to Youngstown residents produced much less than their supporters had hoped and instead benefited those in outlying areas.

Yet despite all of these efforts, Youngstown's economic problems continued to dominate its image. Indeed, the idea that Youngstown was desperate for jobs emerged in almost every story on the industry that eventually succeeded in giving the city an economic boost: prisons. Four prisons were built in the Mahoning Valley between 1992 and 1997, and they made significant contributions to the local economy, boosting payrolls, tax revenues, and overall economic activity. As the *Vindicator* headline noted, "Lockups lead way to a new economy."[95] The development of a prison industry in Youngstown has drawn significant attention from the national press, and these stories almost always make reference to the city's economic struggles. National Public Radio referred to Youngstown as "a rust-belt city long synonymous with steel, more recently with unemployment."[96] NBC's *Dateline* reminded viewers that Youngstown was "so depressed by the collapse of the steel industry it lost half its population in just twenty years."[97] *Sixty Minutes* identified Youngstown as "a former steel town with double-digit unemployment."[98] While Youngstown's economic history was often used as a quick way of defining the place, it is also, in some cases, used to portray Youngstown as desperate and even foolish. Jane Pauley introduced the *Dateline* segment, for example, with this comment: "How would you like to have murderers, rapists, and thieves living in your neighborhood? It's a frightening prospect, even if they're kept behind bars, barbed wire, and under the watchful eyes of prison guards. But, believe it or not, some towns actually welcome prison facilities because of the jobs they create."[99]

When one of the new prisons, the privately owned Northeast Ohio Correctional Center on Youngstown's north side, had a series of problems, including assaults, a murder, and the midday escape of six prisoners, several major news organizations came to investigate. While these reports focus on the malfeasance of the Corrections Corporation of America (CCA), they also use Youngstown's history, its economic struggles, and its national image to portray the city as a victim while ignoring the contentious response within the community. In a *Sixty Minutes* report called "Medium Security, Maximum Problems," Youngstown's history helps to position the community as a hapless victim of yet another outside corporation. *Sixty Minutes* pays no attention to efforts within the community to fight against prison development or to improve conditions within the prisons, however. In many cases, those fighting against the prisons were the same people who fought to save the mills. Among those most active is the local Prison Forum that organized a number of protests against the prisons in the 1990s were Alice and Staughton Lynd, who were also at the forefront of the resistance to plant closings. On the other hand, *Sixty Minutes* suggests that the community may have come to see itself as helpless. The program shows Mayor George McKelvey speculating that "someone in Washington obviously said 'Let's dump on Youngstown. There's nobody there smart enough to even know what we're doing.'" His comment suggests resentment but also some measure of acceptance of the city's image.[100]

Certainly, many in Youngstown bought into the idea that prisons offered economic hope. Despite difficulties with the first CCA prison, many residents were enthusiastic when Traficant began negotiations to have the company build two additional facilities, ironically on the same brownfield sites that were deemed too polluted for any other use. As the article in *Mother Jones* pointed out, "This plan suits many elected officials, who are desperate for an economic boost to a region hardened by the loss of its steel industry." If the CCA expansion had succeeded, one of every fifty residents of the Youngstown-Warren area would be an out-of-state inmate. That would make Youngstown "the private prison capital of the world."[101]

But in April 2001, CCA announced the closing of its Youngstown facility, resulting in the loss of over 500 jobs. The company explained that the closing was necessary because Washington, D.C., did not renew its contract with CCA, and the Federal Bureau of Prisons would relocate the prisoners to other facilities. But not everyone accepted CCA's explanation. Earlier that April, the prison guards at the Northeast Ohio Correctional Center (NOCC) had voted to create an independent union that would be serviced by Teamsters Local 377. Prison reform activist Staughton Lynd contends that the organizing of the prison guards was central to CCA's decision to shut down the NOCC.[102]

CONCLUSION

The images of crime, corruption, and resignation that emerge in media stories about Youngstown in the late 1990s reflect only part of what happened here. News reports expressed fears about the increasing murder rate, concern about business and political corruption, and a tension between hope for the future and desperation about the area's continuing economic struggle. Yet those reports usually focused on the short-term version of the story, largely ignoring the historical roots or complicated sociopolitical contestations that shaped Youngstown's culture. The lingering effects of deindustrialization were consistently downplayed, and class and race divisions were almost entirely ignored.

It is important to understand the relationship between these two sources of struggle in Youngstown. The corporate economic violence of the mill shutdowns of the late 1970s did not attack a community that was in good economic or social health. Rather, deindustrialization exacerbated a process of urban decline that had begun in the 1950s when white workers began to be able to afford suburban homes, and continued in the 1960s when so-called urban renewal projects divided the African-American community. After deindustrialization, arson and demolitions pushed along the process of decay, isolating the poorest members of the community, white and black alike, in neighborhoods that were dotted with abandoned houses and empty lots, while the older communities surrounding the city, such as Struthers and Girard, stagnated, and the southern suburbs of Boardman and Canfield flourished. These developments were rooted in and reinforced race and class divisions that had developed early in the century. Moreover, the community's distrust of institutions and its stubborn, unproductive form of populism grew out of the local history of class conflict, which taught the working class not to trust big business or the government and reinforced the idea that those with limited power could get ahead, or at least protect themselves, with a little extra help from friends with the right connections.

Such erasure creates several problems. First, it contributes to a sense of failure, loss, and helplessness within the community. Local leaders have often complained that Youngstown has a community-wide inferiority complex, and reading media stories about the city, which rarely get beyond blaming the community for its failures, clarifies the source of that attitude. Equally important, when the local community does not understand the source of current problems, it will never find effective solutions. Such a community will see prisons, sports arenas, or legalized gambling as panaceas for long-standing divisions and a deeply rooted culture of corruption. Residents will watch complacently while political leaders are indicted, continue to vote for leaders who are associated with corruption, and feel relieved when no one addresses the deeper problems.

EPILOGUE

❖ ❖ ❖

Community Memory and

Youngstown's Future

Who controls the past now controls the future
Who controls the present now controls the past
Who controls the past now controls the future
Who controls the present now?
Now Testify.
—Rage Against the Machine, "Testify"

In the 1990s, the Youngstown State University football teams won more games than any other NCAA Division IAA school. YSU teams won four national championships, made two additional appearances in the IAA national championship games, and became the only IAA university ever to win over 100 games in a decade. A *Sports Illustrated* story detailed Youngstown's recent history in terms of job loss, continuing high unemployment, poverty, and the high psychological toll that the mill closings had on the area. In the article, team member Chris Sammarone paid tribute to the town's resilience and fortitude, stating, "These are tough people in this city and we represent them by playing football. The people of Youngstown don't give up. Neither do we." In contrast, while YSU coach Jim Tressel proudly boasted that he recruited most of his players from "the state of Youngstown," an area within a sixty-mile radius of the city, he also suggested that he would "like to get people to think about Youngstown, Ohio, as a place where there's a good football team. Not as the place where the steel mills used to be."[1]

Tressel's comment reflects an idea heard often in Youngstown at the start of the twenty-first century: we should forget the past and create a new identity. Yet both *Sports Illustrated* and native son Sammarone recognize that the erasure Tressel advocates is neither possible nor, in the end, desirable. As Sammarone's description of Youngstowners as "tough people" reminds us, even a painful past offers sources of strength for the present and the future. The representations of Youngstown as a site of loss or, more recently, of corruption and criminality have left many individuals feeling a sense of shame, embarrassment, and failure. Others feel cheated by such formulations and lay claim to the better elements of this working-class community—the persistence of family loyalty, the penchant for struggle and dignity, and determination and resilience in the face of adversity. Such are the contradictory images of this community that are constantly being explored and reexamined. Yet finding a way to remember the past that neither idealizes nor dismisses the events and experiences that shaped a place is not simple, especially in a community that has seen so much conflict and so much loss.

Throughout this book, we have argued for the importance of memory in forming the collective identity of a place, yet we do not advocate imagining an idealized version of the past. The idea of community can provide a powerful unifying force for shared struggle and community development. Our interviews with people who grew up in Brier Hill, for example, show how powerful an imagined past of shared poverty in "the old neighborhood" could be. "The Spirit of the Old Neighborhood" continues to exist for the thousands who return to the Brier Hill Italian Fest as a community of memory. Clearly, many former residents have built their identities and their visions of Youngstown on their experiences in Brier Hill, and they recognize that their children do not have the same sense of community spirit. An anonymous second-generation Italian American writing about life in Brier Hill suggests this mix of nostalgia and loss: "Call it a culture, call it tradition, call it roots. I'm not sure what it is. All I do know is that my children have been cheated out of a wonderful piece of our heritage."[2]

At the same time, however, this idealized vision of community has led to the mystification and the concealment of conflict and the alienating effects of work, unemployment, and loss. In identifying themselves so strongly as members of an Italian-American community, Brier Hill residents defined their community as homogeneous, ignoring the fact that both African Americans and other white ethnics lived in the area. At one Brier Hill Fest, the African-American city councilman who represented the section of the city that includes Brier Hill gave a speech in which he claimed his own place in the neighborhood's past, reminding his audience that he, too, had grown up on those streets. When we announced at the Fest that year that we were doing research on Brier Hill and wanted to talk with people about how they remembered the neighborhood, one of the first people to approach us was a German-American man who wanted to make sure we knew that Brier Hill wasn't just Italian. For all their commitment to the idea of Brier Hill, nearly all of those who come back for the Italian Fest each year have moved out of the old neighborhood, many of them during the period when African Americans began to move in.

The ideal of community not only masks difference and the conflict associated with it, but can also gloss over the community's own struggles. Brier Hill residents regularly acknowledge the poverty of the neighborhood, but almost no one ever talks about the difficulty of working in the mills or the working-class struggle to organize unions. Rather, they use their own poverty as evidence of how great their lives were, pointing out how neighbors pulled together to survive hard times.

While this idealization of the past helps former Brier Hill residents define themselves and maintain their commitment to the area, it also, in the long run, undermines the real place they value so highly. In 1999, the Ohio Department of Transportation (ODOT) proposed to build a highway right through the middle of Brier Hill and onto the former sites of the Youngstown Sheet and Tube (Brier Hill Works) and U.S. Steel (Ohio Works).[3] State officials argued that the proposed highway was necessary if the abandoned mill areas were to be redeveloped into industrial parks. While one consultant argued that part of the area that would be destroyed by the new highway might be eligible for inclusion in the National Register of Historic Places, ODOT was not convinced, and it sent in William Hunter, a cultural geographer, to give a second opinion.[4] While Hunter was sympathetic with the idea of saving a significant working-class community, he found that Brier Hill was, as his report was titled, "Historically Significant But No Longer 'Historic.'" His study outlines how the Federal Housing Act of 1949, various urban renewal and "slum clearance" programs, and highway projects had "destroyed the old place of Brier Hill, devalued what remains, and now sets the stage for the next phase of redevelopment."[5] In quoting the original cultural study, he reiterated that this "horribly myopic" program of an earlier era had destroyed "the key social, ecclesiastical, and commercial organizations, and thus remov[ed] a significant portion of the Brier Hill core." The buildings that remain to form the proposed Brier Hill Historic District, Hunter argues, no longer represent the Brier Hill that its former residents remember so fondly. The area's industrial and steel history, immigration, ethnicity and settlement, and the worker neighborhoods have all largely disappeared. In reflecting on his report, Hunter wrote that

> there are historically significant places that have been so transformed by the physical re-creation of the economic landscape as to have lost the ability to tell their very important story. This is the case of Brier Hill, perhaps one of the most historically meaningful places in Ohio, an area that is unquestionably significant for its role in the rise of the United States as an industrial power. But, as the steel industry began to restructure and abandoned the fixed capital in the Mahoning Valley, the vibrant immigrant community of Brier Hill was dismantled by an urban renewal project intended to remedy perceived social problems. The material record of its people was overwrit-

ten and erased. . . . Though Brier Hill is unquestionably significant, the extent of destruction was so great as to prohibit
consideration of the area as a historic district: the story of the
immigrant laborers and their families was so overwritten by
the text of a failed modernist experiment as to be unreadable.[6]

What Hunter does not mention here is the lack of commitment from
former Brier Hill residents to protecting their cherished old neighborhood. Very few people showed up at the several open meetings held
by ODOT to invite comments from the community. While they held
tightly to their community of memory, the real place was being torn
down. Soon, the idealized past is all that will remain of Brier Hill.

This may well be the fate of the larger city of Youngstown. While
some hold on to the memory of shared values, beliefs, and struggles,
the critique of Youngstown and its status as poster child for deindustrialization has discouraged some. Other residents seemed to have
been steeled by the outside criticism and internal conflicts. While
Youngstown as a whole does not have a dedicated corps of individuals who fiercely protect its memory, as in Brier Hill, it is facing some
of the same challenges that have undermined that neighborhood,
though on a broader scale. Like Brier Hill, Youngstown may be vulnerable to disappearance.

Economic and demographic changes constitute a dire threat to the
city, as David Rusk, the former mayor of Albuquerque and leading
urban theorist, has argued. Rusk cites Youngstown as number fourteen on a list of twenty-four American cities that "are beyond the point
of no return." To qualify for this designation, the cities on Rusk's list
shared the following demographic characteristics: 20 percent loss of
population, a minority population exceeding 30 percent, and a per-
person income of less than 70 percent of the income level in surrounding suburban areas. For Rusk, this provided a measure of the neglect
of race and class issues and how it had contributed to urban economic
decline. Youngstown showed clear signs of decline, including rising
poverty rates and increasing concentrations of poor black residents.[7]
This was largely attributed to housing authority policies, white flight,

and the fact that most of the economic growth in the Youngstown metropolitan area was located outside of the city.[8]

In a study of the 2000 census, the Brookings Institution determined that the Youngstown-Warren metropolitan area was one of the ten most segregated areas in the United States.[9] More specifically, the study found that interracial living in Youngstown had increased significantly less than in other metropolitan areas. Researcher Jacob L. Vigdor explained that Youngstown's situation was the direct result "of the number of residents leaving the area and the number of people who, seemingly, refuse to move into the Mahoning Valley." He added that "older, established communities have reputations of being black or white to contend with. . . . In a lot of older cities, once a neighborhood gains a reputation as being either a black neighborhood or being a white neighborhood, it is very hard to change." Lastly, Vigdor explained that while Youngstown does have new housing developments in its suburbs, they are largely devoid of blacks for socioeconomic reasons: "To a large extent, the barriers that remain are not based on race, but on an individual's socioeconomic status. When you get right down to it, there are still pretty large racial differences in income and wealth in this country."[10] Yet, while everyone seems to be aware of the growing inequities, the larger community refuses to address the growing disparities in income and housing or the effects of economic and racial segregation.[11] In essence, a system of geographic, economic, and cultural apartheid has developed in the Youngstown area.

The same is true for the developing Pittsburgh-Cleveland megalopolis to which Youngstown is geographically central. Both Pittsburgh and Cleveland are also facing population loss, increasing minority and poor populations in the city core, and increasing income disparities.[12] For example, according to the 2000 U.S. Census Report, Pittsburgh's population dropped 9.6 percent, and the population of Allegheny County, in which Pittsburgh exists, fell 4.1 percent. Like Youngstown, demographers attributed the decline to "local residents leaving during the decade for better economic opportunities elsewhere; inability to attract many international immigrants; a large eld-

erly population near the end of their life spans; and a low percentage of people of child-bearing age."[13] Yet, as in the Youngstown area,
the suburbs of both cities continue to grow and spread, so much so
that at the start of the twenty-first century, the outer boundaries of
both cities are about thirty minutes by car from the suburbs of Youngstown and Warren. Over time, it appears that the Youngstown metropolitan area will merge with Pittsburgh and Cleveland, creating
a megalopolis that will include large areas of comfortable suburban neighborhoods, where most jobs and commercial activity will be
located, with a system of "reservations" of largely poor and minority
people isolated in urban areas. If this occurs, Youngstown will be
much less a real place, and, like Brier Hill, it will gradually lose its
cultural identity.

Youngstown clearly has a problem with memory. While the history
of work and community here represents important events in the development of unions and responses to deindustrialization, people here
have not learned how to remember the past as at once meaningful and
painful, a source of pride and a tool for understanding community
problems, the basis for identity and the starting place for building a new
identity. Many see the need to end "the mill mentality" and "get over"
the past as preconditions for shaping Youngstown's economic future,
but this attitude is, in part, a failure of memory. In rushing to erase the
difficult parts of Youngstown's history, too many people have also forgotten the powerful events that made Youngstown so important in
American industrial and working-class history. Most important of these
events were the fights for economic and social justice that led to an increasing standard of living for working people and the struggle to save
the mills, which led to improved legislation for workers and their communities throughout the nation. When we forget these battles, as well
as the painful lessons of deindustrialization, we come to see ourselves
as belonging to a community of failure, a place that cannot act in its
own behalf. If we can remember these efforts, and if we understand
clearly how corporate power and business and public corruption have
harmed this community, then we may view ourselves as agents—a
community that has the resources and will to action—and create sig-

nificant positive change. We should remember that Youngstown was not always a victim or a place of loss but also home to robust social organizations and community life. To do otherwise is to practice an ahistoricism that is reinforced in the landscape as industrial and residential structures are torn down and the events associated with those places are forgotten. For as Dolores Hayden says, "even bitter experiences and fights [that] communities have lost need to be remembered—so as not to diminish their importance."[14]

While historian Michael Honey has suggested that "remembering . . . helps us to understand how the world in which we live came to be, and how we too might change it," too many people in Youngstown believe that the only way to move ahead is to forget the past.[15] They misunderstand the meaning of the past. As local artist Bryn Zellers suggests, however, thinking clearly about Youngstown's past is a complicated exercise: "Youngstown's history is not just about the men who worked so hard and risked their lives making steel," but also about those who "stood there with their mouths open while their jobs were being taken away from them." His belief in the importance of remembering and understanding the past is represented dramatically in a 1996 performance art piece titled *Process: Change and Sacrifice*. The performance features sculptural forms taken from the remains of the steel mills, alcohol fires, and Zellers himself, dressed in an asbestos suit and standing before a pulpit, reading a prophetic text about change over a background of pulsing music. In a distorted voice that sounds forceful but also otherworldly, Zellers intones a dark warning about the importance of understanding the past and moving decisively into the future:

We that operate in the present must constantly strive
to maintain a clear vision of the past
so that we might possibly see the future. . . .
Without clear vision of the past which has brought us to the present
Our ability to develop foresight is crippled,
leaving us confused and stagnant. . . .
We must acknowledge and accept without doubt

That each movement forward requires a certain level of change
And with each change something is gained while something is lost.
There is no change without sacrifice.
We must prepare for change.

The performance offers a compelling, dramatic commentary on de-industrialization and the community's response to it. As with much of Zellers's work, the images are dark and angry, and they often seem devoid of hope. Yet for all its darkness, this piece also commemorates many facets of the local steel culture—the heat and danger of the work, the elemental nature of steelmaking, the almost religious power of the massive mill structures, the centrality of steel to this community and its landscape, and the commonality of loss not only of jobs but also of history. In counterpoint to images that reflect the power of steelmaking, the text argues forcefully that we should never forget what happened in Youngstown.[16]

Both forgetting the past and focusing on only the negative elements put a community at risk. As the Palermo (Italy) commissioner of education, Allesandra Siracusa told the visiting Youngstown delegation during the 2000 conference on "Creating a Culture of Lawfulness" that in order for a city to prosper, it must recover its identity by embracing its past and refusing to let others destroy or humiliate it. Community members must understand that cities are the fruit of human relations among people living together, and they must have a sense that their community, including its past, belongs to them.[17] As Zach de la Rocha writes in the Rage Against the Machine song "Testify," "who controls the past now controls the future."

If Youngstown is to be a real community, then, it must understand its past. It must both embrace pride in what was produced here—not just steel but also a strong working-class community—and accept the failure to deal with conflicts involving class and race. It must understand how the history of work and struggle are linked to the landscape and people's ways of remembering. It must never forget the harm inflicted by corporate irresponsibility, yet it must also accept responsibility for tolerating corruption and division. But Youngstown remains unwilling to embrace its past, and thus it cannot begin to address the problems of racial and economic segregation or the need to create new spaces that nurture a real sense of community and diversity.

Youngstown is not alone in this struggle. Rather, the difficulty of understanding the relationship between past, present, and future is part of an international discussion about the meaning of work and place in a postindustrial society. In *Twilight Memories*, Andreas Huyssen argues that late twentieth-century culture is engaged in a "struggle for memory." He sees contemporary culture as both obsessed with memory and beset with amnesia. The contemporary "mnemonic fever" that he diagnoses is "chaotic, fragmentary, and free-floating," an expression of a desire to gain control in a world of ever-faster change and ever-more-confusing technology.[18] We see that confusion in the fragmentary, sometimes contradictory representations of Youngstown as well as in the community's struggle over how to define itself in the future and in the uses of Youngstown in national and international media.

Yet once we understand the contradiction and complexities of memory, we might see a somewhat different view from the Division Street Bridge than we saw at the beginning of the book. The empty fields where mills and homes once stood represent the struggle between workers and corporations to keep the steel mills open, as well as the conflict between preservationists and developers over the use of the land where the mills once stood. Looking at Brier Hill, we might see not just old homes and a now-quiet church, but the persistent conflict in Youngstown over race and ethnicity, evident in abandoned homes where Italian families lived before fleeing to the suburbs in the 1950s and 1960s, and also evident in the annual Brier Hill Italian Fest that restages the neighborhood's past but ignores its very different present. Looking at the county jail and the YSU stadium, we see not just a changed economy but a central tension over how the city sees itself: as a place of growth (spurred on by an increasingly well-educated population) or as a place of resignation, where a local and national crime problem looks like an employment opportunity. Work and conflict continue to shape this landscape, a struggle made even more complicated by the tension over how to remember the past.

Yet memory has not yet disappeared here. Not long ago, standing in the DeBartolo Stadium Club looking down over the city, a friend commented that what he saw below was not a mental health clinic or university parking lots, but the neighborhood where he and his friends had played as children. What looks like development to some looks like loss and erasure to others. Like any community, Youngstown is constructed out of the experiences and memories of the people who live here, and as the landscape and representations that preserve memory change, much is being lost.

NOTES

INTRODUCTION
Remembering Youngstown

Epigraph: "Youngstown" by Bruce Springsteen. Copyright © 1995 by Bruce Springsteen (ASCAP). Reprinted by permission.

1. Here and throughout the book, our references to Youngstown usually encompass the whole steelmaking district of the Mahoning Valley, which includes Youngstown, Warren, and the many small communities surrounding these cities as well as Sharon, Pennsylvania.

2. Robert N. Bellah et al., *Habits of the Heart: Individualism and Commitment in American Life* (Berkeley: University of California Press, 1985), 153.

3. Ibid.

4. *Creating a Culture of Lawfulness: The Palermo, Sicily, Renaissance,* conference booklet, United Nations and the Sicilian Renaissance Institute, 2000.

5. Julie Grant, "Youngstown, Ohio, Moves to Combat Organized Crime," *Morning Edition,* National Public Radio, 11 December 2000.

6. Bellah et al., *Habits of the Heart,* 153.

7. More than any city in the nation, Youngstown pays attention to what is said about it. After all, it is "the media capital of the United States." According to the advertising firm Young and Rubicam, who report on media usage in the 209 U.S. media markets, Youngstown residents "spend more time with their televisions, radios, newspapers, and magazines than anywhere else." Every day, the average Youngstown resident watches television for four hours and twenty minutes (10 percent more than the national average). They listen to the radio for three hours and thirty-one minutes (5 percent more), and they spend eighteen minutes reading magazines (12 percent less) and forty-one minutes with newspapers (21 percent more). The total time a Youngstown resident spends with all media is eight hours and fifty minutes each day, compared with the na-

tional average of eight hours and three minutes. See Joe Schwartz, "America's Media Capital," *American Demographics* (July 1992): 52.

8. Springsteen's comments to Griel Marcus's students is paraphrased in "Notebook," *Chronicle of Higher Education* (12 January 2001): 37.

CHAPTER 1
Reading the Landscape: Conflict and the Production of Place

Epigraph from Dolores Hayden, *The Power of Place: Urban Landscapes as Public History* (Cambridge: MIT Press, 1996), 9

1. Dolores Hayden, *The Power of Place: Urban Landscapes as Public History* (Cambridge: MIT Press, 1996), 20.

2. Donald Mitchell, *Lie of the Land: Migrant Workers and the California Landscape* (Minneapolis: University of Minnesota Press, 1996), 6.

3. George Revill, "Reading *Rosehill:* Community, Identity, and Inner-City Derby," in *Place and the Politics of Identity,* ed. Michael Keith and Steve Pile (London: Routledge, 1993), 120.

4. Joseph G. Butler Jr., *The History of Youngstown and the Mahoning Valley, Ohio* (Chicago and New York: American Historical Society, 1921), 710.

5. For fuller discussion of settlement patterns in the Mahoning Valley, see David T. Stephens, Alexander T. Bobersky, and Joseph Cencia, "The Yankee Frontier in Northern Ohio: 1796–1850," *Pioneer America Society Transactions* (1994): 1–10.

6. D. J. Lake, *Atlas of Mahoning County, Ohio* (Philadelphia: Titus, Simmons & Titus, 1874).

7. Howard C. Aley, *A Heritage to Share: The Bicentennial History of Youngstown and the Mahoning Valley, Ohio* (Youngstown, Ohio: Bicentennial Commission of Youngstown and Mahoning Valley, 1975), 66.

8. *Mahoning Vindicator,* 31 January 1873, 5.

9. *Mahoning Vindicator,* 24 January 1874, 5.

10. "A Letter from an Operator," *Miner and Manufacturer,* 31 January 1873, 1.

11. "Miners in Turmoil," *Miner and Manufacturer,* 31 January 1873, 4.

12. Ibid., 4.

13. *Mahoning Vindicator,* 7 February 1873, 5.

14. "Miners," *Miner and Manufacturer,* 4.

15. Bridgett M. Williams, *The Legacy of Mill Creek Park: A Biography of Volney Rogers* (Youngstown, Ohio: Youngstown Lithographing Company, 1992), 34.

16. David T. Stephens, "Youngstown: The Decline of a Steelmaking Giant," in *A Geography of Ohio,* ed. Leonard Peacefull (Kent, Ohio: Kent State University Press, 1996), 200.

17. For a map of Youngstown in this period, see the panoramic map by A. Ruger, "Panoramic View of the City of Youngstown, County Seat of Mahoning Co., Ohio," (Madison, Wis.: Ruger & Stoner, 1882). Library of Congress, American Memory, g4084y pm007121. Online: http:// memory.loc.gov/cgi-bin/map_item.pl?data=/gmd408/g4084/ g4084y/ m007130.sid&style=gmd&itemLink=D?gmd:2:./temp ~ammem_6x07::@@@mdb=gmd,gmd,gmd,gmd&title=Panoramic+ view+of+the+city+of+Youngstown,+county+seat+of+Mahoning+Co.,+ Ohio+ 1882.+

18. *Youngstown Telegram,* 20 September 1918, 1. Furnaces were typically named for the wives or daughters of company presidents, and in many cases, the person for whom the furnace was named also had the honor of lighting it.

19. Rebecca Rogers, *Worker Housing Neighborhood Survey, Youngstown, Ohio, Part One* (Youngstown, Ohio: Community Development Agency Report, 1992), 16; U.S. Department of Commerce, *U.S. Census of Population,* 1900–1960 (Washington, D.C.: U.S. Government Printing Office, 1900–1960); Stephens, "Youngstown," 200.

20. Donna DeBlasio, "'A Splendid Place to Live': Housing and the Youngstown Sheet and Tube Company" (conference presentation, Great Lakes American Studies Association, March 1998), 2.

21. Rogers, *Worker Housing,* 15.

22. Phillip S. Foner, *On the Eve of America's Entrance into World War I,* vol. 6 of History of the Labor Movement in the United States series (New York: International Publishers, 1947), 30.

23. John A. Fitch, "Arson and American Citizenship: East Youngstown and the Aliens Who Set the Fire," *Survey* (22 January 1916), 479.

24. "Strike Spreads and Mob Rule Reigns in Village," *Youngstown Vindicator,* 7 January 1917, 1.

25. DeBlasio, "A Splendid Place to Live," 3; Aley, *A Heritage to Share,* 206–207.

26. Joseph G. Butler Jr., *Recollections of Men and Events: An Autobiography* (New York: G. P. Putnam's Sons, 1927), 243.

27. "Grand Jury Indicts Big Steel Companies," *Youngstown Vindicator,* 8 March 1916, 3.

28. Ibid., 3.

29. "Judge Anderson Quashes Steel Indictments: Motion to Quash Steel Indictments Was Sustained," *Youngstown Vindicator,* 28 March 1916, 1.

30. Chester M. Wright, quoted in Foner, *On the Eve*, 40.

31. Peter Gottlieb, "Steel Strike of 1919," in *Labor Conflict in the United States: An Encyclopedia*, ed. Ronald Filippelli (New York: Garland Publishing, 1990), 501–502.

32. William Jenkins, *Steel Valley Klan: The Ku Klux Klan in Ohio's Mahoning Valley* (Kent, Ohio: Kent State University Press, 1990).

33. Ibid., 119–120.

34. Leo Jennings II and Leo Jennings III, interview by authors, Youngstown, Ohio, 1 October 1999.

35. Gabriel Palmer-Fernandez, director, James Dale Ethics Center, interview by authors, Youngstown, Ohio, 21 August 1999.

36. Sam Donnorummo, interview by Donna DeBlasio, Oral History Collection, Youngstown Historical Center for Industry and Labor, Youngstown, Ohio, 4 April 1991.

37. Jim Davis, interview by Donna DeBlasio, Oral History Collection, Youngstown Center for Industry and Labor, Youngstown, Ohio, 26 September 1991.

38. John Fitzgerald, interview by Donna DeBlasio, Oral History Collection, Youngstown Historical Center for Industry and Labor, Youngstown, Ohio, 4 April 1991.

39. Oras Vines, interview by Donna DeBlasio, Oral History Collection, Youngstown Historical Center for Industry and Labor, Youngstown, Ohio, 1 April 1991.

40. Edward Stonework Jr., "Depression Experience of Blacks," interview by John A. Parker, Youngstown State University, History Department, Oral History Program, item number 1259, 18 July 1989.

41. Richard Shale, *Idora Park: The Last Ride of Summer* (Jefferson, Ohio: Amusement Park Journal, 1999).

42. *Youngstown Telegram*, 4 September 1918, 4.

43. DeBlasio, "A Splendid Place to Live," 5.

44. Ibid., 16, 11.

45. Ibid., 13.

46. Ibid., 14.

47. Aley, *A Heritage to Share*, 285.

48. Joseph L. Heffernan, "The Hungry City," *Atlantic Monthly*, May 1932, 541–543.

49. Peter Gottlieb, "Steel Strike of 1937," in *Labor Conflict in the United States: An Encyclopedia*, ed. Ronald Filippelli (New York: Garland Publishing, 1990), 509.

50. Irving Bernstein, *Turbulent Years: A History of the American Worker*

(Boston: Houghton Mifflin, 1970), 479–480; Ronald Filippelli, *Labor in the USA* (New York: Alfred A. Knopf, 1984), 191.

51. For a full discussion of the events in Youngstown during the "Little Steel" strike, see United States Senate, Seventy-fifth Congress, *Violations of Free Speech and Rights of Labor: Hearings before the Subcommittee on Education and Labor* (Washington, D.C.: U.S. Government Printing Office, 1939), vols. 26–34.

52. For fuller discussion of the gains and struggles of the steel unions during the postwar period, see Jack Metzgar, *Striking Steel: Solidarity Remembered* (Philadelphia: Temple University Press, 2000).

53. Maeva Marcus, *Truman and the Steel Seizure Case: The Limits of Presidential Power* (New York: Columbia University Press, 1977).

54. Metzgar, *Striking Steel.*

55. For discussions of the postwar period as a time of decline in working-class identity, see Daniel Bell, *The End of Ideology* (Glencoe, Ill.: Free Press, 1960); Clark Kerr, Charles M. Myers, John Dunlop, and Frederick H. Harbison, *Industrialism and Industrial Man* (London: Oxford University Press, 1962); and Arthur M. Schlesinger Jr., *The Vital Center: The Politics of Freedom* (Boston: Houghton Mifflin, 1949).

56. John Turco, "Fifties: Growth of Suburbs, University Highlighted Decade," *Youngstown Vindicator,* 4 July 1999, A4.

57. Joseph E. Koch, "The Puerto Ricans Come to Youngstown," *Commonweal* (9 October 1953), 9.

58. Robert Bruno, *Steelworker Alley: How Class Works in Youngstown* (Ithaca, N.Y.: ILR/Cornell University Press, 1999), 33–34.

59. Shale, *Idora Park,* 99.

60. J. Philip Richley, interview by Donna DeBlasio, Oral History Collection, Youngstown Historical Center of Industry and Labor, Youngstown, Ohio, 6 December 1991.

61. Lizabeth Cohen, "From Town Center to Shopping Center: The Reconfiguration of the Community Marketplace in Postwar America," in *His and Hers: Gender, Consumption, and Technology,* ed. Roger Horowitz and Arwen Mohun (Charlottesville, Va.: University Press of Virginia, 1998), 191.

62. Fred and Josephine Ross, interview by authors, Youngstown, Ohio, 22 October 1998.

63. John N. Ingham, *The Iron Barons: A Social Analysis of American Urban Elites, 1874–1965* (Westport, Conn.: Greenwood Press, 1978), 203.

64. John Kobler, "Crime Town, USA," *Saturday Evening Post,* 9 March 1963: 71–76.

65. Harry Meshel, interview by authors, Youngstown, Ohio, 10 September 1999.

66. These estimates are based on average manufacturing wages, loss of steel jobs, and the average number of hours worked.

67. See Stephens, "Youngstown," 1996, 201.

68. Ira C. Magaziner and Robert B. Reich, *Minding America's Business: The Decline and Rise of the American Economy* (New York: Harcourt Brace and Jovanovich, 1982), 155–168.

69. Staughton Lynd, *The Fight Against Shutdowns: Youngstown's Steel Mill Closings* (San Pedro, Calif.: Singlejack Books, 1982), 24–25.

70. Scott Camp, *Worker Responses to Plant Closings: Steelworkers in Johnstown and Youngstown* (New York: Garland Publishing, 1995).

71. John Russo, "Changes in the Unionized Construction Industry," in *Proceedings of the Forty-eighth Annual Meeting, Industrial Relations Research Association Series,* ed. Paula Voos (Madison, Wis.: Industrial Relations Research Association, 1996), 123.

72. Ellen J. Sullivan, "Bankruptcy Filings in Area Show Small Decline in 1985," *Youngstown Vindicator,* 1 January 1986, B12; Karen Guy, "Bankruptcy Boom Means Recession," *Youngstown Vindicator,* 18 February 1991, A1-3; Denise Dick, "Bankruptcy Court Sees Sharp Rise in '97 Filings," *Youngstown Vindicator,* 21 March 1998, B1-2.

73. Urban League Study Committee, *A Study of Economic and Cultural Activities as They Relate to Minority People in the Youngstown Area* (Youngstown, Ohio: Youngstown Community Corporation, 1966), 3.

74. John Russo, *A Needs Assessment of Parkview Counseling Center* (Youngstown, Ohio: Parkview Counseling Center, 1984).

75. John Russo, "Lordstown Strike of 1972," in *Labor Conflict in the United States: An Encyclopedia,* ed. Ronald Filippelli (New York: Garland Publishing, 1990), 284.

76. The events at Lordstown were intensely studied by the media and the government. As a result, the U.S. Department of Health, Education, and Welfare released a 1973 study entitled *Work in America* in which the term the "Lordstown Syndrome" was used as a catchall phrase for worker responses to fragmented, alienated, boring, and repetitive work.

77. John Russo, "Integrated Production or Systematic Disinvestment: The Restructuring of Packard Electric" (conference presentation, Facing North/Facing South: A Multidisciplinary Conference on U.S./Canadian/ Mexican Relations after NAFTA, 14 May 1994).

78. Thomas Shipka, "Recollections of the Formation and Evolution of the YSU-OEA," *The Advocate: Special Edition* (1996).

79. Roger Smith, "Lockups Lead Way to New Economy," *Youngstown Vindicator*, 27 June 1999, A1-4.

80. Dale Maharidge and Mike Williamson, *Journey to Nowhere: The Saga of the New Underclass* (New York: Hyperion, 1996), 192.

81. George Denny, "Segregation Spells Disaster, Expert Says," *Youngstown Vindicator*, 1 December 1995, A4.

82. "Youngstown Prison," *All Things Considered*, National Public Radio, 27 March 1998, Lexis-Nexis Transcript #98032705-212; "House of Correction?" *Dateline*, NBC News, 11 October 1998, NBC News Transcripts; "Medium Security, Maximum Problems," *Sixty Minutes*, CBS News, 2 May 1999, Burrelle's Information Services.

83. Roger Smith, "Escapes Weigh Heavily against Benefits," *Youngstown Vindicator*, 27 June 1999, A3.

84. Denny, "Segregation," A4.

CHAPTER 2
Steel Town

Epigraph from *Steel Town* (Washington, D.C.: U.S. Office of War Information, Overseas Bureau, 1945).

1. *Youngstown and the Mahoning Valley* (Youngstown: Youngstown Area Chamber of Commerce, 1933), 9.

2. Nicholas U. Comito, *Youngstown in Pen and Pencil* (New York: Robert W. Kelly, 1934).

3. Howard C. Aley, *Working Together We Serve the World: A Book of Supplementary Reading Materials Devoted to an Understanding of the Kinds of Work and the Variety of Products Found in the Four-County Industrial Area Embracing Mahoning, Trumbull, Columbiana, [sic] Counties and Alliance in Ohio, and Mercer County, Pennsylvania* (Industrial Information Institute and the Schools Advisory Committee, 1950), 43.

4. Stephen V. Ward, *Selling Places: The Marketing and Promotion of Towns and Cities, 1850–2000* (London: E & FN Spon, 1998), 163–168.

5. *Youngstown, the City of Progress: A Natural Center of Manufacture and Distribution* (Youngstown: Youngstown Area Chamber of Commerce, 1913).

6. Comito, *Pen and Pencil*.

7. In a similar vein, a nine-volume set of short books of photographs, *Art Work of Youngstown* (Chicago: Gravure Illustration, 1927), offers

images of the Butler Institute of American Art, local churches, and impressive homes, highlighting the prosperity and modernity of the city. Interestingly, *Art Work of Youngstown* didn't include a single steel mill image.

8. *Youngstown: The City of Homes,* brochure, ca. 1931.

9. "The Youngstown Federation of Women's Clubs," *Town Talk,* December 1930, 26.

10. *Youngstown, Ohio: City of Steel Mills and Parks* (Chicago: Curt Teich & Co., 1939).

11. "Youngstown," Detroit Publishing Company Photograph Collection, Library of Congress Prints and Photographs Division, online. Available http://lcweb2.loc.gov/ammem/detroit/dethome.html. Digital ID det 4a28742. 22 August 2000.

12. "Panoramic View of Youngstown, OH," Taking the Long View: Panoramic Photographs, 1851–1991, Library of Congress Prints and Photographs Division, online. Available http://memory.loc.gov/ammem/pnhtml/pnhome.html. Digital ID pan 6a15348. 22 August 2000.

13. Youngstown Historical Center for Industry and Labor, Youngstown Sheet and Tube Audiovisual Archives, 1907–1952; Container 0140-4, Folder 58.

14. Aley, *Working Together,* 40.

15. Ibid.

16. *Youngstown Grows with Ohio,* Youngstown Sesquicentennial Committee, 1953.

17. *Fifty Years in Steel: The Story of the Youngstown Sheet and Tube Company: This Is America* (Youngstown: Youngstown Sheet and Tube, 1950); Youngstown Sheet and Tube Company, *Letter to Youngstown* (Cleveland: Cinecraft Productions, 1961), film.

18. Youngstown Sheet and Tube calendars, 1949, 1953, 1962, Mahoning Valley Historical Society.

19. *Men Who Make Steel* (Cleveland: Cinecraft Productions, n.d.), film.

20. *The Men and Machines of Modern Steelmaking* (Sharon, Penn.: Sharon Steel Corporation, 1968).

21. Kenneth Patchen, *The Collected Poems of Kenneth Patchen* (New York: New Directions, 1968), 281.

22. Ibid., 282, ellipses in original.

23. Ibid., 398–399.

24. Martha McCloskey, *Mills,* 1936. Butler Institute of American Art, 945-W-104, 1945 museum purchase.

25. Albert Parella, *View from the Bridge,* n.d., Butler Institute of American Art, 965-W-141.

26. George Breckner, *Mill Entrance*, 1953, Butler Institute of American Art, 954-O-104, 1954 museum purchase.

27. Michael McGovern, *Labor Lyrics and Other Poems* (Youngstown: Vindicator Press, 1899), 3, 14, 37.

28. Ibid., 14, 37, 14.

29. Ibid., 133.

30. Ibid., 4–5, 7.

31. Carl Sandburg, "Smoke and Steel," in *Smoke and Steel* (New York: Harcourt, Brace, 1920), 5.

32. Ibid., 4, 6.

33. Ibid., 6, 7.

34. Ibid., 8.

35. Philip R. Yannella, *The Other Carl Sandburg* (Jackson, Miss.: University Press of Mississippi, 1996), 144–146.

36. *Steel Town* (Washington, D.C.: U.S. Office of War Information, Overseas Bureau, 1945).

37. Howard C. Aley, *Our Neighbors Tell Us about Their Work: A Book of Supplementary Reading Material Designed to Promote an Understanding of How People Earn a Living in the Four-County Area Embracing Mahoning, Trumbull, Columbiana [sic] Counties in Ohio, and Mercer County, Pennsylvania* (Industrial Information Institute and the Schools Advisory Committee, 1949), 5.

38. Ibid., 25–26.

39. Arlette Gatewood, quoted in *Workers Remember: Fifty Years of Labor*, 20 October 1994, videotape, Youngstown Historical Center for Industry and Labor, Ohio Historical Society.

40. Fred A. Fortunato, "Youngstown Steel Strike Project," interview by Philip Bracy, Youngstown, Ohio, 6 January 1983, Youngstown State University Oral History Program, O.H. 0222.

41. "A Prescription," *Bulletin*, 15 January 1922, 5.

42. "The Right Kind of Work the Very Best Aid to Well-Being," *Youngstown Vindicator* 17 August 1918.

43. *Men Who Make Steel*.

44. McGovern, *Labor Lyrics*, 133.

45. James J. Donnelly, "Labor Day," *Bulletin*, 15 September 1921, 14.

46. Jamie Heron, "Steel—America's National Cream," *Bulletin*, 15 March 1922, 14.

47. Aley, *Working Together*, 42, 44, 82.

48. Fortunato, "Youngstown Steel Strike Project," 26; Dan Thomas, "Steel Industry Labor and Management," interview by Emmett C. Shaffer, 1 August 1974, Youngstown State University Oral History Program, O.H. 5, 2; Augustine F. Izzo, "Personal Experience," interview by Andrew

Russ, 14 November 1988, Youngstown State University Oral History Program, O.H. 1214, 22.

49. Joe Gavini, interview by authors, Youngstown, Ohio, 27 July 2000.

50. "Dedication Service for Ten Clerestory Windows," brochure, St. John's Episcopal Church, 1 May 1955, mimeograph.

51. James J. Donnelly, "The Boys of the Open Hearth," *Bulletin*, 15 September 1921, 7.

52. "Back of It All," *Bulletin*, March 1932, 13.

53. *Men Who Make Steel.*

54. Advertisement, Home Savings and Loan Company, *Youngstown Vindicator*, 3 September 1962, A3.

55. Youngstown Sheet and Tube, *Letter to Youngstown*, 1961.

56. Cartoon, *Youngstown Vindicator*, 4 September 1927, 6A.

57. Advertisement, *Youngstown Vindicator*, 1 September 1935, A6.

58. Advertisement, *Youngstown Vindicator*, 6 September 1936, A4.

59. Advertisement, *Youngstown Vindicator*, 6 September 1936, A11.

60. Advertisement, *Youngstown Vindicator*, 1 September 1935, A4.

61. Grover Mace, interview by Bernice Mercer, Youngstown, Ohio, 14 May and 28 May 1981, Youngstown State University Oral History Program, O.H. 1082, 5, 10.

62. Archie Nelson, "Personal Experience," interview by Andrew Russ, 26 October 1988, Youngstown State University Oral History Program, O.H. 1216.

63. E. W. Hudson, "How a Steel Worker Views the Meaning of CIO," cartoon, *Steel Labor*, 6 March 1937, 5.

64. "Organized Labor Sets a New Light and Meaning to the Life of Mankind," *Steel Labor*, 5 September 1936, 1.

65. Advertisement, *Steel Labor*, 19 December 1936, 8.

66. Advertisement, Republic Steel Corporation, *Youngstown Vindicator*, 20 August 1946, A5.

67. Advertisement, *Youngstown Vindicator*, 6 September 1953, Rotagravure section.

68. Advertisement, Hall Painting Company, *Youngstown Vindicator*, 2 September 1956, B3.

69. "A Thought for Labor Day," *Youngstown Vindicator*, 1 September 1958, 22.

70. "Also, the Day to Count Our Blessings," *Youngstown Vindicator*, 6 September 1949, 13.

71. Sandburg, "Smoke and Steel," 6.

72. Patchen, *Collected Poems*, 292.

73. Ibid., 384.

74. Michael McGovern, "The Dinner Pail," *Youngstown Vindicator,* 24 September 1900, 4.

75. "About the Dinner Pail," *Youngstown Vindicator,* 19 September 1900, 4.

76. Oswald Greig, "The Dinner-Pail Brigade," *Youngstown Vindicator,* 28 August 1918, 6.

77. McGovern, "The Dinner Pail," 7.

78. Rene Bache, "Labor Fears Dumping of Aliens," *Youngstown Vindicator,* 4 September 1921, 7C.

79. Editorial, *Youngstown Telegram,* 3 January 1916, 8.

80. Irving Bernstein, *Turbulent Years: A History of the American Worker, 1933–1941* (Boston: Houghton Mifflin, 1970), 478.

81. "Three Killed, Nineteen Shot, Town Set Afire, Ohio Militia Out," *New York Times,* 8 January 1916, sec. 1, 1.

82. "Loot Is Found on Foreigners: About Thirty Suspicious Characters Are Arrested by Local Police," *Youngstown Vindicator,* 8 January 1916, 1.

83. Editorial, *Youngstown Telegram,* 8 January 1916, 8.

84. "Our Debt to Mr. Gary," *Youngstown Telegram,* 13 October 1919, 4.

85. "A Common View of the New American," *Youngstown Vindicator,* 12 October 1919, 9D.

86. Editorial, *Youngstown Telegram,* 13 October 1919, 8.

87. George P. West, "Youngstown," *New Republic,* 29 January 1916, 331, 332.

88. Mary Heaton Vorse, "The Tories Attack through Steel," *New Republic,* quoted in *Rebel Pen: The Writings of Mary Heaton Vorse*, ed. Dee Garrison (New York: Monthly Review Press, 1985), 202.

89. Vorse, "The Tories Attack," 208.

90. Mary Heaton Vorse, "Labor's Challenge," *Photo History* 1, no. 2 (July 1937): 61

91. Rose M. Stein, "It's War in Youngstown," *Nation,* 3 July 1937, 12–13.

92. William Gropper, "Gropper Visits Youngstown," *Nation,* 3 July 1937, 14–15.

93. Howard E. Wooden, catalog notes, Butler Institute of American Art Web site, http://www.butlerart.com/pc_book/pages/william_gropper_1897.htm, 9 November 2000.

94. William Gropper, *Youngstown Strike,* 1937, Butler Institute of American Art, 1985 museum purchase, 985-0-106.

95. Editorial, *Youngstown Vindicator,* 4 September 1950, 12.

96. Editorial, *Youngstown Vindicator,* 7 September 1959, B2.

97. Letters to the Editor, *Youngstown Vindicator,* 31 August 1958, D7; 3 September 1961, D8; 19 August 1962, B10; 2 September 1962, C16.

98. "Youngstown Ohio: A Steel Town on Strike," *Time,* 12 October 1959, 22.

CHAPTER 3

Deindustrialization and the Struggle over Memory

Epigraph from Carol Greenwald and Dorie Krauss, *Shout Youngstown* (Boston, Mass.: Century III Teleproductions, 1984).

1. "Steel Mill Outlook Improves in District," *Youngstown Vindicator,* 16 September 1977, A16.

2. Sergio Lalli, "Campbell Works More Than Jobs; Steel Way of Life Is Disappearing," *Youngstown Vindicator,* 26 September 1977, A5.

3. Mark Shields, "The Pain of Youngstown," *Washington Post,* 26 October 1984, A23.

4. John Martin, "Steel 1980," in *Overtime: Punchin' Out with the Mill Hunk Herald Magazine (1979–1989)* (Pittsburgh, Penn.: Piece of the Hunk Publishers and Albuquerque: West End Press, 1989), 9.

5. Teresa Anderson, "Mike Bibich and Youngstown, Ohio," in *Overtime,* 46.

6. Frank Rose, "Carroll Megginson," *Real Men* (Garden City, N.Y.: Doubleday, 1980), 105.

7. Ibid., 106.

8. Ibid., 125.

9. Ibid., 129, 130.

10. Ibid., 136.

11. Quoted in exhibit brochure, *Youngstown Steel: A Tribute to the American Open-Hearth,* Butler Institute of American Art, 1986.

12. We're grateful to the Sheely-Lee Law Library of the Dickinson School of Law for loaning its collection of photographs by George Bennett.

13. *The Steelmakers,* George Segal, Youngstown Historical Center for Industry and Labor, Ohio Historical Society.

14. Ibid.

15. Ibid.

16. Dale Maharidge and Michael Williamson, *Journey to Nowhere: The Saga of the New Underclass* (1985; reprint with introduction by Bruce Springsteen, New York: Hyperion, 1996), 11.

17. Ibid., 12.

18. Ibid., 18.

19. Ibid., 23.

20. "Youngstown" by Bruce Springsteen. Copyright © 1995 by Bruce Springsteen (ASCAP). Reprinted by permission.

21. Nicholas Dawidoff, "The Pop Populist," *New York Times Magazine,* 26 January 1997, 33.

22. Bryn Zellers, interview with authors, Youngstown, Ohio, 7 September 1997.

23. M. Lisa Shattuck, "Open Hearth," in *Mahoning Valley Poetry,* ed. Julie Brown and Robert Brown (Bristolville, Ohio: Bacchae Press, 1993), 110–111.

24. Kelly Bancroft, "My Grandfather," *Mahoning Valley Poetry,* 9.

25. Joe Gorman, "Days Since Last Accident," *Mahoning Valley Poetry,* 46.

26. Betty Lambert, *Personal Statement* and *Certain Death,* 1999.

27. Lalli, "Campbell Works," A5.

28. "S&T Workers See Future as Bleak," *Youngstown Vindicator,* 20 September 1977, A1.

29. "Loss of S&T Taxes to Hurt Area," *Youngstown Vindicator,* 20 September 1977, A1.

30. Leon Stennis, "Churches Try to Shun Gloom of S&T Decision," *Youngstown Vindicator,* 24 September 1977, A7.

31. Editorial, *Youngstown Vindicator,* 20 September 1977, A10.

32. "Steel Firm to Close Ohio Unit," *Washington Post,* 20 September 1977, D8.

33. Bill Richards, "From the Mine to Factory, Steel Is Having Troubles," *Washington Post,* 24 September 1977, A1.

34. Shields, "Pain of Youngstown."

35. Peter Kilborn, "The Twilight of Smokestack America," *New York Times,* 8 May 1983, sec. 3, 1.

36. James M. Perry, "Down and Out: Idle Mills, a Dearth of Hope Are Features of Ohio's Steel Towns," *Wall Street Journal,* 20 January 1983, 1, 14.

37. Quoted in "Songs on Bruce Springsteen's New Album Inspired by 'Journey to Nowhere.'" *CBS This Morning* (New York: CBS News, 22 January 1996).

38. Jeff Ortenzio, "Degrees of Gray in Youngstown," *Mahoning Valley Poetry,* 88.

39. Joe D'Angelo and Sam D'Angelo, "Ten Years After," *Sister Ray: To Spite My Face* (New York: Resonance 19010-2, 1990).

40. *George Dombeck: Paintings 1975–1988,* exhibit catalog, Butler Institute of American Art, 1988. 25.

41. Ibid., 29.

42. James Jeffrey Higgins, *Images of the Rust Belt* (Kent, Ohio: Kent State University Press, 1999), 6.

43. Ibid., ix, 6.

44. *Steel Town Portraits: Exhibition of Paintings, Prints, Drawings by Agis Salpukas,* exhibit brochure, Youngstown Historical Center for Industry and Labor, 1993.

45. *Patchwork of Poverty* (Catholic Conference of Ohio and Classic Teleproductions, 1990).

46. Bill Donovan, *Michael Harrington and Today's Other America: Corporate Power and Inequality,* 1999.

47. *CBS This Morning,* "Springsteen's New Album."

48. Bob Dyer, "The Boss Tunes in to Youngstown," *Akron Beacon Journal,* 4 December 1995, A1.

49. *Nightly Business Report* (Miami: Community Television Foundation of South Florida, 10 July 1998).

50. Editorial, *Youngstown Vindicator,* 20 September 1977, A10.

51. *News Bulletin,* October 1977, 3.

52. Susanna McBee, "Youngstown's Vital Signs Encouraging after Plant Shutdown; Youngstown Didn't Die, after All, When Steel Plant Shut Its Doors," *Washington Post,* 19 November 1978, A23.

53. John Russo, "Saturn's Rings: What the GM Saturn Project Is Really About," *Labor Research Review* 5, no. 2 (fall 1986): 67–77.

54. George Welker, "Steel Missed, Hearth and Soul," *Youngstown Vindicator,* 14 September 1997, A1, A4; George Welker, "American Steel Has Come Back Stronger Than Ever, Experts Say," *Youngstown Vindicator,* 14 September 1997, A4; "Mill Land, Called 'Brownfields,' Produces Green," *Youngstown Vindicator,* 14 September 1997, A1, A5.

55. Lawrence Quinn, "250 Go to D.C. with Petitions," *Youngstown Vindicator,* 23 September 1977, A1.

56. Janie E. Jenkins, "Reopening of Time Capsule in 2076 May Find Steel Gone," *Youngstown Vindicator,* 25 September 1977, A2.

57. Dennis LaRue, "How One Monday in September Changed Our Lives," *Youngstown Vindicator,* 25 September 1977, A12.

58. Marge Smotrila, Annabelle Bodnar, and Edward Dailey, "Letters," *Youngstown Vindicator,* 25 September 1977, B20.

59. Editorial, *Youngstown Vindicator,* 26 September 1977, A12.

60. Michael J. Katula Jr., "Campbell Mayor Pleads for Calm," *Youngstown Vindicator,* 26 September 1977, A13.

61. Marc Siegel, producer and director, with Dan Cordtz, correspondent, *The Fight Against Black Monday,* McGraw-Hill Films, ABC News, 1978. Audiovisual collection, Youngstown Historical Center for Industry and Labor, Ohio Historical Society.

62. Mike Stout, "Flowers of the Working Class," *Working Class Reminiscing and Vision* (Homestead, Penn.: Blue Collar Records, 1996).

63. Bryn Zellers, interview with authors, Youngstown, Ohio, 7 September 1997.

64. Greenwald and Kraus, *Shout Youngstown.*

65. Staughton Lynd, *The Fight against Shutdowns: Youngstown's Steel Mill Closings* (San Pedro, Calif.: Singlejack Books, 1982), 11.

66. Ibid., 225.

67. Staughton and Alice Lynd, eds., *The New Rank and File* (Ithaca, N.Y.: ILR/Cornell University Press, 2000), 122. The book offers interviews with a number of activists, including many who were active in the Youngstown struggle.

68. Charles McCollester, telephone interview by authors, 4 December 2000. According to McCollester, the new organization was forged when John Barbero compared what was happening in Youngstown with his experience as a marine who was part of the first contingent to enter Hiroshima. Barbero likened the impact of deindustrialization of Youngstown to "radiation sickness," where fellow workers, neighbors, and neighborhoods began to simply disappear. By focusing on the conference on the "human tragedy," Barbero provided "the great moral statement" that brought together the disparate group.

69. Staughton Lynd, telephone interview by author, 5 December 2000. See also Mike Stout, "Reindustrialization from Below: The Steel Valley Authority," *Labor Research Review* 5, no. 2. (fall 1986): 18–33.

70. The Ohio Public Interest Campaign was involved in community and grassroots organizing and later became affiliated with Citizen Action. It is now called Ohio Citizen Action.

71. June Lucas, telephone interview by authors, 1 December 2000. Robert Hagan, telephone interview by authors, 1 December 2000.

72. *A Conversation with Bishop James Malone,* videotaped interview by Father Richard Murphy, Youngstown, Ohio, 21 March 1997.

73. The museum won a major citation as part of *Progressive Architecture*'s awards program. See *Progressive Architecture* 69, no. 1 (January 1988): 122–123.

74. Philip Arcidi, "Steel Industry Enshrined: Youngstown Museum, Youngstown, Ohio," *Progressive Architecture* 1, no. 3 (March 1990): 84.

75. Andrew Muhr, "The (Empty) Steel Museum," *Newsweek,* 30 October 1989, 84.

76. Donna DeBlasio, interview by authors, Youngstown, Ohio, 2 May 2000.

77. Curtis Minor, "Exhibition Reviews: By the Sweat of Their Brow: Forging the Steel Valley," *Journal of American History* 80, no. 3 (December 1993): 1,020.

78. Mike Wallace, *Mickey Mouse History and other Essays on American Memory* (Philadelphia: Temple University Press, 1996), 92–93.

79. Ibid., 98.

80. Miner, "Exhibition Reviews," 1,024.

81. Jeff Gammage, "Razing a Symbol of an Ohio Town's Prosperous Past," *Philadelphia Inquirer* 16 December 1996, A3.

82. Ibid.

83. James Allgren, interview by authors, Youngstown, Ohio, 26 June 2000.

84. For more information, see the Tod Engine Web site, http://home town.aol.com/todengine/todengine.html.

85. The Brier Hill Italian Fest: "The Spirit of the Family," Festival Program, September 1993, 1.

86. First Annual Brier Hill Italian Fest, "The Spirit of the Old Neighborhood," Festival Program, September 1992, 9.

87. Bob Black, *Brier Hill Italian Fest* (Youngstown: WKBN, 15 August 1997).

88. Dan Pecchio and Mary Frances Carol, interview by authors, Youngstown, Ohio, 20 June 2000. Both Pecchio and Carol grew up in Brier Hill and are in their mid-seventies.

89. Fred and Josephine Ross, interview by authors, Youngstown, Ohio, 22 October 1998.

90. Sam Camens and Joe Gavini, interview by authors, Youngstown, Ohio, 11 July 2000.

CHAPTER 4
From "Steel Town" to a "Nice Place to Do Time"

Epigraph from Kathy Kiely, "Is Ohio's Traficant Too Colorful for Congress?" *USA Today,* 23 February 2000, 8A.

1. Joe Williams, "Mob-Apprentice Movie Has Oedipal Undertones," *St. Louis Post-Dispatch,* 26 March 1999, E3.

2. Kevin Dressor, cover illustration, "Welcome to Youngstown: A Story of the Mafia, the FBI, a Congressman and the Most Crooked City in America," *New Republic,* 10 and 17 July 2000.

3. Amanda Garrett, "High Crime, Low Hopes in Youngstown," *Rocky Mountain News,* 7 January 1996, 20A.

4. Chris Whitley, "Homicide Rate Remains High," *Youngstown Vindicator,* 28 November 1999, A1–A3.

5. Elizabeth Marchak, "Youngstown Black Women Suffer Reign of Violence," *Plain Dealer,* 14 March 2000, A1.

6. Peter Williams, *The Human Factor: Youngstown USA* (Instructional Television Service, TVS Television Limited, 1992).

7. William Julius Wilson, *When Work Disappears: The World of the New Urban Poor* (New York: Alfred A. Knopf, 1997), xiii–xxiii.

8. C. Allen Pierce, interview by authors, Youngstown, Ohio, 11 July 2000. See also Latisha Bunkley, "Youth Who Kill: A Case Study Approach" (master's thesis, Youngstown State University, 1999); C. Allen Pierce, "Epidemic Theory as Applied to Incidence of Homicides" (paper presented at the thirty-fourth annual meeting of the Academy of Criminal Justice Sciences, Louisville, Kentucky, 14 March 1997); Christopher T. Lowenkamp and C. Allen Pierce, "Comparative Analysis between High and Low Homicide Rate Cities" (paper presented at the thirty-fifth annual meeting of the Academy of Criminal Justice Sciences, Albuquerque, New Mexico, 13 March 1998).

9. Richard Bee and Yih-wu Liu, "An Analysis of Crime and Economic Conditions in a Declining Area," *Akron Business and Economic Review* 15, no. 4 (winter 1984): 25–29. Also see Richard Bee and Yih-wu Liu, "Modeling Criminal Activity in an Area of Economic Decline," *The American Journal of Economics and Sociology* 42, no. 4 (October 1983): 385–392.

10. Wilson, "When Work Disappears," xviii.

11. Pierce, interview.

12. Mark Niquette, "Mob's Pull in Valley Is an 'Investment' in Microsoft," *Youngstown Vindicator,* 7 March 1999, A1–A3.

13. Bruce Nelson, "Race Relations in the Mill: Steelworkers and Unionism in Youngstown" (presentation, Center for Working-Class Studies lecture series, 13 May 1996).

14. Homer Warren, interview by authors, Youngstown, Ohio, 5 June 2000.

15. Sarah Brown-Clark, interview by authors, Youngstown, Ohio, 21 August 2000.

16. Consent Decree I, United States District Court for the Northern District of Alabama Southern Division, Civil Action No. 74 P339, United States of America, Department of Labor, *Equal Employment Opportunity Commission v. Allegheny Ludlum Corporation; Armco Steel Corporation;*

Bethlehem Steel Corporation; Jones and Laughlin Steel Corporation; National Steel Corporation; Republic Steel Corporation; United States Steel Corporation; Wheeling-Pittsburgh Steel Corporation; Youngstown Sheet and Tube Company; and United Steelworkers of America, AFL-CIO-CLC, 12 April 1974.

17. Jolie Solomon with Bruce Shenitz and Daniel McMinn, "Mickey's Secret Life," *Newsweek,* 31 August 1992, 70.

18. Jim Gilmore, Paul Judge, and Paul Solman, "How to Steal $500 Million," *Frontline* (Washington, D.C.: Public Broadcasting Service, 8 November 1994).

19. Solomon, "Mickey's Secret Life."

20. Ibid.

21. Marcus Gleisser, "Ex-Football Player Pleads Guilty to Jury Tampering," *Plain Dealer,* 6 August 1996, 4C.

22. Gilmore, Judge, and Solman, "$500 Million."

23. Ibid.

24. Solomon, "Mickey's Secret Life."

25. Editorial, "Like Father, Like Son—Monuses Are Committed to Area," *Youngstown/Warren Business Journal,* mid-March 1989, sec. 1, 4.

26. Don Hanni Jr., "Monus' Contributions to the Valley Worth Recalling," *Youngstown Vindicator,* August 7, 2000, 4.

27. The Cafaro Corporation, another local mall developer, endured similar activities from the son of the company founder, William Cafaro. While not made public, the company suffered from the misappropriation of funds and poor judgment of J. J. Cafaro involving business enterprises outside the core family business. He was subsequently expelled from the family business by his father and brother and left the area.

28. Martin Smith and Matthew Kennedy, "Edward J. DeBartolo Sr.," *Pittsburgh Press,* 9 October 1983, special section.

29. "DeBartolo Fete to Benefit YSU Raises $500,000," *Youngstown Vindicator,* 16 June 1984, A1.

30. Smith and Kennedy, "DeBartolo Sr."

31. Ibid.

32. Ibid.

33. Dan Moldea, *Interference: How Organized Crime Influences Professional Football* (New York: Morrow, 1989), 287–291.

34. Thomas George, "Pro Football; For the Forty-Niners, Being in the Hunt Is Simply Not Good Enough," *New York Times,* 11 November 1994, B10.

35. Dave Goldberg, "Eddie DeBartolo: An Owner on the Move," *Associated Press,* 25 January 1990.

36. "Sports News," *Associated Press*, 29 January 1995.

37. Dennis Georgatos, "Sports News," Associated Press, 24 July 1992.

38. John Eckhouse, "'91 Talk of Forty-Niners Sale Reported, but DeBartolo Claims Team Isn't on Block," *San Francisco Chronicle*, 2 February 1992, A1.

39. Christopher Palmeri, "Horse Sense," *Forbes*, 24 October 1994, 19.

40. Smith and Kennedy, "DeBartolo Sr."

41. Manuel Roig-Franzia, "DeBartolto Plea Deal Pressures Edwards: Forty-Niners Chief Testifies to Payoff," *Times-Picayune*, 7 October 1998, A1.

42. Gordon Forbes, "Developing New Interests: Pro Football Only Thing Missing for Tampa's Mall Man," *USA Today*, 28 June 2000, 3C.

43. "The Forbes 400: Divided We Stand," *Forbes*, 11 October 1999, 308–310.

44. Laurie P. Cohen, "Edward DeBartolo Jr. Tried to Go It Alone, but All Bets Are Off," *Wall Street Journal*, 19 February 1998, A1.

45. Ann Killon, "Forty-Niners' New Owner Speaks Up," *San Jose Mercury News*, 1 August 2000, A1.

46. Ibid.

47. Niquette, "Mob's Pull in Valley," A-1.

48. Francis X. Clines, "Fighting to Help an Ohio City Shed Its Image as 'Crimetown, U.S.A.,'" *New York Times*, 11 April 2000, sec. 1, 20. Kiely, "Ohio's Traficant."

49. "The Ten Most Corrupt Cities in America," *George*, March 1998.

50. David Grann, "Crimetown, USA: The City That Fell in Love with the Mob," *New Republic*, 10 and 17 July 2000, 23.

51. Kiely, "Ohio's Traficant."

52. Jeff Glasser, "The Sopranos Come to Youngstown, Ohio: The Feds Target a Local Hero in a Shady Town," *U.S. News & World Report*, 6 March 2000, 28–29.

53. Kiely, "Ohio's Traficant."

54. James F. McCarty, "Traficant Plays Familiar Role, " *Cleveland Plain Dealer*, 6 February 2000, 1B.

55. Ibid.

56. Patricia Meade, "FBI Official: Voters Stem Corruption," *Vindicator*, 11 November 1999, A1–2.

57. Clines, "Fighting to Help an Ohio City."

58. Patricia Meade, "Traficant Vows to Fight," *Youngstown Vindicator*, 5 May 2001, 1A.

59. *Time* Magazine, 14 May 2001, page 15.

60. James McCarty and Sabrina Eaton, "Mover-and-Shaker Is Feds' Key Witness in Traficant Case," *Cleveland Plain Dealer*, 20 May 2001, A1.

61. Jason Vest, "Congressman Corruption?" *The American Prospect* online, http://www.americanprospect.com/print-friendly/webfeatures/2001/05/vest-j-05-11.html.

62. William Claiborne, "A Rust Belt Democrat Will Not Go Gently," *Washington Post,* 26 February 2000, A3.

63. Ibid.

64. Mark Rollenhagen, "Trial Shows Mob Still a Concern in Youngstown; Strollo Racketeering Case Starts Tuesday," *Cleveland Plain Dealer,* 14 February 1999, 1B.

65. Rick Porello, *To Kill an Irishman: The War that Crippled the Mafia* (Cleveland: Next Hat Press, 1998), 184.

66. Ibid.

67. John Goodall, "When the Law Was the Jungle," *Youngstown Vindicator,* 30 April 2000, B-3.

68. Edward Allen, *Merchants of Menace—The Mafia: A Study of Organized Crime* (Springfield, Ill.: Charles C. Thomas, 1962), 68.

69. Ibid., 158

70. Goodall, "When the Law Was the Jungle."

71. Rose Hanson, "Scholar Blames Mob for Apathy," *Tribune Chronicle,* 21 March 2000.

72. This number is very low, as it involves only the direct loss of the fires. When water and smoke damage is calculated, the figures are much higher. For information prior to 1980, see David Stephens, "Arson: The City Burns" (paper presented at the annual conference of the Association of American Geographers, Denver, Colo., 24 April 1983).

73. The statistical information was developed from fire department records and FBI reports by Tim McGarry, with the assistance of Robert Sharp, chief arson investigator.

74. John O'Neil, Tim McGarry, Dante Barber, and Martin Conti, interview by authors, Youngstown, Ohio, 29 February 2000; Tim McGarry and Bob Sharp, interview by authors, Youngstown, Ohio, 5 July 2000. All those interviewed are current or former officials of the Youngstown Fire Department.

75. According to the firefighters, the most common technique involved nothing more than gasoline-filled garbage bags usually hung from the ceiling. This "fire bomb" technique allowed the arsonist time to set small fires and then escape the building before the accelerants ignited. These fires could not be easily extinguished, threatened the lives of firefighters, and resulted in the structural collapse of the house or roof (or both). If the roof collapsed, insurance companies were likely to total the house.

76. Niquette, "Mob's Pull in Valley."

77. Claiborne, "Rust Belt Democrat."

78. "Traficant Easily Survives Primary: Rival Prepares for Battle," *Beacon Journal Online*, 8 March 2000. Available http://www.ohio.com/bj/news/ohio/docs/026570.htm, 9 March 2000.

79. Diane Evans, "Neighbors Make City Look Good," *Akron Beacon Journal*, 25 March 2001, F1.

80. "The Mahoning Valley: An Economic Resource Profile" (Youngstown: Mahoning Valley Economic Development Corporation, 1997), 2.

81. Jon Baker, "Being in Spotlight Hasn't Always Been Bright for Mahoning Valley," *Youngstown Vindicator*, 7 November 1999, A4.

82. "The Mahoning Valley," 2, 8.

83. Ibid., 7.

84. Ohio Bureau of Employment Services, *Annual Trends in Employment Covered under Ohio Unemployment Compensation Law* (Columbus, 1998). The total employment and industry sector statistics have been drawn from data from the *Annual Trends* for Trumbull and Mahoning Counties.

85. Holly Burnett, interview by authors, Youngstown, Ohio, 3 August 2000.

86. *These Hundred Years: A Chronicle of the Twentieth Century* (Youngstown: Vindicator Printing Company, 2000), 91.

87. Frank Akpadock, "Patrick Ungaro, Brownfield Redevelopment, and Revitalization of Youngstown, Ohio," in *Governing Middle-Size Cities: Studies in Mayoral Leadership*, ed. James R. Bowers and Wilbur C. Rich (Boulder, Colo.: Lynne Rienner, 1999), 167–168.

88. Roy R. Weil and Mary H. Shaw, eds., *Canoeing Guide: Western Pennsylvania, Northern West Virginia*, 7th ed. (Pittsburgh: American Youth Hostels, 1983), 92.

89. Akpadock, "Brownfield Redevelopment," 177–178.

90. "Mill Land, Called 'Brownfields,' Produce Green," *Youngstown Vindicator*, 14 September 1997, A1–5.

91. "The Mahoning Valley."

92. Quoted in Akpadock, "Brownfield Redevelopment," 179.

93. Thomas Maraffa, interview by authors, Youngstown, Ohio, 14 May 1998.

94. Thomas Finnery Jr., interview by authors, Youngstown, Ohio, 28 June 2000.

95. Roger G. Smith, "Lockups Lead the Way to a New Economy," *Youngstown Vindicator*, 27 June 1999, A1–A3.

96. Vincent Duffy and Linda Wertheimer, "Youngstown Escape," *All Things Considered*, National Public Radio, 30 July 1998, Transcript #98073011-212.

97. Jane Pauley, "House of Correction? Community Outrage over Profit-Driven Prison in Youngstown, Ohio," *Dateline,* NBC News, 11 October 1998, NBC News Transcripts.

98. Ed Bradley, "Medium Security, Maximum Problems," *Sixty Minutes,* CBS News, 2 May 1999.

99. Pauley, "House of Correction?"

100. Bradley, "Medium Security, Maximum Problems."

101. Barry Yoeman, "Steel Town Lockdown," *Mother Jones,* May/June 2000, 40.

102. Arthur Santana, "D.C. Scatters Inmates from Troubled Ohio Prison," *Washington Post,* 11 May 2001, A24. Vest, "Congressman Corruption?" *The American Prospect* on-line.

EPILOGUE
Community Memory and Youngstown's Future

Epigraph from Zach de la Rocha, "Testify," *The Battle of Los Angeles* (Los Angeles: Sony/Epic, 1999).

1. "Town Pride," *Sports Illustrated,* 17 October 1994, 86–87.

2. *The Joy of Growing Up Italian in Brier Hill,* pamphlet distributed at the Fourteenth Annual Brier Hill Reunion.

3. Marc Perrota, Kevin Coleman, and Deborah L. Dobson-Brown with contributions by William Hunter, *Phase II Architectural Assessment of (MAH/TRU-711-0.00/0.00, PID No. 7386) Eight Properties (Brier Hill Area, MAH-1436-4, MAH-1437-4, MAH-280-4, MAH-1438-4, MAH-123-4, TRU-2658-24, TRU-2660-24) in the City of Youngstown, Mahoning County, and City of Girard, Trumbull County Ohio,* 9 September 1999.

4. William M. Hunter, "Review of Phase II History Architecture Report," Ohio Department of Transportation, Office of Environmental Services, interoffice communication to Paul Graham, 17 May 1999.

5. William M. Hunter, "Historically Significant But No Longer 'Historic': The Case of Brier Hill," a summary of the report to Ohio Department of Transportation, March 1999.

6. William M. Hunter, "Brier Hill Report: A Website Summary for the General Public," Center for Working-Class Studies, Youngstown State University, Youngstown, Ohio, June 2000.

7. Youngstown State University Center for Urban Studies, *Youngstown: State of the City* (Youngstown: Center for Urban Studies, 1995), 1–2.

Also see David Rusk, *Cities without Suburbs* (Washington: Woodrow Wilson Center Press, 1993).

8. George Denny, "Segregation Spells Disaster, Expert Says," *Youngstown Vindicator,* 1 December 1995, A4.

9. Edward L. Glaser, Jacob L. Vigdor, and Terry Sanford, *Racial Segregation in the 2000 Census: Promising News,* Center on Urban and Metropolitan Policy (Washington, D.C.: Brookings Institution, 2001).

10. "Separated Living Has Many Causes," *Youngstown Vindicator,* 29 May 2001, A2.

11. Denny, "Segregation Spells Disaster," A4. According to David Rusk, Youngstown could reverse its economic and social situations through regional cooperation led by coalitions of state legislators with common goals involving revenue sharing, fair-share housing, and land-use planning.

12. Rusk, *Cities without Suburbs,* appendix A-1.

13. Gary Rothstein, "Census 2000," *Pittsburgh Post-Gazette,* 10 March 2001, A-1.

14. Dolores Hayden, *The Power of Place: Urban Landscapes as Public History* (Cambridge: MIT Press, 1996), 9.

15. Michael Keith Honey, *Black Workers Remember: An Oral History of Segregation, Unionism, and the Freedom Struggle* (Berkeley, Calif.: University of California Press, 1999), 13.

16. Bryn Zellers, *Process: Change and Sacrifice,* Trumbull Art Gallery, 29 June 1996.

17. Allesandra Siracusa, "Educating for Citizenship: Reconstructing the Identity of Our City" (presentation at Creating a Culture of Lawfulness: The Palermo, Italy, Renaissance, 14 December 2000).

18. Andreas Huyssen, *Twilight Memories: Marking Time in a Culture of Amnesia* (New York: Routledge, 1995), 5, 7.

INDEX

ABC News, 170
AFL-CIO. *See* American Federation of Labor–Congress of Industrial Organizations
African Americans, 10, 13, 16, 22, 33
  businesses, 198–199, 200
  and crime, 64, 194, 197–198
  health, 194
  home ownership, 41, 42
  jobs, 32, 43, 51, 53, 198
  and mill closures, 53, 200
  and murders, 194–195, 197–198, 223
  neighborhood housing, 32–33, 42, 199, 241
  population, 25–26, 27 (table), 198
  segregation, 53, 65, 95
  and suburbs, 42
  wages, 41
  women, 194, 199
Agee, Rita, 195
Akpadock, Frank, 231
Akron (Ohio), 152
Akron Beacon Journal, 161, 227
Alexander, George, 216
Aley, Howard C., 21, 79, 93
Allen, Edward, 220
Allgren, James, 183
Alperovitz, Gar, 49
Aluminum industry, 47
American dream, 110, 143

American Federation of Labor, 28, 121, 122
American Federation of Labor–Congress of Industrial Organizations (AFL-CIO), 57
Americanism, 109, 117
Americanization, 36, 74
American Labor Year Book, 29
American Legion, 30
American plan, 30
American Prospect, 217
Anderson, Teresa, 135
"Anna Karenina and the Love-Sick River" (Patchen), 118
Anxiety (Zellers sculpture), 146, 147 (photo)
Arcidi, Philip, 179
Arena, Andrew, 215–216
Arms Museum, 13
Arson, 51, 222–226
Atlantic Monthly, 38
Aug, Stephen, 161, 162
Austintown (Ohio), 64–65, 233
Auto industry, 54–57, 162
Autoworkers, 55–56, 59

Bancroft, Kelly, 148
Bankruptcy, 51
Barbero, John, 132, 171, 174, 175, 177
Bars, 33, 191, 225
BBC. *See* British Broadcasting Corporation
Beeghly, Nancy, 205
Bellah, Robert N., 3, 4

Bennett, George, 137, 138
Bergles, Steve, 205
Bernstein, Adam, 191
Bethlehem Steel, 37
Bibich, Mike, 135
Black, Bob, 186
Black Monday (1977), 48, 166
Blast Furnace (Salpukas painting), 158
Blast furnaces, 1, 19. *See also* Steelmaking
Boarding houses, 26
Boardman (Ohio), 233, 237
Bolsheviks, 29, 109
Bootlegging, 31
Breckner, George, 87
Brier Hill neighborhood, 32, 41, 45, 101–102, 240–243, 248
    estate, 18, 19, 20, 26
    Italian Fest, 58, 178, 184–187, 241, 248
Brier Hill Steel Company, 24
Brier Hill Works, 1, 9, 10, 37, 47, 50, 53, 66, 137, 140, 164, 173
British Broadcasting Corporation (BBC), 195
Brookings Institution, 244
Brown-Clark, Sarah, 199, 200
Brownfield redevelopment, 231–233, 235
Bruno, Robert, 42, 45
Buckeye Land Company (Youngstown Sheet and Tube), 31, 34, 35 (illus.), 37
Bulletin (Youngstown Sheet and Tube paper), 96, 97, 105, 106
Burnett, Holly, 231
Butler, Joseph, Jr., 29
Butler Institute of American Art, 13, 14 (photo), 29, 87–88, 137, 154
By the Sweat of Their Brow: Forging the Steel Valley (Ohio Historical Center for Industry and Labor display), 180

Cafaro family, 44, 102, 268n27
Cafaro, John J., 217
Camens, Sam, 187, 188
Camens, Sam, Steelworkers' Center, 187–188
Camp, Scott, 50
Campbell (Ohio), 33, 34, 53, 150, 169–170, 171
Campbell Works, 12, 25, 36, 37, 47, 50, 53, 64, 131, 133, 174
Camp Tuff Enuff, 203
Canfield (Ohio), 233, 237
Cargill (agribusiness), 53
Carnegie Steel, 24, 34
Carol, Mary Frances, 186
Carter, Jimmy, 152, 218
CASTLO (Campbell, Struthers, and Lowellville) project, 53
Cathedral of St. Columba, 179
Catholic churches, 23, 26, 32
    and steelworkers, 100–102, 168
Catholic Conference of Ohio, 158–159
CBS This Morning (television program), 160–161
CCA. *See* Corrections Corporation of America
Census (2000), 244
Centers for Disease Control and Prevention, 194
Certain Death (Lambert sculpture), 149
Chapin, James, 159
Charcoal, 19
Chinese, 22, 121
CIO. *See* Congress of Industrial Organizations
Civic culture, 4
Class conflict, 5–6, 15, 21, 24, 30–31, 68, 130, 218
    and labor and management, 120–121
    and labor organization, 37–41
    in suburbs, 45

Cleveland, 244, 245
Cleveland Plain Dealer, 194, 214, 215, 219, 233
Clines, Francis X., 216
Clinton, Bill, 218
Coal mines, 18, 19, 21–22
Coca Cola (company), 204
Cohen, Lizabeth, 44
Cold War sentiments, 83. *See also* Communists
Collective bargaining, 37, 42, 176
Colorado Rockies (baseball team), 203
Communists, 29, 38, 109, 117
Community of memory, 3
    conflicting, 4–5, 68, 245–246, 248–249
    and crime and corruption, 3–4, 8, 245
    and landscape, 17, 66, 246, 249
    and memory of place, 66, 130, 159, 178–188, 240–243, 245
Company workers' organizations, 111
Company unions, 38–39
Congress of Industrial Organizations (CIO), 112, 126. *See also* American Federation of Labor–Congress of Industrial Organizations
Constitutive narrative, 2–3, 4, 7–8
Consumerism, 79
Cordz, Dan, 170
Corporate paternalism, 39
Corporate power, 16, 39–40, 159
Corrections Corporation of America (CCA), 60, 62, 63, 64, 235–236
Crabbe, William, 151
"Creating a Culture of Lawfulness" (2000 conference), 247

Crime and corruption, 3–4, 8, 31, 46–47, 51, 64, 65, 159, 190–198
    white-collar, 191, 201–213
    See also Community of memory; Organized crime

D'Angelo, Sam, 153
Daniels, Ron, 169, 174, 175
Dateline (television program), 64, 234
Davey, Martin L., 40
Davis, James, 32–33, 175
Dawidoff, Nicholas, 145
"Days Since Last Accident" (Gorman), 148–149
DeBartolo, Edward, Jr., 202, 208–213
DeBartolo, Edward, Sr., 202, 206–208
DeBartolo, Edward J., Corporation, 206, 208, 211
DeBartolo family, 13, 44, 211, 212, 213
DeBartolo-York, Denise, 211, 212
DeBlasio, Donna, 34, 180–181
DeGennaro family. *See* Jennings brothers
"Degrees of Gray in Youngstown" (Ortenzio), 152–153
Deindustrialization, 3, 4, 48, 68, 132, 151, 159, 189, 236–237
    and activism, 132, 167–178
    and boosterism, 133, 163–167
    and constitutive narrative, 4, 8
    reconceptualized, 182
    See also Crime and corruption; Steel mills, closures; Work, loss of
De la Rocha, Zach, 247
Delphi Packard Electric, 162
Democratic Party, 217–218
Denver (Colo.), 38
Detroit (Mich.), 152

Detroit Publishing Company
Photograph Collection, 75–76
"Dinner-Pail Brigade, The"
(Greig), 120
"Dinner pail" poems, 119–120
Dombeck, George, 154–155
Donnelly, James J., 97
Donnorummo, Sam, 32
Donovan, Bill, 159, 160
Drug dealing, 195, 197, 203
Dyer, Bob, 161

East Liverpool (Ohio), 155, 156
Ecumenical Coalition of the
Mahoning Valley, 49–50, 170,
173, 177, 178, 218
Edge cities, 44, 46
Edwards, Edwin, 211–212
Eminent domain, 50, 162, 177
English-language courses, 36
Environmental Protection
Agency (EPA), 49, 227
EPA. *See* Environmental
Protection Agency
Ethnic diversity, 42

"Family Portrait" (Patchen), 85–86
FBI. *See* Federal Bureau of
Investigation
Federal Bureau of Investigation
(FBI), 46–47, 65, 215–216
Federal Bureau of Prisons, 236
Federal Organized Crime Strike
Force, 219
*Fifty Years in Steel: The Story of the
Youngstown Sheet and Tube
Company: This Is America*, 81
*Fight Against Youngstown, The:
Youngstown's Steel Mill
Closings* (S. Lynd), 176
Fitch, John A., 28
Fitzgerald, John "Denny," 33
"Flowers of the Working Class"
(song), 171

Forbes magazine, 212
Fortunato, Fred A., 95, 99
Frontline (PBS documentary), 202,
203, 204, 205

Gains, Paul, 216
Gambling, 31, 210, 220, 221
Gammage, Jeff, 182
Gangs, 197
Gary, Elbert, 124
Gatewood, Arlette, 95
Gavini, Joe, 175, 188
General Motors (GM), 54–57,
161–162, 165
General Motors Assembly
Division (GMAD), 56
George magazine, 213
Germans, 20, 26, 32, 121, 241
Ghost of Tom Joad, The
(Springsteen), 144
Girard (Ohio), 237
Girdler, Thomas, 39
GM. *See* General Motors
GMAD. *See* General Motors
Assembly Division
Gompers, Samuel, 81, 83, 121, 149
Gorman, Joe, 148–149
Government loan programs
discrimination, 41
Graham, Jim, 217
Grant, Rosalee, 223
Grant, Ulysses S., 117
Graves, Michael, 14, 178–179, 181
Great Depression (1930s), 37, 38–
41
Greeks, 25
Greenwald, Carol, 173, 176
Greig, Oswald, 120
Gropper, William, 126–128
Gun sales, 197

*Habits of the Heart: Individualism
and Commitment in American
Life* (Bellah et al.), 3

Hagan, Robert, 177
Hall Painting Company, 117
Hanni, Don, Jr., 205–206, 218, 219
Hanson, J. M., 125
Hayden, Dolores, 17, 246
Health care, 194
Heffernan, Joseph, 38
Henderson, Charles, 220
Higgins, James Jeffrey, 155, 156, 157
Highways, 43
Hispanics, 42, 65
Historical sites, 4, 16
Homage to Ed Mann (Man of Sorrows) (sculpture), 171–173
Honey, Michael Keith, 246
"Horatio Alger myth," 205
Hornack, Jay, 177
Horsecars, 26
"How a Steel Worker Views the Meaning of CIO" *(Steel Labor),* 112–113, 114 (illus.)
Hubbard (Ohio), 155
Hudson, E. W., 112
Hudson, Rufus, 183
Human Factor, The (television documentary), 195, 197
Hungarians, 25, 26, 32
Hunter, Jack C., 151
Hunter, William M., 242
Huyssen, Andreas, 248

Idora Park (amusement park), 13, 14, 33, 43
Images of the Rust Belt (Higgins), 155–157
Immigrants, 10, 20, 22, 23, 24, 25, 26, 28
  and AFL, 121
  Catholic, 31
  churches, 23, 26, 32, 33, 42, 184
  image of, 123–124
  and jobs, 32, 90, 98
  and strikes, 124
  See also Working class; Youngstown, racial and ethnic conflict
Industrial Information Institute, 79, 94
Industrial parks, 53, 60, 233
Industry Week magazine, 229, 230
Ingham, John, 46
Inland Steel, 37
Irish, 20, 26, 31, 32, 33
Isaac, Ray, 204
Italians, 10, 25, 26, 28, 31, 32, 33, 42, 121, 241
  workers and Catholic churches, 100–102, 184
Izzo, Augustine F., 99

Jaminet, Raymond J., and Partners, 178
Janis, Jay, 171
Japanese, 121
JBFPA. *See* Jeannette Blast Furnace Preservation Association
Jeanette ("Jenny") Blast Furnace, 1, 2, 9, 10, 11 (photo), 16, 24, 54, 58, 145, 155, 167, 182–183
Jeannette Blast Furnace Preservation Association (JBFPA), 182–184
Jenkins, William, 31
Jennings brothers, 31
Jews, 20
Journal of American History, 181
Journey to Nowhere: The Saga of the New Underclass (Maharidge), 6, 143–144, 152, 160
Jungle Inn, 220, 221

Kadilak, John, 151
Kahn, Si, 174, 175
Katula, Michael J., Jr., 169–170
Ketchum, Robert Glenn, 156

Kilborn, Peter, 152
Kirwan, Michael, 220
Kosa, Victor, 100
Krauss, Dorie, 173, 176
Kristol, Irving, 159
Ku Klux Klan, 26, 30–31, 72, 109, 121

Labor Lyrics and Other Poems
    (McGovern), 89–90, 92
Labor-management conflict, 21–22,
    37–38, 56, 60, 68, 74, 129–130
    and housing, 34
    and unions, 95–96, 99, 107–110
    See also Strikes
Labor organization, 21–22, 112–
    116
    and foreign born, 30–31
    gains, 41, 99–100
    and Great Depression, 38–40
    and NLRB, 37
    and racial divisions, 95
    by teaching faculty, 57–58
Ladies Professional Golf
    Association (LPGA), 203, 205
Lalli, Sergio, 133–134
Lambert, Betty, 149
Last Days of Youngstown Steel
    (Bennett), 137–139
Letter to Youngstown
    (Youngstown Sheet and Tube
    film), 81, 106–107
Lie of the Land, The (Mitchell), 61
Lithuanians, 28
"Little Steel" companies, 37, 39
Lordstown (Ohio), 54
    GM plant, 53 (photo), 161–162
"Lordstown Syndrome," 56
Louisiana Downs racetrack, 206,
    210
Lowellville (Ohio), 53
LPGA. *See* Ladies Professional
    Golf Association
LTV (formerly Republic Steel
    Company), 180

Lucas, June, 174, 177
Lykes Corporation, 48–49, 164
Lynd, Alice, 62, 235
Lynd, Staughton, 49, 62, 174, 176–
    177, 235

Mace, Grover, 111–112
Maciose, Thomas M., 207
Maharidge, Dale, 143, 160
Mahoning River, 19, 232
Mahoning Valley Economic
    Development Corporation,
    229, 232
Mahoning Valley Historical
    Society, 13
Mahoning Vindicator
    (Youngstown), 21, 22
Malls, 44, 200, 206
Malone, James (bishop), 177–178
Mann, Ed, 171–173, 174, 175, 177
Maquiladora section (Mexico),
    57
Maraffa, Thomas, 233
Marshall, Joe, and Joe, Jr., 143–
    144, 160
Martin, Dean, 221
Martin, John, 135
"May I Ask You a Question, Mr.
    Youngstown Sheet and
    Tube?" (Patchen), 84–85
McCloskey, Martha, 86
McCollester, Charles, 177
McDonald Steel (U.S. Steel), 180
McDonough Museum of Art
    (YSU), 13
McEwen, Mark, 161
McGovern, Michael, 89–90, 92,
    97, 119–121
McKelvey, George, 4, 64, 235
McMahon, Ken, 163
Mechanics of Youngstown, 21
Megginson, Carroll, 135, 136–139
Memory. *See* Community of
    memory

Index

Men and Machines of Modern Steelmaking, The (Sharon Steel Corporation), 85, 85 (illus.), 88
Mental health, 53
Men Who Make Steel (Republic film), 84, 88, 97, 106
Meshel, Harry, 47
Metzenbaum, Howard, 177
Metzgar, Jack, 41
Michael Harrington and Today's Other America: Corporate Power and Inequality (film), 159–160
Middle class, 31, 41, 160, 197, 198, 220
Mill Creek Park, 13, 15, 23, 70, 72, 77, 78 (illus.)
Mill Entrance (Breckner painting), 87
Mill Hunk Herald (journal), 135
Mills (McCloskey painting), 86
Miner and Manufacturer (miners' union newspaper), 21, 22
Miners' and Laborers' Benevolent Association, 21
Minor, Curtis, 181, 182
Mitchell, Don, 15, 61
Mob activities, 31, 46, 191, 225
Mock, Tom, 227
Modarelli, Dominick "Dee Dee," 184
Mohawk Valley formula, 39, 122
Mondale, Walter, 218
Monus, Michael (Mickey), 202–206, 212, 213
Mon Valley Unemployed Committees, 177
Mother Jones, 227–229, 235
"My Workingman" (McGovern), 90, 97

Nation, 126
National Center for Economic Alternatives, 49
National Conference of Catholic Bishops, 178
National Guard (Ohio), 40
Nationalism, 83
National Labor Relations Board (NLRB), 37, 40
National Public Radio, 64, 234
National Steel Company, 24
Nelson, Archie, 112
Nepotism, 222
New Castle (Pa.), 30
"New localism," 231
New Republic, 125, 191, 192 (illus.), 213
Newspaper Guild, 57
Newspaper strike (1962), 57
Newsweek, 180, 202, 203, 205
New York Times, 152, 157, 209, 216
New York Times Magazine, 145
Nightly Business Report (television program), 161–162
Niles (Ohio), 31, 39, 44, 46, 233
NLRB. *See* National Labor Relations Board
NOCC. *See* Northeast Ohio Correctional Center
Northeast Ohio Correctional Center (NOCC), 234–235, 236
North Star Steel, 10, 12, 53
Nurses' strike, 57

ODOT. *See* Ohio Department of Transportation
Ohio Bureau of Employment Sevices, 47
Ohio Department of Transportation (ODOT), 241–243
Ohio Education Association, 57
Ohio Historical Center for Industry and Labor, 178–182
Ohio Historical Society (OHS), 178, 180, 183
Ohio Public Interest Campaign, 177

Ohio's Mahoning Valley: An Economic Resource Profile (Mahoning Valley Economic Development Corporation), 229–230

OHS. *See* Ohio Historical Society

Olah, Steven, 219

Olmstead, Frederick Law, 23

"100% Americanism," 109

O'Nesti, Charles, 216, 225

"Open Hearth" (Shattuck), 148

Oral histories, 94–96, 107, 111, 180–181

"Orange Bears, The" (Patchen), 119

Organized crime, 46–47, 65, 197, 213–227

influence on judiciary, 197

Ortenzio, Jeff, 152, 153

Other Carl Sandburg, The (Yannella), 92

Our Lady of Mt. Carmel church, 102

Our Neighbors Tell Us about Their Work (Aley), 93–94

Packard Electric (GM), 56–57

Palermo (Sicily), 3–4, 247

Panic (Zellers sculture), 146

Parella, Albert, 86

Parkview Counseling Center, 53

Patchen, Kenneth, 84–86, 118–119

Patchwork of Poverty (film), 159

Pauley, Jane, 234

Pecchio, Dan, 186

Pennsylvania and Ohio Canal, 19

Perry, James M., 152

Phar Mor (company), 202, 203, 204, 206

Philadelphia Inquirer, 182

Photo History, 126

Pierce, C. Allen, 193, 196

Pig iron, 19

Pittsburgh (Pa.), 25, 177

Pittsburgh–Cleveland megalopolis, 244, 245

Pittsburgh Penguins (sports team), 206

Pittsburgh Press, 207

Plant closing legislation (1988), 50, 162, 177

Platt, Ken, Jr. and Sr., 144 (photo)

Poles, 26, 28, 33

Policy, Carmen, 209, 210, 219–220

Pollution, 10, 49

Population

balkanization, 31–32

shift, 4, 41–42, 44

See also under Youngstown

Populist politics, 218

Porello, Rick, 219

Postindustrial era, 8, 156. *See also* Youngstown, economy (1990s)

Poverty, 33

"Prescription, A" (poem), 96

Princeton University, 8

Prison Forum, 235

Prisons. *See under* Youngstown

Process: Change and Sacrifice (Zellers performance art), 246–247

Protestant churches, 23, 26, 102–105, 184

Public housing, 10, 42, 198

Public schools, 197

Public sector jobs, 222

"Puddler poet." *See* McGovern, Michael

Puerto Ricans, 42

Purnell, Frank, 39

Racial and ethnic conflict. *See under* Youngstown

Racketeer Influenced and Corrupt Organization Act (1970), 216

Railway Conductors' union, 121

Rand, James H., 122
Reagan, Ronald, 152, 218, 231
Real estate, 51
Real Men (Rose), 135–137
Redburn, Steve, 164
Red scare (1950s), 117
Regional Guide (Burnett), 230–231
Remington Rand, 122
Republic Rubber, 34
Republic Steel Company (now
    LTV), 12, 24, 37, 47, 58, 71,
    79, 125
  as antiunion, 39, 40
  promotional materials, 83–84,
    88, 115–116
  working conditions, 28
Restaurants, 33
Revill, George, 18
Richley, J. Philip, 43–44, 164
Riverboat casino, 210, 211
RMI Titanium, 58, 59
Rocky Mountain News (Denver),
    191
Roderick, David, 173
Rogers, Rebecca, 26
Rogers, Volney, 22–23
"Role of Civil Society in
    Countering Organized
    Crime: Global Implications
    of the Palermo, Sicily,
    Renaissance, The" (UN
    Symposium), 3–4
Rollins, J. Richard, 182
Romanians, 33
Rose, Frank, 135–136
Ross, Fred, 45, 187
Ross, Josephine, 45, 187
Rusk, David, 63, 65, 243
Rust Belt, 50, 132, 155, 157, 181

Salpukas, Agis, 157–158
Salt, 19
Salt Springs Road Industrial
    Park, 60, 233

Sammarone, Chris, 239, 240
Sandburg, Carl, 90–92, 118
San Francisco Forty-Niners (sports
    team), 206, 208–210, 211
Saturday Evening Post, 46
Schools Advisory Committee
    (Industrial Informational
    Institute), 94
School segregation, 65
Segal, George, 139–143
Serbs, 28
Sharon Steel Corporation, 83–84,
    85
Shattuck, M. Lisa, 148
Shields, Mark, 134
Shipka, Al, 57
Shipka, Tom, 57, 134, 150, 188
Shout Youngstown (film), 173–176
Shutes, Mark, 219, 222
Simon Corporation, 206
Simon–DeBartolo Property
    Group, 210–211
Simon Property Group, 210, 211
Sinter, 12
Siracusa, Allesandra, 247
Sister Ray band, 153
Sixty Minutes (television
    program), 64, 214, 235
Six Ways to Sunday (film), 191
Slag, 233
Sloss Furnaces National Historic
    Landmark (Birmingham,
    Ala.), 182
Slovaks, 25, 26, 32, 33, 121
Smith, Roger, 165
"Smoke and Steel" (Sandburg),
    91, 117
Smokey Hollow neighborhood,
    102
Social clubs, 32
Southern Park Mall, 211
"Spontaneous insubordination,"
    56
Sporting News, 209

Sports Illustrated, 239, 240
Springsteen, Bruce, 8, 66, 144–145, 160, 161. *See also* "Youngstown"
St. Anthony's Catholic Church, 184, 185
  school, 100–101
St. John's Episcopal Church, 102–105
St. Joseph (patron saint of workers), 100–101, 102, 103 (photo)
"St. Joseph—A Spiritual Force of Labor" (sculpture), 102, 103 (photo)
St. Louis Post-Dispatch, 191
St. Nicholas Church (Struthers), 168
St. Rocco (patron saint), 184
St. Rocco Episcopal Church, 184
"Steel—America's National Cream" (poem), 97–98
Steel Labor (SWOC weekly), 112–115, 116 (illus.)
Steelmakers, The (Segal sculpture), 139, 140 (photo), 143
Steelmaking
  and environmental concerns, 76–77, 169
  image of, 70–77, 79, 80–81, 84, 107, 135–136, 137, 139–142
  painting of, 100
  photos, 137–139
  technology, 81, 83, 107
Steel mills, 12
  antiunion activities, 39-41
  closures, 1–2, 3, 41, 47–51, 53, 131–132, 150, 168–169
  early, 19–20
  and economic development, 47
  employment, 69
  and government contracts, 34
  and housing, 30, 34–37
  images of, 77–84, 106, 146, 155, 163, 180

  investment, 48
  modernization, 48, 49
  profits, 122
  and technology, 48, 107
  torn down, 1, 10, 16–17
  transformations, 53
Steel Mill South (Dombeck painting), 154 (photo)
Steel museum. *See* Ohio Historical Center for Industry and Labor
Steel Town (film), 92–93, 195
Steel Valley Authority, 177
Steel Valley News (Youngstown), 57
Steelworkers, 12 (map)
  benefits, 2, 40, 41
  class conflict, 16, 29–33, 89
  and closures, 50, 53, 54, 132
  drawings of, 126–128
  house ownership, 2, 34, 41, 73
  housing, 28, 30, 34–37, 41
  housing differences, 36
  identity and image, 84–121, 124, 132, 135, 137–139 (*see also* Working class, in art, film and poetry)
  neighborhoods, 10
  and other jobs, 134
  skilled and unskilled, 32, 36, 89, 90, 105
  strike (1916), 14, 28–30, 123–125
  strike (1937), 37, 39–40, 99, 125–128
  strike (1952), 40
  strike (1959), 128–129
  strike (1995), 59
  wages, 30, 40, 98, 99
  and workers' rights, 2, 40, 41, 175, 200
  working conditions, 28, 29–30, 99, 118–119
  See also under Catholic churches

Steel Workers Organizing Committee (SWOC), 37, 40, 112, 115
Stein, Rose M., 126
Stennis, Leon, 151
Stephens, David, 222
Stonework, Edward, Jr., 33
Stout, Mike, 171, 173
Streetcars, 5, 26
Strikebreakers, 120–121
Strikes, 57, 111, 121–129
  1865, 21
  1869, 21
  1873, 21–22, 30
  1916, 14, 28–30, 123–125
  1937 ("Little Steel"), 37, 39–40, 99, 125–128
  1952, 40, 99
  1959, 128–129
  1972, 56
  1990s, 59–60
Striking Steel: Solidarity Remembered (Metzger), 41
Strollo, Lenny, 65, 216
Struthers (Ohio), 33, 34, 36, 53, 157, 168, 237
Suburbanization, 41–42
Sullivan, William, Jr., 164, 170
Superior Beverage Company, 59–60
Survey (Youngstown), 28
SWOC. *See* Steel Workers Organizing Committee

Tax abatements, 232, 233
Teachers' strike, 57–58
Teamsters union, 59, 60
Technology, 81, 83, 107
"Ten Years Later" (song), 153
"Testify" (song), 239, 247
Thistledown racetrack, 206
Thomas, Dan, 99
Thomas, Mary Jeannette, 24
Thomas Steel Company, 24

Three Hundred Years: A Chronicle of the Twentieth Century (Vindicator Printing Company), 231
Timber, 19
Time magazine, 128–129, 217
Tod, David, 18, 19, 20
Tod Engine, 183–184
Together We Serve the World (Aley), 79
Town Talk (magazine), 74
Traficant, James A., Jr., 64, 65, 193, 213–219
Tressel, Jim, 239–240
TriState Conference on Steel (1979), 177
Trolleys, 23
Truman, Harry, 40
Truscon Steel, 71–72
Twilight Memories: Marking Time in a Culture of Amnesia (Huyssen), 248

Unemployment, 38, 40, 47, 50–51, 52 (table), 72, 131, 194, 196
Ungaro, Patrick, 183, 213, 226
Unions. *See* Labor organization
United Auto Workers Local 1112, 217
United Nations, 3
U.S. Bishops Pastoral Letter on the Economy (1985), 178
U.S. News & World Report, 213, 214
USA Today, 211, 213, 214
U.S. Steel (now USX), 9, 12, 24, 34, 50, 58
  and closings, 173
  McDonald Works, 39, 47
  Ohio Works, 24, 39, 47, 53, 100, 174, 199, 242
  Real Estate, 53
USX (formerly U.S. Steel), 53

United Steel Workers of America (USWA), 43, 59, 115, 171, 176
  Local 1330, 100, 187
Urban renewal program, 43
USWA. *See* United Steelworkers of America

Vasquez, Bob, 175
Venture magazine, 203
Vest, Jason, 217
View from the Bridge (Parella painting), 86
Vines, Oras, 33
Vorse, Mary Heaton, 125–126

Wallace, Mike, 181–182
Wall Street Journal, 152, 210, 212
Walters, Randy, 227
Ward, Stephen V., 70
Warehouse distribution facilities, 60
Warren, Homer, 198
Warren (Ohio), 12, 39, 45 (photo), 58, 162, 215, 227, 229, 244
Washington Post, 134, 151, 164, 219, 227
Water pollution, 232
WBL. *See* World Basketball League
WCI Steel, 12, 58–59, 229
Welfare capitalism, 30
Welsh, 20, 26, 32
"We're Still Here" (song), 174
Westlake Crossings, 199
Westlake Terrace (public housing), 198–199, 200
When Work Disappears: The World of the New Urban Poor (Wilson), 196
Williams, Joe, 191
Williamson, Michael, 143, 152, 160
Wilson, William Julius, 196, 201
Work, 8, 55, 248
  loss of, 133–150
  meaning of, 156

and personal development, 96–97
and productivity and virtue, 97–99, 101
and religion, 100–105
representations of, 67, 68, 96–102, 121–129
and shared identity, 90–92, 129
and social organization, 15, 69, 89, 90, 129–130
Working class, 5–6
  in art, film, and poetry, 84–92, 97, 118–121, 126–128, 132–133, 135, 139–150, 152–153, 154–159, 171–176
  conflict, 20–21, 29–30
  corruption, 219–220
  foreign-born, 27 (table), 30, 32, 36, 42, 99, 109 (*see also* Immigrants)
  housing, 20, 36, 41, 73
  identity and image, 41, 55, 110–112, 247
  labor force, 52 (table), 89 (*see also* Auto workers; Steelworkers)
  native born, 30, 32, 36
  out migration, 197
  solidarity, 89, 120
  standard of living (1950s), 41
  in suburbs, 43–45
  white, 3, 32, 42, 107, 109
  women, 56–57
  See also Ohio Historical Center for Industry and Labor
"Workingman on the 'Dinner pail,' The" (McGovern), 119–120
Working Together We Serve the World: A Book of Supplementary Reading Materials (Aley), 98, 257n3
Works Progress Administration (WPA), 100
World Basketball League (WBL), 202, 204

WPA. *See* Works Progress Administration

Yannella, Philip R., 92
YMCA. *See* Young Men's Christian Association
York, Ed, 56
Young, John, 10, 20
Young Men's Christian Association (YMCA), 36
Youngstown (Ohio), 9, 45 (map), 76–77 (photo)
  abandoned property, 51, 153, 161, 191, 226
  area, 5, 13, 18, 151, 230, 244, 251n1
  as beyond the point of no return, 243–244
  bridges, 13, 25
  businesses and civil clubs, 110
  churches, 23, 26, 32, 49, 151, 179
  city council, 39–40, 220
  community identity, 3, 9, 15, 17, 67, 92 93, 150, 189, 226, 237, 246, 247–248, 249 (*see also* Community of memory)
  as "Crime Town, USA," 46, 63, 191 (*see also* Crime and corruption)
  downtown, 13, 25, 38, 44, 61, 76–77 (photo)
  East, 26, 28–30 (*see also* Campbell)
  ecological recovery, 10, 12, 161
  economic future (*see* Brownfield redevelopment; Deindustrialization)
  and economic restructuring, resistance to, 7, 16
  economy (1900–1970s), 2–3, 4, 7, 24–25, 37–39
  economy (1970s–1990s), 4–5, 7–8, 50–51, 53–58, 131, 196–197, 200–201
  economy (1990s), 2, 4, 13, 48, 51, 58–65, 66, 161, 230, 233–234
  economy (2000), 57, 132
  and federal government, 169, 171, 174, 231, 235–236
  Fire Department, 223, 224
  founder, 19, 20
  housing, 10, 17, 20, 22, 25, 26, 28, 226
  mayors (*see* Heffernan, Joseph; Henderson, Charles; Hunter, Jack C.; McKelvey, George; Richley, J. Philip; Ungaro, Patrick)
  as media market, 5, 251n7
  murder rate, 193–194, 197
  museums, 13, 178–182
  neighborhoods, 10, 13, 15, 26, 31, 32–33, 34, 42, 43, 46, 51, 64–65, 102, 199–200
  parks, 23
  population, 22, 24, 25–26, 27 (table), 109, 196, 227, 244–245
  poverty rate, 200–201
  power relations, 5–6, 15, 16, 20, 22–23, 30–31, 69, 74, 130
  prisons, 13, 60–64, 161, 190, 227–229, 234–236
  racial and ethnic conflict, 6, 15–16, 22, 24, 26, 31–33, 36, 42, 45–46, 53, 65, 74, 95, 121 (*see also* Class conflict; Crime and corruption)
  representations of, 6–7, 18, 69–77, 79–88, 227–234
  representative (*see* Traficant, James A., Jr.)
  sports teams, 202–203
  as "Steel Town, USA," 67, 69
  suburbs, 41–42, 43, 44–46, 54–55, 64, 200, 233–234, 244, 245
  transportation, 23, 25, 26, 43, 44, 54, 199–200, 241–243

"Youngstown" (song), 1, 2, 5, 6, 17

Youngstown, 1953 (sesquicentennial commemoration folio), 79–80

"Youngstown: The City of Homes" (brochure), 72–73

Youngstown/Warren Business Journal, 205

Youngstown/Warren Chamber of Commerce, 227, 230

Youngstown Area Arts Council, 139

Youngstown Area Chamber of Commerce, 163

Youngstown Association of Insurance Agents, 110

Youngstown Charity Organization Society, 125

Youngstown Commerce Park, 233–234

Youngstown Empire News Service, 220

Youngstown Federation of Women's Clubs, 74

Youngstown Garden Club, 110

Youngstown Grows with Ohio (centerfold), 80 (illus.)

Youngstown Historical Center for Industry and Labor, 14, 17, 142, 178, 179 (photo)

Youngstown in Pen and Pencil (Comito), 70, 71 (illus.), 74–75, 77, 130

Youngstown International Institute, 36

Youngstown Pride (sports team), 202–203, 206

Youngstown Sheet and Tube Company, 1, 9, 12, 24–25, 29, 37
    as antiunion, 39, 123

    closures, 47, 48, 131, 150–151, 162
    and the environment, 76–77
    promotional material, 79–83, 96, 107, 180
    and suburbs, 44
    taxes, 151, 231
    worker housing, 34–37
    working conditions, 28

Youngstown Sheet and Tube v. Sawyer (1952), 40–41

Youngstown State University (YSU), 13, 51, 57–58, 199, 219
    Cushwa Center for Entrepreneurship, 183
    football team, 204, 239–240
    Monus Chair of Entrepreneurship, 203
    Urban Studies Center, 65

Youngstown Steel: A Tribute to the American Open-Hearth (Butler Institute of American Art exhibit), 137–139

Youngstown Steel Company, 24

Youngstown Strike (Gropper painting), 127–128

Youngstown Telegram, 24, 122, 123

Youngstown Vindicator, 28, 61, 96, 119, 120, 123, 169
    on crime, 193, 205–206, 220, 221
    on economic recovery, 166–167, 231, 232, 234
    labor ads and cartoons, 107–109, 115, 117
    and steelworker job loss, 133–134
    strike (1962), 57
    on unionism, 128

YSU. *See* Youngstown State University

Zellers, Bryn, 17, 146, 171–173, 246–247